Strategic Talent Management

With contributions from leading scholars and practitioners, this *Cambridge Companion* examines the topical issue of talent management from a strategic perspective, mapping out insights from a number of related fields including strategy, organisational learning, marketing, and supply chain management. The authors examine the challenges faced when viewing talent management in a global context, showing how both comparative and international HRM thinking have become increasingly important when, for example, managing talent in emerging markets, or trying to globalise the talent management function. The book concludes with a valuable summary of key learning points about talent management for both practitioners and researchers, as well as a discussion of the most fruitful areas for future research. This *Companion* will be an essential resource for academic researchers, graduate students, and practitioners of global strategic talent management.

PAUL SPARROW is the Director of the Centre for Performance-led HR and Professor of International Human Resource Management at Lancaster University Management School. He has consulted with major multinationals, public sector organisations and inter-governmental agencies and was an Expert Advisory Panel member to the UK Government's Sector Skills Development Agency. His research interests include cross-cultural and international HRM, HR strategy, cognition at work and changes in the employment relationship. From 2008–2012, he was voted amongst the Top 15 Most Influential HR Thinkers by *Human Resources* magazine.

HUGH SCULLION is Professor of International Management at NUI Galway, Ireland. He has published in leading North American and European journals including the *Academy of Management Journal, Journal of World Business, Human Resource Management Journal* and *International Human Resource Management Journal*, and he has published a number of books in the area of International HRM. He has acted as consultant to multinational companies in Europe and Asia.

IBRAIZ TARIQUE is an Associate Professor of HRM and Director of Global HRM Programs at the Lubin School of Business, Pace University, New York City campus. His research interests are in IHRM, GTM, and investments in human capital. He has published in the *International Journal of Human Resource Management, Journal of World Business,* and *International Journal of Training and Development.* He has presented numerous papers at the Annual AOM Meetings and is the co-author of "International Human Resource Management: Policies and Practices for Multinational Enterprises", a comprehensive textbook in IHRM.

CAMBRIDGE COMPANIONS TO MANAGEMENT

SERIES EDITORS:

Professor Cary Cooper CBE, *Lancaster University Management School*
Professor Jone L. Pearce, *University of California, Irvine*

ADVISORY BOARD:

Professor Linda Argote, *Carnegie Mellon University*
Professor Michael Hitt, *Texas A&M University*
Professor Peter McKiernan, *St Andrew's University*
Professor James Quick, *University of Texas*
Professor Dean Tjosvold, *Lingnan University, Hong Kong*

Cambridge Companions to Management provide an essential resource for academics, graduate students and reflective business practitioners seeking cutting-edge perspectives on managing people in organizations. Each *Companion* integrates the latest academic thinking with contemporary business practice, dealing with real-world issues facing organizations and individuals in the workplace, and demonstrating how and why practice has changed over time. World-class editors and contributors write with unrivalled depth on managing people and organizations in today's global business environment, making the series a truly international resource.

TITLES PUBLISHED:

Brief *Diversity at Work*
Cappelli *Employment Relations*
Cooper, Pandey and Quick *Downsizing*
Pearce *Status in Management and Organizations*
Saunders, Skinner, Dietz, Gillespie and Lewicki *Organizational Trust*
Sitkin, Cardinal and Bijlsma-Frankema *Organizational Control*
Smith, Bhattacharya Vogel and Levine *Global Challenges in Responsible Business*
Tjosvold and Wisse *Power and Interdependence in Organizations*

FORTHCOMING IN THIS SERIES:

Palmer, Greenwood and Smith-Crowe *Organizational Wrongdoing*
Reb and Atkins *Mindfulness in Organizations*

Strategic Talent Management

Contemporary Issues in International Context

Edited by

PAUL SPARROW

HUGH SCULLION

and

IBRAIZ TARIQUE

CAMBRIDGE
UNIVERSITY PRESS

CAMBRIDGE
UNIVERSITY PRESS

University Printing House, Cambridge CB2 8BS, United Kingdom

Cambridge University Press is part of the University of Cambridge.

It furthers the University's mission by disseminating knowledge in the pursuit of education, learning and research at the highest international levels of excellence.

www.cambridge.org
Information on this title: www.cambridge.org/9781107032101

© Cambridge University Press 2014

First published 2014

Printed in the United Kingdom by Clays, St Ives plc

A catalogue record for this publication is available from the British Library

Library of Congress Cataloguing in Publication data
Strategic talent management : contemporary issues in international context / edited by Paul Sparrow, Hugh Scullion, Ibraiz Tarique.
    pages   cm. – (Cambridge companions to management)
ISBN 978-1-107-03210-1 (Hardback)
1. Personnel management.   2. Employee motivation.   3. Creative ability in business.
I. Sparrow, Paul, editor of compilation.   II. Scullion, Hugh, editor of compilation.
III. Tarique, Ibraiz, editor of compilation.
HF5549.S8866 2014
658.3–dc23   2014005287

ISBN 978-1-107-03210-1 Hardback

Dedications

To Denise, thanks for all your support and love. Hugh
To Sue, as always, who sees me through my writing. Paul

Contents

Figures

Tables

Contributors

JOHN W. BOUDREAU is Professor of Business and Research Director at the Center for Effective Organizations of the Marshall School of Business, University of Southern California.

CLIFF BOWMAN is Professor of Strategic Management, Cranfield School of Management.

PETER CAPPELLI is the George W. Taylor Professor of Management at the Wharton School University of Pennsylvania, and Director of Wharton's Center for Human Resources.

JEAN-LUC CERDIN is Professor of Management at ESSEC, Cergy-Pontoise, France.

JONATHAN DOH is Professor, Management & Operations, and holds the Herbert G. Rammrath Endowed Chair in International Business. He is Director, Center for Global Leadership at Villanova University.

ELAINE FARNDALE is Assistant Professor at the School of Labor and Employment Relations at the Pennsylvania State University.

MARTIN HIRD was Executive Director at the Centre for Performance-Led HR at Lancaster University and formerly a Fellow at the Centre for Leadership Studies at Exeter University.

J. R. KELLER is Doctoral Researcher at Wharton's Center for Human Resources.

EDWARD E. LAWLER III is Director, Center for Effective Organizations, and Distinguished Professor of Business in the Marshall School of Business, University of Southern California.

GREG LINDEN is Research Associate at the Institute for Business Innovation at Haas School of Business, University of California, Berkeley.

GRAEME MARTIN is Chair and Professor of Management in the Graduate School of Natural Resources Law, Policy and Management at the University of Dundee, and formerly Director of the Centre for Reputation Management through People at the University of Glasgow.

RANDALL SCHULER is Professor II, Human Resource International Management and Founder, Center for Global Strategic Human Resource Management in the Department of Human Resource Management at the School of Management and Labor Relations, Rutgers University.

HUGH SCULLION is Professor of International Management at NUI Galway, Ireland.

RICHARD SMITH heads Accenture's Global Leadership Development practice out of Singapore and teaches global talent management at Singapore Management University.

PAUL SPARROW is Director of the Centre for Performance-led HR and Professor of International HRM at Lancaster University.

STEPHEN STUMPF is Professor and the Fred J. Springer Endowed Chair in Business Leadership, Villanova University, Villanova School of Business.

IBRAIZ TARIQUE is Associate Professor of Human Resources Management and Director of Global HRM Programs at the Lubin School of Business, Pace University.

DAVID J. TEECE is Chairman and CEO of the Berkeley Research Group, and Thomas W. Tusher Chair in Global Business at the Haas School of Business, University of California, Berkeley.

WALTER G. TYMON, Jr. is Associate Professor, Management and Operations at the Center for Global Leadership at the Villanova School of Business.

Foreword

In any gathering of human resources professionals today their conversation is dominated by questions of strategic talent management. These professionals and their executives want to know how they can more effectively acquire and manage the talent their organizations need to meet their current client and customer needs, as well as be staffed for the demands they expect to be facing. This is without question the most pressing practical challenge in human resources management today throughout the world. However, this cacophony of practical questions and ad hoc advice makes it difficult to know what to trust. People use the word "talent" to mean very different things. For example, does talent management refer only to elite employees, or is every employee in the organization talent? Further, is talent management just old human resources management under a new name? Such questions, and the circumstances that make any one approach useful or not, are not well understood. Scholars have only recently begun to provide the clarity and coherence necessary to the effective application of strategic talent management in organizations, as is reflected in the numerous recent journal special issues on the topic. However, such collections of divergent perspectives do nothing to bring coherence to the subject.

Here Paul Sparrow, Hugh Scullion, and Ibraiz Tarique address this challenge by collecting the growing body of systematic research and integrating it into a coherent framework. Making a compelling case that talent management places strategy at the center of employee hiring and management retention, and that there is a range of useful innovations and programs, developing one strategy is the driving objective. This volume makes it clear there is indeed something new and important happening under the umbrella called strategic human resources management. Yet this book does not shy from addressing the competing ideas and interpretations of talent, but lets the disputants make their cases in their own words. The editors then go on to explain where each perspective has the most value, using the differences to explain and illustrate rather than taking any one perspective and seeking to impose it on others. This volume contains contributions from (and has value to) those in fields as diverse as strategy, organizational learning, organizational behavior, marketing, supply-chain management, as well as human resources management. Further, it has a global focus, recognizing that the most challenging talent management is in far-flung global firms and non-governmental organizations.

This volume will be of interest to practitioners because it will help them to distinguish armchair speculation from what has been systematically tested, as well as providing a framework for strategic human resources management that will aid them in sorting out all of the conflicting views flooding the practitioner literature. Management scholars now have a credible resource they can use to design their own studies of talent management, as well as use in their teaching and advice. We congratulate the authors for presenting and developing such a diverse set of perspectives on strategic talent management, and hope this ambitious work spurs the further development of this critical yet nascent area of scholarship.

Series editors:
Cary Cooper,
Lancaster University Management School;
Jone L. Pearce,
University of California, Irvine, and
London School of Economics and Political Science.

Acknowledgements

I would like to thank the many managers and specialists working in the field whose experiences and attempts to grapple with the problems of talent management have stirred my interest. I am also indebted to the editorial team at Cambridge University Press, and to my friends and colleagues in the international human resource management field whose ideas have always influenced me.

Paul Sparrow

I would like to acknowledge the guidance, support and mentoring of Professor Randall Schuler of Rutgers University over the past 25 years.

Hugh Scullion

I would like to thank my family and mentors for their guidance and endless support. I am grateful to my international human resource management friends and colleagues for their assistance and encouragement.

Ibraiz Tarique

PART I

Mapping the field of strategic talent management

1 | Introduction: challenges for the field of strategic talent management

PAUL SPARROW, HUGH SCULLION, AND IBRAIZ TARIQUE

1.1 Introduction: why this book?

The origins of this book can be traced back to a symposium held in Chicago at the 2009 US Academy of Management on the topic of *Global Talent Management: Understanding the Contours of the Field and the Challenges for HRM*. A group of academics from the UK, the United States, Ireland, Finland, the Netherlands, and Australia got together to explore what they felt were the emerging challenges in this field, which was in the infancy stage of development. Under the umbrella term of global human resource management (GHRM), they identified the need to understand an increasingly wide range of challenges, including a changing set of academic contours that were being placed around their field, and a range of innovations in practice. Their historical interest in how organizations exported talented expatriates around the world had been taken over by the need to look at multiple resourcing options – organizations were now combining the use of assignments with efforts to localize management across new global operations. They were capitalizing on international commuters and business travel, short-term assignments, international projects, knowledge management exchanges, building centers of expertise, moving people from countries or regions into these centers and then exporting them back out again, using passive recruitment to pick up potential talent in globalized labor markets or global cities, and attracting skilled migrants. In short, they were trying to build skills and capabilities around the world. They might not be managing these multiple ways of moving talent and their insight around the world very strategically, but by default this was what they were doing. Who knows how to solve these sorts of problems? Were the new contours of talent management making it a branch of knowledge management, global leadership, and international human resource management (IHRM) strategy, we asked?

Organizations were looking at important locations around the world, such as emerging markets or into regional hubs of expertise, and they were thinking more long term about what they needed to do to build up their organizational capabilities in these locations. They were partnering with other talent across organizations in these locations, sending in their own expertise to carry out very specific tasks rather than just to manage the locals, making judgments about the speed at which they could ramp up their business offerings in these markets, moving them from a simple to a more full-service business model as the demand justified it. They were thinking about the pace at which they could move from providing the skills and insight to support this from their central operations toward a situation where this capability existed locally. They were looking to make investments in building an employer brand and mapping the local talent markets before they needed to actually switch on their traditional resourcing activity. Who knows how to solve these problems? Were the new contours of talent management also really making it a branch of strategy, operations management, and marketing, we asked?

For those of us who worked closely with organizations and their human resource management (HRM) functions, it was clear that practitioners were equally grappling with what this meant for their own expertise. While some were not really doing much more than repackaging traditional resourcing and career management activity under the label of talent management, others were setting up networks of practitioners from a range of disciplines to work on important projects linked to these challenges, or innovating their practices. This was clearly not easy for them to do – line managers did not always understand the need to start operating differently. There was also a degree of disquiet among practitioners by this time – the consequences of the global financial crisis were becoming evident and many practitioners looked to their internal systems and wondered if those they were classifying as talent really were as talented as we might wish. Were their tools, technologies, and mindsets tuned into the real task at hand?

Moreover, were they structured in the right way to do anything about this? Who really should own talent management if it had to solve these increasingly cross-functional problems? The HRM function seemed to have taken control of designing the talent-management processes, but line managers actually owned these processes – and the people who were deemed to be talent – and had the ability to either engage or totally switch off this talent. The need to integrate a whole range of processes potentially associated with talent management – from planning, searching, locating, attracting, sourcing, assigning and deploying, tasking, coaching, building, developing, retaining, internalizing the learning, and exporting – raised questions about whether those with the traditional recruitment, selection, development, and career-management skills really were the best equipped to do this? In any event, were the challenges of talent management something that needed to be managed by other people than human resources (HR), either given the cost pressures of the recession or for other managerial reasons? The chief executive officer (CEO)? The chief operating officer (COO)? The capability directors? The major business divisions?

At the symposium, the question that arose was, do we really need to build a new field of management here? Should we build bridges between the IHRM specialists who deal with the management of globalization and those who understand how HRM operates differently across countries? Should we build bridges between the people who know how to solve the strategic and organizational capability, distribution of global resources, knowledge management, and organizational learning challenges that organizations were having to deal with?

Would this lead to the development of a new field of management? Will it loosen up academic constraints, and in creating new bedfellows, lead to more fruitful paths of research? Will this field be of any value to practitioners? Is there a need to lay out a new education syllabus for those who wish to contribute to talent management?

It is in the context of this history, this intellectual but also pragmatic quest, that we wish to position this book. Is it time to build organizational functions and academic insights that truly deserve the title of *strategic talent management*?

1.2 The challenges at hand: competing definitions and interpretations

Talent management might not even be the best starting point. It has become a topic of central interest to practitioners and academics alike. Yet, despite over a decade of debate about the importance of talent management for success in what is an increasingly competitive global business environment, the concept of talent management is still lacking in definition and theoretical development. There are also many debates and criticisms about the way it is applied in practice. Putting to one side more strategic concerns for a moment, there is already a host of practical but rather important questions being asked.

- Is talent management primarily concerned with how best to handle an elite, or selected, group of employees who have exceptional skills, the potential to handle greater responsibility, and the likelihood of significant organizational impact? For advocates of this exclusive approach, the issue is how to differentiate the level of attention and resources given to this elite. An exclusive approach is based on the notion of workforce differentiation, which involves using a differentiated HR architecture (Becker, Huselid, and Beatty, 2009; Sparrow, 2012).
- Should everybody be seen as talent? For advocates of the "all employees have talents" stance, then talent management should be about that set of HR practices that enables the identification, exploitation, and optimization of the generic capabilities of all employees. The key question is, should an organization provide all employees with the same opportunity to succeed within the organization?
- Is talent management just a new term for the existing HR function – a relabelling of, and substitute for, many traditional activities such as succession planning, human resource planning, and leadership development?
- Is talent management more about critical roles, not just critical people?
- Is talent management best served through the use of a focused set of metrics that can be used to evidence the most effective and efficient use of human capital? For those who take this stance, talent management becomes a form of economics.

To many people, the field continues to suffer from both theoretical and practical limitations. Many of the currently available texts in the area of talent management are simply descriptive of practices and organizations that seemed to have had some success at one point in time – that may be presented as the heroes of practice – and yet a few years later the same organizations are used as case studies of how easy it is to get it all wrong. Much of our practice and underlying models and theories still seem to lack rigor. But to make such a statement is perhaps too critical. There has been a groundswell of interest and attention given to the topic, and in this renewed interest, there lies the opportunity to strengthen our understanding and improve our practice.

The growth of an academic interest, for example, is evidenced by a number of special issues that have been published, independent of and since that 2009 symposium. These have started to delineate the topical research issues, and build a community of academics. The pursuit of global talent management has been covered in the *Journal of World Business* (Scullion, Collings, and Caligiuri, 2010), European perspectives covered in the *European Journal of International Management* (Collings, Scullion, and Vaiman, 2011), Asia-Pacific perspectives covered in the *Asia Pacific Journal of Human Resources* (McDonnell, Collings, and Burgess, 2012), and most recently a general review of debate has been covered in the *International Journal of Human Resource Management* (Vaiman and Collings, 2013). In the latter, Vaiman and Collings (2013) drew attention to four challenges that remain: understanding the conceptual and intellectual boundaries of talent management; the practice of talent management in different national contexts; in different types of organizations; and understanding which elements of talent management are the most effective for organizational performance.

Not surprisingly, given the relatively recent history of this field, once academic reviews began to be conducted, they argued (and continue to argue) that there is still no precise definition of what is meant by talent management and that this is slowing down the development of the field (Lewis and Heckman, 2006; Collings and Mellahi, 2009; Iles, Chuai, and Preece, 2010; Tarique and Schuler, 2010; Garavan, Carbery, and Rock, 2012).

There is still no consensus around the intellectual boundaries that will help us understand the topic (Collings, Scullion, and Vaiman, 2011) and there is also a view that, as is often the case, discussions around the practice of talent management have been dominated by both study of Anglo-Saxon organizations and by analysis of US academics (Scullion and Collings, 2011). In particular, the effectiveness of and types of talent-management activities have yet to be fully understood in different national contexts and in different types of organizations (Scullion and Collings, 2011; Stahl *et al.*, 2012).

Despite these concerns, as outlined in the next chapter, there have been some significant contributions to the conceptual development of talent management and there is a growing understanding of the different ways in which talent management is defined and conducted in different organizations and contexts (Cappelli, 2008; Collings and Mellahi, 2009). Further, recent reviews suggest the emergence of more cohesive talent-management frameworks (Dickmann and Baruch, 2011; Valverde, Scullion, and Ryan, 2013).

Recent academic debate has also asked whether the field is still in a stage of infancy or whether it has reached a stage of adolescence (Collings, Scullion, and Vaiman, 2011; Thunnissen, Boselie, and Fruytier, 2013). It has also asked whether, indeed, it is time to question "the tablets and stone" upon which practice is based (Sparrow, Hird, and Balain, 2011).

In support of the charge of infancy, Thunnissen, Boselie and Fruytier's (2013) search of the academic literature from 2001 to 2012 found that over 170,000 hits on Google Scholar could be boiled down to 62 documents on the subject, 43 of which were peer-reviewed articles in international journals, one-third of which present some empirical evidence (mainly only since 2010), and talking mainly about the scope and scale of talent-management challenges faced by organizations (rather than actual practice), or they reflect single case studies, or views from a particular geography. The other two-thirds are either conceptual or review-based (i.e., trying to define a field). Hence the conclusion: "the majority of the academic literature is still conceptual, trying to respond to the question of what talent management is" (Thunnissen, Boselie, and Fruytier, 2013: 1749).

But we should remember that the infancy versus adolescence debate is a traditionalist critique. It is one that is applied to any new discipline. If everything depends on context, it argues (which it generally does no matter what aspect of management we talk about), then isn't it time that the field of talent management accepts the impact of context and internalizes this context into its rhetoric? This is a fair point, and much of this book lays out exactly what these contextual considerations need to be.

But the traditionalist critique has a positive and a negative aspect to it. On the one hand, it legitimately asks that a new discipline begin to ground itself in pre-existing knowledge, providing a counterbalance from other areas of research.

On the other hand, it can be a gravitational force that acts against innovation, because at its heart it asks that one ideology (the rhetoric of talent management) starts to espouse the existing academic status quo – the functional research interests and perspectives of academics who may be equally grounded in their own ideologies!

Therefore the more reflective practitioner is sitting in a difficult space. They realize that their fellow practitioners are cautioning against the ideology of some consultants or service providers, or the mindless adoption of best-practice ideas, but then they can also see that the academic debate may be equally politicized or in danger of being driven by ideologies.

Meanwhile, in the real world, events happen, their people and organizations need managing, and someone has to make some decisions and do something about the management of talent.

1.3 The structure of this book

This book therefore draws on recent theoretical contributions in the area and presents a current and critical review of the key issues in the field. As authors we map out the territory that the field covers in the opening and closing chapters, and contribute to some of the issues in chapters in between. But we also draw on contributions from the leading figures in the field. We aim to provide practitioners, students, and researchers alike with a well-grounded and critical overview of the key issues surrounding talent management. We think there are a number of questions that now need to be answered.

1. It is clear that we need to bring strategy back into assessment of what makes individuals talented. What do strategists think about the debates about talent management?
2. In making such assessments, we need to answer the "talent for what" question. We noted the importance of what we called "business model capital". What should be the role of expert knowledge in the assessment of talent?
3. Talent management also involves the potential for more strategic workforce planning, especially around the creation of more extended and reliable talent pipelines. How should talent-management functions best think about such issues in an era of high levels of uncertainty?
4. It is clear that the field of talent management has expanded the role and contribution of HRM functions, but that it also brings in a language from other related management disciplines – notably marketing. How should the field of talent management best draw

upon these concepts when articulating concepts such as employee-value propositions or employer brands?

5. Given the competing models of talent management that exist, what are the issues surrounding the formation and alignment of talent-management strategies? How should organizations think about the configuration of talent-management practices that they need to put in place?

6. The talent-management agenda increasingly is driven by inter-national dimensions. What challenges does this create for the convergence–divergence of best practice across international oper-ations, and what impact will the growth of emerging markets have on global models of talent management?

7. How then do firms accommodate competing dynamics of global integration and local responsiveness into the structures of the talent function?

To answer each of these questions we have invited contributions from leading scholars working on the talent-management problems and issues they are grappling with. The book follows a clear structure in terms of the sequence of the issues examined. It is organized into three parts, each of which addresses a separate agenda. We lay out the contribution of each chapter a little later in this chapter, but begin by explaining the overall design of the book.

In Part I, which includes this chapter, we cover the necessary territory to ground our understanding of strategic talent management. In this chapter we lay out a brief history of how practice has developed and how some important differences in understanding began to emerge. We outline the routemap for the whole book, moving from early debate about talent management in domestic settings, through to explanations about what a more strategic use of talent management might mean, and finally the evolution of talent-management interests as they deal with more global issues. In Chapter 2 we then look in much more detail at the competing philosophies associated with the study and practice in talent management, explaining where these ideas came from and the assumptions on which they are based. Part I is intended to help lay out some answers to the following.

- What are the existing contours of the field of talent management?
- How did we get to these contours?
- What are the questions and challenges that dominate existing practice?

Suitably equipped with this historical and current understanding, in Part II we address questions about the scope of the field and its future intellectual boundaries. The field is full of contrasts. Throughout this book we argue that the field of talent management on the one hand brings with it the promise of helping HRM functions address some strategically important problems. But on the other hand, it also brings with it a degree of hype about some of its practices, naivety in some of its assumptions, and simplicity in the narrowness of some of its proposed solutions. There has been increasing critical questioning about the field by both academics and practitioners alike, yet at the same time, there is increasing advocacy that, teething-problems apart, the issue of talent management presents us with the opportunity to engineer a new field of HRM. Part II is intended to help lay out some answers to the following.

- What are the contours of this new field if it is to sustain?
- What must be some of its underlying theory?
- What should be its disciplinary base?

We have purposefully tried to broaden out the debates around talent management by bringing in insights from related fields. If we wish to talk about such a thing as strategic talent management, why not ask strategists what they think about talent? If we wish to argue that talent is critical to the pursuit of innovation, and that talent has unique abilities and business insight, then why not ask those who know about the economics of innovation and the microfoundations of organizational performance what they understand the contribution of the expert talent to be? If we wish to talk about the creation of talent pipelines and ensure the reliability of such pipelines, then what can we learn from operations management about creating such supply chains? Given that we bandy around ideas such as employer branding, employee-value propositions, or talent-market mapping, then should we not look to the fields of marketing to understand how brands work and how such ideas work, or need to be adapted, then thinking about people? In the opening chapters, then, we attempt to expand the field of talent management, and firm up its ideas, by taking us all back to the disciplines that originally owned some of the ideas that have been co-opted by us as practitioners, consultants, or academics. It will be evident from what we say that as first suspected back in 2009, we firmly believe that talent management is a "bridge" field – and that it needs to be taught and practiced in a cross-disciplinary way. Talent management should not just be the preserve of HR functions.

However, there is another reason why talent management needs to be thought about more widely. We continue to globalize our organizations and the management of a global organization remains a major challenge. This is the focus of Part III, which looks at the challenges of global talent management. There are a number of reasons why it is important to incorporate a global context into our understanding of the field. There is a growing recognition of the key role played by globally competent leadership and managerial talent in the success of the globalizing organizations. However, these organizations are also facing significant problems in recruiting and retaining the necessary managerial talent, expert talent, or more intermediate levels of skills needed for their global operations. There are changes in both demand and supply factors. On the one hand there is a need for highly mobile elites of management to perform "boundary spanning" roles – helping to build the social networks that facilitate the exchanges of knowledge necessary to support globalization. These organizations also need the sort of talent that has the competences needed to be able to manage in a global context. Many organizations continue to report shortages of global managerial talent, particularly in the emerging markets, which significantly constrains their ability to implement their globalization strategies. This globalization of talent management brings with it the requirement to create new HRM tools and methods. It often creates the need to set up new processes of functional integration, aimed at providing the necessary coordination systems to support global integration. Therefore we need to incorporate the broadening out of talent management brought about by the global agenda at the same time as addressing the new insights from related management fields.

1.4 A brief history: the functional roots of talent management

We have to begin somewhere, and a sensible starting point is to look at the functional roots from which the practice of talent management has developed. In this opening chapter we begin by laying out this development, along with the way that practitioner concerns have developed, and track the parallel development of academic interests.

We provide an overview of the practitioner and the academic debates about the field. We need to understand not only the different academic and consulting trajectories that were developing, but the way that those who had to listen to the message or who were initiating their own practices – the HR functions inside organizations – were themselves structured. Were they able to receive the messages that were being sent? Did their internal structures lead to faithful adoption or rejection of ideas, creative adaptation, or ill-informed redirection? Both the literature on talent management (Silzer and Dowell, 2010) and the organizational structures through which talent-management specialists work, have evolved through a series of identifiable stages.

There was, even in those early days, a split in the trajectory followed by academics, HR practitioners, and consultants. In one direction we saw efforts to demonstrate return on investment on human capital. The intellectual roots of talent management were originally in the HR planning movement of the 1980s and 1990s, with its focus on forecasting of staffing needs to meet business needs, planning and managing staffing needs, succession planning, and short-term management development moves.

In the other we saw the integration of resourcing and career development traditions into a life-cycle perspective, applied in the first instance to a small group of high-value managers. By the late 1990s and early 2000s we saw the use of talent management as a label in its own right, with debate focusing on how organizations could develop, sustain, and manage talent pools; engrain a talent mindset in the culture of an organization; align various HR programs and processes to the needs of talent; and understand the time needed to pursue talent strategies that balanced recruitment versus the development of talent. In parallel with the emergence of the HR function as a strategic business partner, it was argued that organizations should see talent as a strategic resource and source of competitive advantage (Silzer and Dowell, 2010).

Reflecting the human capital tradition, claims were being made that investment in talented employees resulted in significant financial benefit for organizations (Gubman, 1998). Drawing upon HR accounting traditions, Fitz-enz (2000) argued that management books were either ignoring, avoiding, or throwing gratuitous or simplistic platitudes at the question of human value in business environments. The ever-present threat of talent shortages, particularly across the emerging markets, discussed from the 1990s onwards, was for Fitz-enz not solvable just by attending to productivity, which was a by-product, but only by addressing the fundamentals of fulfillment at work, based on knowledge and feedback on achievement. Human-capital planning required an integration of five core elements: planning, acquiring, maintaining, developing, and retaining.

Two capabilities were deemed important in converting this human capital planning cycle into a talent-management system.

1. Measuring the impact that human capital (talent) had on the ability to execute an organization's business processes evaluating through truly analyzing best practices. The impact of talent on processes needed to be analyzed in terms of whether this impact helped reduce operating expense and product or service costs, did it shorten the cycle time of important processes, could people do more with less through the methods involved, were the number of errors or defects reduced, were customers or employees more satisfied, and so forth. The original discussion of human-capital planning was about the demonstration of lean, efficient, and effective performance through the efforts of talent – not the more lazy and fairy-tale (Fitz-enz) practice of bench-marking.

2. The use of the forward-looking skills of trending, forecasting, and predicting. These were deemed necessary for identifying relationships and patterns, fallacies in trends, finding meaning in variables and their predictable consequences while avoiding mixing up linkage and correlation with causation, identifying data sensors (data that tip you off to the emergence of a problem or opportunity). An example definition today, from Cappelli (2008), coming from this human-capital perspective, defines talent management as the process through which employers anticipate and meet their needs for human capital.

Fitz-enz (2000) saw this requirement to forecast, plan, and ensure a continuous pipeline of talent, as a necessary yet dangerous art, but a manageable one. He cautioned:

the latest flawed attempt at validity centers on gathering management attitudes toward a set of mixed, arbitrary, often overlapping, subjective issues, simultaneously ignoring quantitative performance records, and then promising to draw correlations with creation of shareholder value. This is one of the most blatant ruses I've seen. (p. 164)

But in terms of common practice, for most organizations the origins of talent management lay in two earlier HR activities – recruitment and career development. Recruitment of all levels of employees has been a key HR activity for many years, but a conscious focus upon career development was a later development, occurring around the late 1980s and early 1990s. The bringing together of recruitment and career development responsibilities led to the development of a life-cycle approach, and many of the definitions still used today reflect this thought process. So, for the American Productivity and Quality Center (2004) talent management was defined as involving cradle-to-grave processes to recruit, develop, and retain employees within an organization. Or for Avedon and Scholes (2010) talent management is an integrated set of processes and procedures used in an organization to attract, onboard, retain, develop, move, and exit talent, to achieve strategic objectives.

Structurally, a role emerged in some larger organizations that focused upon the general stewardship of a cadre of senior managers and directors, typically the top 500 employees. The responsibilities for these heads of resourcing included senior employee role rotation, development of the senior cadre, identifying those members of the cadre with the highest potential for board-level roles, and, where considered necessary, the exits of low-performing members. A definition typical of this more focused effort would be from the UK's Chartered Institute of Personnel and Development, which defines talent management as "the systematic attraction, identification, development, engagement/retention and deployment of those individuals who through their potential have a positive immediate or long-term impact on organizational performance" (CIPD, 2008).

During this period, then, when one looked inside organizations, it was often the head of resourcing role that was the one that was developing into that of talent director (Sparrow, Hird, and Balain, 2011). These emerging talent directors became important players in the HR hierarchy, because CEOs, and the boards they led, became increasingly aware of the need to possess talented employees in terms of competitive advantage. The portfolio of responsibilities for many talent directors included high-potential identification, succession planning, critical role analysis, external search and recruitment, executive strength benchmarking, and in some organizations performance management and strategic workforce planning. A key output for many talent directors was the periodic production of talent review reports for the board to assess the overall level of competitive advantage. Still a subfunction of HRM, talent management began to emerge and develop its own identity as the internal talent teams inside organizations looked for frameworks that would aid the categorization of all their managerial employees, in particular, frameworks that would identify and highlight so-called high potentials. For the majority of organizations talent management came to operate around a few core technologies and tools – notably systems that categorize people as talented based on evaluations of their performance and potential.

At the same time there was a growing emphasis upon what we later note was called the war for talent. This emphasis, which was based on claims about shareholder value, eclipsed the human-capital management movement for a few years, but had a significant impact on the newly emerging talent directors. Michaels, Handfield-Jones, and Axelrod (2001) in their book *The War For Talent* argued that corporate leaders needed to be obsessed with talent, and hold a deep-seated belief and mindset that having better talent at all levels enabled an organization to outperform its competitors. Talent management was to be a central focus of their activity. They would set the standards for progression, become actively involved in decisions, drive a probing review process, instill a culture that manages talent, invest money in talented people, and would hold themselves accountable for the pool of talent and the actions of this pool. Talent management was therefore *not* about having sophisticated HR processes concerned with succession planning, recruitment, and compensation, it was argued, but rather having HR systems that differentiated and affirmed the status of talent, hiring assumed talented people, and paying them more than they thought they were worth.

1.5 Part I: the growth of more critical agendas and the reemergence of "strategic" talent management

Part I of the book then asks that we must begin by accepting that there is immense variability in the way the technology of talent management is being used. When you ground talent management in reality, by exploring organizations' talent-management strategies, or the assumptions that their talent directors make, although on the surface they may be using many of the same tools and technologies, the talent systems they operate may in reality be very different.

Talent management might be referring to the talents that very effective people have, to the individuals who have such talents, or to groups and pools of such people, or indeed used collectively to refer to the entire employee population. It might be referring to specific processes or component practices involved in the management of the above. It might be seen as an outcome of such processes, or a goal of the HR strategy, or an achievement the rest of the organization will hold the HR function to account for (Silzer and Dowell, 2010). Collings and Mellahi (2009), in a very helpful review of approaches, boiled this down to four different philosophies, or approaches, that have come to dominate discussion of talent management. These can be called the key people, key practices, key positions, and key strategic pools approaches, and each one has helped shape mainstream thinking in the area.

We look at and explain each of these philosophies in Chapter 2. We link them back to the debates on which they are based, and the assumptions they make about how organizational effectiveness is created. We surface both the explicit and the hidden assumptions that are associated with each perspective on talent management and raise some of the key critiques in the field, such as debates about whether it is individual stars or teams and systems that most impact organizational effectiveness, or whether elite versus egalitarian approaches are best. But importantly, this chapter also raises the question of "talent for what"? We argue that the answer requires that two bellwether judgments be made about the knowledge possessed by talent:

1. is the individual capable of high-quality strategic thought?
2. does the "capital" that they possess enable them to make a potential contribution to value creation?

Perhaps realising that they would be hard pressed to make such a judgment, practitioners themselves also became more questioning of their achievements:

as practitioners in this area we have both bought into this notion, and worked for many years to make it happen. We have worked with CEOs, undertaking extensive talent reviews. We have worked with psychologists assessing people's capability. We have worked with technology specialists to introduce databases to capture skills across the workforce. We have worked with "the talent" as coaches. We have worked with recruiters to scour the market for more talent. And yet when we reflected on the difference this activity was really making we felt that it was still not enough... the struggle was systemic... in truth, we had metaphorically put sticking plasters over the obvious issues without really getting to the root cause of the problem... it felt to us that organizations were operating in a talent "doom loop". (Davies and Kourdi, 2010: p. 3).

Their critique of their own practice was that talent management needs to be about knowledge, innovation, and relationships today rather than executive potential tomorrow. The vital many were as important as the special few. The interdependence between people within and across organizations is critical. Individuals control when and who they share their potential with, so the idea that organizations can manage talent is an outdated conceit. Finally, the social dimension matters more than the capability and resources of individuals. We need to manage how talent works – the whole ecology of an organization and its ability to create social capital.

For Sparrow, Hird, and Balain (2011) it was "time to question the tablets of stone". They teased out differences in the underlying philosophies, providers, practices, and principals. The *philosophy* reflects basic assumptions that are made about the nature of talent management and its link to organizational effectiveness – the type of talent differentiation and segmentation to be pursued, focus, levels of transparency, functional ownership and allocation of responsibilities, and the extent of risk taking involved in the talent system. As detailed in the next section, there are a number of different schools of thought that have influenced talent directors. For some talent is seen as being just about top elites, for others it applies to all employees as a rebranded form of people management. Yet others see talent management as a branch of human-capital management, building and utilizing sophisticated metrics to capture the efficiency and effectiveness of their HRM. However, there is immense variability of practice.

At a practical level organizations have relied on different service *providers* – with occupational psychologists, search consultants, and HR development consultants all playing a major role. However, each provider brings their own models of potential, leadership, and human capability, and thinks about questions of potential, talent deployment, career advancement, and career derailment with different models. So the assessment and development models – the competence systems used to capture the nature of human capital – can be a product of historical and professional practice.

The scope of *practices* that may be bundled together by organizations under the label or umbrella of talent management varies. In some instances key practices may by shaped by external providers – or they might reflect internal design assumptions. Organizations might create formal and explicit links between talent-management systems and performance-management and rewards systems, or they might have kept such systems separate, at least formally. Some organizations have put immense effort into enriching some of the lynchpin tools, such as how they categorize employees into different talent segments, with only a few members of the organization deemed sophisticated enough to understand and pronounce on the tools (rather like a guild or priesthood). Others are content to use fairly simple and pragmatic tools, with little shaping of line management behavior built into their operations.

Finally, there are differences in the attention to underlying *principles* – the fundamental or primary truth or rule of action and conduct – that the talent-management system is supposed to serve. After the global financial service crisis, for example, a number of organizations began to re-stress the corporate values that talent managers were supposed to possess and display, re-specified the underlying leadership models, or re-stressed social purposes. Talent management becomes a vehicle for creating important behavioral outcomes through the display of values, behaviors, and other social indicators. Organizations and now being encouraged to incorporate principals of risk management into their talent-management processes (Cascio and Boudreau, 2010, 2012).

They are being exhorted to give renewed attention to the leadership model that underpins their assessment of talent – creating linkage between talent management and efforts to foster specific concepts or brands of leadership, such as authentic leadership (Avolio and Gardner, 2005; Cooper, Scandura, and Schriesheim, 2005; Gardner, Avolio, and Walumbwa, 2005; Goffee and Jones, 2005; Brown and Treviño, 2006); or sustainable leadership (Senge, 2008; Hind, Wilson, and Lenssen, 2009; Kakabadse, Kakabadse, and Lee-Davies, 2009). For other organizations their talent-management systems serve a social purpose – such as promoting social mobility.

Most talent directors, when asked, acknowledge that talent management, as practiced by HR professionals, is an artform, not a science. Managers balance competing demands and priorities depending on the circumstances their firm faces. Although often imperfect, they combine different ideas about talent management into their HR systems, trading off priorities. But for all organizations, talent management was always intended to be about strategy.

Amid the uncertainty of the economic crisis, we have seen a return of the word "strategic" in association with talent management. The term *"strategic talent management"* – the focus of this book – began to be used much more by the late 2000s, with discussion focusing on how talent strategies can better be integrated with business strategy, how business planning and operations cycles may be better linked to talent planning cycles, thereby helping change talent management into a core business process. The topic of talent management was also moving closer to related challenges of engaging talent.

Cheese, Thomas, and Craig (2008), reflecting their work while at Accenture, defined human talent (in a business context) as "the combined capacity and will of people to achieve an organization's goals – is a productive resource... with a unique capacity to add value to an organization (p. 1)". The management of talent needed organizations to understand how to discover it, develop it, deploy it, and *motivate and energise it* (our italics). Schiemann (2009), writing on behalf of the Society for Human Resource Management in the United States, also complained of unfocused activities, woefully inadequate measures in a nascent field, and a failure to accept that talent management is not just a business issue, but a social issue. Again the need for a change in the rules of the game and for talent management to capture the engagement issue (through what he called a need for people equity) was raised.

Questions were being raised about who should have operational responsibility for talent management. For Cheese, Thomas, and Craig (2008), this broadened remit had to be handled strategically and was therefore:

too important to be assigned only to specialist functions and regulated by specialist processes... they need a holistic approach. (p. 1)

Talent was also becoming a more critical and complex issue because:

the conditions faced by every organization in the search for talent are changing with astonishing rapidity... familiar talent pools are shrinking, new ones emerging, new technologies are transforming the nature of work... new elements are arriving in the global mix with new attitudes and ambitions. (p. 2)

The field, they argued, needed to provide more guidance on how to look at talent more strategically.

Cheese, Thomas, and Craig (2008) saw the terms talent and human capital as broadly interchangeable, while noting that human capital tends to be the preferred language if one is talking about strategic, financial, and economic matters, but is out of favor because it somehow sounds more impersonal than talent. The relationship between HRM and talent management represents an unfinished evolution, akin to that seen in the management of quality and information technology.

A more strategic approach to talent management requires the "multiplication of talent", an effort achieved by combining and recombining knowledge, skills, and competences throughout the organization, and one of the understated processes in enabling this is more thoughtful deployment of talent. This in turn requires closer match between employees' talent and the strategic goals of the organization, expanding an organization's capabilities by leveraging the contribution of projects through individuals' strengths, perspectives, and experiences, and encouraging and enabling the sharing of knowledge to encourage continuous renewal.

For Silzer and Dowell (2010) the label "strategic" could only be earned if talent-management processes:

- identify and deliver individuals who had individual competences that enhanced or established competitive advantage and played a crucial role in identifying, developing, and protecting core organizational capabilities
- identify different talent for different strategies – aligning talent profiles more specifically to both near-term and far-term organizational demands
- find global talent and pursue talent strategies that supported entering and surviving in other geographic markets.

For Avedon and Scholes (2010) the label strategic talent management requires processes that enable the organization to decode which talent pools are the most valuable, and these typically fall into four broad categories.

1. Leadership talent: enabling a flow of leaders with appropriate competences through all career stages (early career, mid career, and late career).

2. Talent for strategic functions: key functions of critical importance to the strategy at a given time, often technical specialists but also hybrid roles that become central to the effective delivery of a new business model, or in the pursuit of different strategic foci such as innovation, operational excellence, customer intimacy, or globalization.
3. Talent for strategic technologies: ensuring access to new educational disciplines and start-up activities.
4. Talent for strategic geographies: covering mature through to emerging markets.

This is no different to taking a market-segmentation approach, where investments vary in relation to the strategic importance to the organization: good development for all, great development for some.

Senior executives also have some concerns about the performance of HR in relation to talent management. In a survey of 418 executives run by the Economist Intelligence Unit, research conducted on behalf of KPMG (KPMG, 2012), 81% thought an effective talent-management strategy was key to competitive success, and 59% believed it would become more important strategically in the future. However, just 17% thought HR did a good job at demonstrating its value to business, and only 25% felt their own HR function excelled at core issues such as sourcing and retaining key talent globally, supporting a virtual and flexible workforce, and supporting the greater globalization of the business.

Cheese, Thomas, and Craig (2008) also attributed the need for a more strategic understanding of talent to the shifting global economic context: new paradigms for growth; an economic revolution that is changing the nature of work and value; a need to embrace diversity because of shifting populations and ageing workforces; and the parallel existence of global abundance but local scarcities of talent. As the label of strategic talent management began to be used, the opportunity arose to broaden out and integrate a number of related activities. Talent management began to be seen in the context of managing organizational capabilities. Organizations began to think about links between talent management and the development and exploitation of an employer brand. They began to think about links between talent management and strategic workforce planning. Finally, they began to align talent management with efforts at globalization.

However, beyond noting that flexibility over the pool of candidates in a talent pool is called for, and that the pool should be refreshed depending on whether the strategy might be, for example, to grow in emerging markets, or some other strategic priority, little has been said in the talent-management literature about the problem of strategic alignment. We have to look to other literatures to gain some insight into this. Hence the need for Part II of this book.

1.6 Part II: redefining the intellectual boundaries of strategic talent management

In the opening to Part II, Cliff Bowman and Martin Hird in Chapter 3 pick up on the challenge we have set to bring strategy back into assessment of what makes individuals talented. In outlining what strategists think about the debates about talent management, they present a critique of many of the assumptions made by talent-management practitioners – especially those who adopt an elite model. They surface many of the key assumptions that we make about talent management, and then, by drawing upon research from the field of strategic management and the understanding it has developed around a resource-based view of the firm, they question whether it is really possible for organizations to actually "manage" talent. The chapter addresses the following fundamental questions.

- Are the most valuable and firm-specific capabilities to which talent contribute more easily built rather than bought?
- To what extent are organizational capabilities the result more of the collective interactions and interconnections between talent?
- By building on what we know about strategy, can we improve the practice of talent management?

In Chapter 4, Greg Linden and David J. Teece pick up on the ideas from the resource-based view of the firm articulated by Cliff Bowman and Martin Hird, and explain how it can be developed through an understanding of the dynamic-capabilities framework to identify different categories of experts. They argue that the field gives far too much importance to the notion of general management potential and underplays the value of expert knowledge. The chapter raises the following questions.

- What does a broader understanding of the firm's strategy, capabilities, and potential tell us about the importance of expert talent?

- Does expert talent need to be managed and kept stimulated in different ways to general management talent?
- Can research from the field of organizational learning, strategy, and innovation management help us better understand whether talent have appropriate strategic understanding and ability?

In Chapter 5, Joseph R. Keller and Peter Cappelli build on another type of risk. Traditional workforce-planning models are based on assumptions of predictability, stability, and control. These assumptions do not hold in an environment characterized by uncertainty in supply and demand. They address two fundamental questions.

1. How do organizations ensure a sufficient supply of human capital when both demand and supply are uncertain?
2. What are the different human-capital sourcing strategies available to firms, and when should each be used?

To answer these questions practitioners must look to ideas from outside HRM from the field of operations management.

Chapter 6, by Graeme Martin and Jean-Luc Cerdin, as with the preceding chapter, also takes as its starting point the challenge of managing talent pipelines. It is clear that the field of talent management has expanded the role and contribution of HRM functions, but this also brings in a language from other related management disciplines – notably marketing. It addresses important questions that flow from this development.

- How should the field of talent management best draw upon these concepts when articulating concepts such as employee-value propositions or employer brands?
- Have HRM professionals, in co-opting ideas like these, truly understood the underlying marketing research – have the ideas been transposed sensibly?
- Where should these new multidisciplinary talent-management professionals best sit in the organization – does it make sense to site a talent-management function still within HRM structures?
- Once you accept notions of employer brand, how do you work these ideas through into the longer term career management of talent?

In the final chapter in Part II, Chapter 7, Ibraiz Tarique and Randall Schuler help answer these questions by concentrating on the four generic processes of talent attraction, retention, development, and mobilization (the planning for and positioning of talent). In the context of the need to manage talent on a global basis, they point out that not only are there different interpretations of talent management but there are also different theoretical assumptions, derived from ideas such as high-performance work systems, employee differentiation, human capital theory, and portfolio models of performance potential. This chapter addresses the following questions.

- What are the different configurations of practice that can be engineered across these generic talent-management processes?
- What are the issues surrounding the formation and alignment of talent-management strategies?
- When operating on a global basis, do organizations assume there is such a thing as best practice when they try and manage the talent strategy on a global basis?
- Or do they believe that the problems of convergence and divergence in IHRM practices also apply to the talent system?
- Are there different conceptions of talent-management practice across these regions?

1.7 A globalization of the talent-management agenda

Chapter 7 then starts to take us into a talent-management agenda that is driven increasingly by international dimensions. This takes us into Part III of the book. Globalization creates challenges for the field of talent management in dealing with the convergence–divergence of best practice across international operations, and also dealing with the growth of emerging markets. However, the way in which talent should be (or by default currently is) managed, depends upon the countries in which a global firm operates, and the nature of its strategic priorities. Moreover, although firms might recognize the importance of talent management, the way in which they actually implement it may still be poor (Vaiman, Scullion, and Collings, 2012).

Beyond the distinctions found in the domestic talent-management literature, a number of writers have also argued recently that global talent management has become of increasing strategic importance to organizations (Scullion, Collings, and Caligiuri, 2010; Tarique and Schuler, 2010; Schuler, Jackson, and Tarique, 2011). For Sparrow

(2007) it has been the globalization of labor markets that has led to an interesting development, in which academics from a number of fields related to international management have begun to come together, particularly from the mid 2000s onwards, to address global talent-management issues.

A number of factors have led to this growth of interest of talent management in a broader international context.

- An intensification of competition between multinational enterprises (MNEs), leading to an increased importance of innovation and learning across borders, in turn much dependent upon the quality of leadership talent (Black, Morrison, and Gregerson, 2000; Scullion and Starkey, 2000; Collings, Scullion, and Morley, 2007).
- A shift in the competition between employers for talent from the country level to regional labor markets and different parts of a global network of talent (Sparrow, Brewster, and Harris, 2004).
- An increase in demand for expatriates with the capability to develop new markets, access to specialized talent to assist the execution of overseas projects and to develop emerging markets, managers with distinctive competences and a desire to manage in culturally complex and geographically distant countries; and the need for highly mobile elites of management to perform boundary-spanning roles to help build social networks and facilitate the exchange of knowledge necessary to support globalization (Li and Scullion, 2006, 2010; Farndale, Scullion, and Sparrow, 2010).
- Shortages of such capable leadership talent in many geographies and local labor markets, coupled with rapid shifts in demographic profiles that are impacting the supply of labor, the retention of key knowledge and capability, and the depth and breadth of future talent pipelines (Tarique and Schuler, 2010).
- The globalization of a number of professional labor markets (such as healthcare and information technology), the shift toward skills-related immigration systems, higher levels of international migration into domestic labor markets, and the growth of reverse migration patterns for returnee immigrants bringing skills and networks back to home markets (Clark, Stewart, and Clark, 2006; Tung and Lazarova, 2006, 2007; Sparrow, 2007; Solimano, 2010).
- Growing demand for alternative forms of international assignments such as short-term assignments, commuter assignments, and the like

(Collings, Scullion, and Morley, 2007; Mayrhofer, Reichel, and Sparrow, 2012).

Whether we look at talent management in relation to different stages of globalization (Sparrow, Brewster, and Harris, 2004), or across countries (Collings, Scullion, and Vaiman 2011; McDonnell, Collings, and Burgess, 2012), it becomes apparent that there are many differences in the understanding of, definition of, meaning in, and goals of talent management.

For Scullion, Collings, and Caligiuri (2010):

Global talent management includes all organizational activities for the purpose of attracting, selecting, developing and retaining the best employees in the most strategic roles (those roles are necessary to achieve organizational strategic priorities) on a global scale. Global talent management takes into account the differences in both organizations' global strategic priorities and the differences across national contexts for how talent should be managed in the countries where they operate. (Scullion, Collings, and Caligiuri, 2010: p. 106)

Tarique and Schuler (2010) see it as a subset of international HRM policies and practices focused on attraction, retention, development, and mobilization, that are systematically linked to manage with the strategic direction of a multinational enterprise. In their recent review of the literature on global talent management (GTM) they suggested that one can categorize GTM as a "bridge field" where important issues, problems, and ideas discussed by HR managers and professionals are examined by the academic IHRM community.

The first global perspective that we address in the book is talent management when seen across different geographical contexts. Not surprisingly, given the level of interest in talent management, the comparative HRM academics have moved into the field. This raises important questions.

- What does talent management look like in different national contexts?
- Is it a concept that has any resonance beyond its Anglo-Saxon origins?

We know, for example, that in the European context, the diverse national business systems, industrial structures, and different institutional arrangements likely have an impact on the attractiveness (or not) of a concept such as talent management, and certainly an impact on the way it might be operationalized by organizations (Collings and Scullion, 2011; Collings, Scullion, and Vaiman, 2011). Certainly, across Europe the "power" that talent might have varies. Graduates in countries such as Greece and Spain, for example, have little opportunity in their local labor markets, making generic talk about organizations having to respond to the desires and tastes of the younger generation somewhat fanciful. So too do the skills needs and demands of the economies.

So, the particular organizational challenges that a talent-management strategy has to solve are very country and national labor market specific. For example, a study of talent-management practices in 58 Polish organizations (Skuza, Scullion, and McDonnell, 2013) showed there was still little evidence of Polish practice converging with Western models. There were differences in the intensity of challenge to do with talent identification, development, or evaluation between the domestically owned and foreign-owned organizations, and the practices used for each aspect of talent management reflected: the typical industrial structure and historical traditions rather then the practices prescribed in best practice or academic books; the limited power and influence of HR functions; a cultural emphasis on personal and private networks and on the collective rather than on individual success; and biases (high potentials are a threat to your own hard-fought-for position). Valverde, Scullion, and Ryan (2013) found very little awareness of the practice or rhetoric of talent management among medium-sized organizations in Spain.

Similarly, Festing, Schäfer, and Scullion (2013) point out that the nature of talent management and practices associated with it of course vary by type of firm (they looked at small- and medium-sized enterprises, SMEs) and national context (they looked at Germany). In Germany, immediate realities of relatively low levels of unemployment and support, high levels of skilled migration, and longer term characteristics such as an emphasis on education, vocational qualifications, and a development orientation, coupled with key elements of a social market economy, create a specific set of practices and challenges (Festing, Schäfer, and Scullion, 2013). Attracting key skills and talent is a challenge for German SMEs, but they lack for example the brand recognition for a more global approach to sourcing to automatically be successful. However, reflective of national cultural and institutional influences, a common effect across the 700 SMEs was that organizations took a more collective and inclusive view on talent management aimed at targeting all or most employees, rather than the more elitist approach seen in other cultures or in MNEs. Among German SMEs, 54% focused their talent-management activities on all employees, 29% cited technical experts as the most important target group, 10% focused on senior management and executives, and 8% concentrated on high-potential talent. Each firm pursued different combinations of these activities.

We devote two chapters in this book to reflect on these arguments and to consider talent management across different geographical contexts. In Chapter 8, John W. Boudreau and Edward E. Lawler III look at the strategic context in the largest emerging market – that of China – through comparison of practices with those in the United States.

- Is there any evidence to suggest whether there is any convergence around best practices or not?
- How involved in strategy are Chinese and US HR leaders?
- What are the important contingencies from strategy – such as management focus – that impact the HR practices adopted?
- Are these different strategies associated with the degree to which HR engages in strategic activities and spends time on strategy?

Then, in Chapter 9, Jonathan Doh, Richard Smith, Stephen Stumpf, and Walter Tymon look at the challenges of regional patterns in the emerging markets of India and China. Growth in emerging markets and the changing balance of power from developed to emerging economies has considerable implications for human capital and talent-management strategies. There is both a changing balance of economic power from developed to developing countries and a new geographical demography, giving rise to the potential for enormous talent pools. Despite the increased national-level focus on skills development and the global financial crisis, talent shortages remain a real concern in countries such as India and China.

- What are the talent-management challenges in India and China?
- How are organizations formalizing and institutionalizing talent practices?
- How are they responding to the unique social and cultural settings of these countries?
- What is the nature of the talent-management challenges in the emerging markets and how do these challenges vary across these markets?

There is of course a second global perspective that needs to be addressed. What is the role of talent management when it is seen as part of the globalization process? A number of research programs, generally those observing actual practice within multinational corporations (MNCs), have, however, shown that although there are very strong institutional and cultural pressures that make the pursuit of talent management subject to the dictates of local country-level practices, there increasingly are strong pressures toward the use of talent management as a globally integrating set of practices (Sparrow, Brewster, and Harris, 2004; Guthridge and Komm, 2008; Stahl *et al.*, 2012). These studies provide some qualified support for the convergence perspective in IHRM.

Sparrow, Brewster, and Harris (2004) placed global talent management under strategies aimed at the development of organizational capabilities on a global scale, as organizations went through more and more globalization. They argued that:

- within global organizations where there were quite different levels of HR sophistication across the businesses, this limited the pace at which global themes could be deeply applied and brought into play
- despite the best intentions, many organizations find it difficult to maintain a focus on such initiatives on a global scale.

The intentions of organizations that were globalizing their HRM were, however, becoming explicit. There were a number of integration mechanisms being mobilized within HRM, notably: competency and values models, employer branding, talent management, and performance management. These were used as global themes to legitimize global coordinated and consistent practice.

However, although we can see the sorts of policies and practices being used to try and create more globally integrated talent management, we still know little about the ways in which corporate HR functions must manage these global talent-management activities.

- How then do organizations accommodate the competing dynamics of local responsiveness, made evident in Chapters 8 and 9, with the pressures for global integration outlined above?
- How do they incorporate these demands into the structures of the talent function?

The challenges that corporate HRM functions face in attempting to manage these tensions are picked up by Paul Sparrow, Elaine Farndale, and Hugh Scullion in Chapter 10. In the last of the issues-based chapters, they look at the challenges faced by organizations – and specifically their corporate headquarters (HQs) and international-mobility functions – in their attempts to globalize their HR architecture.

- Can we use notions of global integration and local responsiveness to signal the challenges faced by corporate functions in balancing their global talent-management practices?
- Should talent management deliver a degree of vertical (global) integration *within* businesses across the internal labor (talent) markets, between the strategy, business model, and structure through to the talent-management practices?
- Can talent management create horizontal integration across operating divisions in order to shape requisite levels of transfer of knowledge and individuals across businesses?
- What are the most important roles for corporate HR functions to bring about this vertical and horizontal integration?

To conclude, this book therefore takes us through a fascinating journey that both practitioners and academics have undertaken. It asks a range of important questions about the future shape of the field, and it uses the various analyses to identify the messages for practice. We bring the book to a close in Chapter 11. In this chapter we summarize the learning across the three parts of the book and from the various contributions. We argue that strategic talent management is best seen as a bridge field, and we explain some of the important connections that are now being made, and those that should form the basis of the forward research agenda.

The themes covered in this book will help to understand and contextualize talent-management strategies in the context of global strategies. The book makes a unique contribution to the literature by providing some development in the theoretical underpinning of talent-management systems, exploring the interplay between different lenses on talent-management systems from across a range of academic fields, and by considering the challenges associated with implementing a talent-management strategy in an international context.

References

American Productivity and Quality Center (2004). *Talent Management: From Competencies To Organizational Performance. Final report.* Houston, TE: American Productivity and Quality Center.

Avendon, M. J. and Scholes, G. (2010). Building competitive advantage through integrated talent management. In R. Silzer and B. E. Dowell (eds.) *Strategy-driven Talent Management: a Leadership Imperative.* San Franciscio, CA: Jossey-Bass–Society for Industrial and Organizational Psychology, pp. 73–122.

Avolio, B. J. and Gardner, W. L. (2005). Authentic leadership development: getting to the root of positive forms of leadership. *Leadership Quarterly*, 16, 315–38.

Becker, B. E., Huselid, M. A., and Beatty, R. W. (2009). *The Differentiated Workforce : Transforming Talent into Strategic Impact.* Boston, MA: Harvard Business Press.

Black, J. S., Morrison, A. J., and Gregerson, H. B. (2000). *Global Explorers: The Next Generation of Leaders.* New York, NY: Routledge.

Brown, M. E. and Treviño, L. K. (2006). Ethical leadership: A review and future directions. *Leadership Quarterly*, 17, 595–616.

Cappelli, P. (2008). *Talent on Demand: Managing Talent in an Age of Uncertainty.* Boston, MA: Harvard Business Press.

Cascio, W. F. and Boudreau, J. W. (2010). *Investing in People: Financial Impact of Human Resource Initiatives.* New York, NY: Financial Times Press.

  (2012). *A Short Introduction to Strategic Human Resource Management.* Cambridge: Cambridge University Press.

Cheese, P., Thomas, R. J., and Craig, E. (2008). *The Talent Powered Organization: Strategies for Globalization, Talent Management and High Performance.* London: Kogan Page.

CIPD (2008). Talent management: design, implementation and evaluation. *CIPD Online Practical Tool.* London: CIPD.

Clark, P. F., Stewart, J. B., and Clark, D. A. (2006). The globalization of the labor market for health-care professionals. *International Labor Review*, 145, 37–64.

Collings, D. G. and Mellahi, K. (2009). Strategic talent management: a review and research agenda. *Human Resource Management Review*, 19 (4), 304–13.

Collings, D. G., Scullion, H., and Morley, M. (2007). Changing patterns of global staffing in the multinational enterprise: challenges to the conventional expatriate assignment. *Journal of World Business*, 42 (2), 198–213.

Collings, D. G., Scullion, H., and Vaiman, V. (2011). European perspectives on talent management. *European Journal of International Management*, 5 (5), 453–62.

Cooper, C. L., Scandura, T. A., and Schriesheim, C. A. (2005). Looking forward but learning from our past: potential challenges to developing authentic leadership theory and authentic leaders. *Leadership Quarterly*, 16, 474–93.

Davies, J. and Kourdi, J. (2010). *The Truth About Talent*. Chichester: Wiley.

Dickmann, M. and Baruch, Y. (2011). *Global Careers*. New York, NY: Routledge.

Farndale, E., Scullion, H., and Sparrow, P. (2010). The role of the corporate human resource function in global talent management. *Journal of World Business*, 45 (2), 161–8.

Festing, M., Schäfer, L., and Scullion, H. (2013). Talent management in medium-sized German companies: an explorative study and agenda for future research. *International Journal of Human Resource Management*, 24 (9), 1872–93.

Fitz-enz, J. (2000). *The Return on Investment of Human Capital: Measuring the Economic Value of Employee Performance*. New York, NY: American Management Association.

Garavan, T. N., Carbery, R., and Rock, A. (2012). Managing talent development: definition, scope and architecture. *European Journal of Training and Development*, 36 (1), 5–24.

Gardner, W. L., Avolio, B. J., and Walumbwa, F.O. (eds.) (2005). *Authentic Leadership Theory and Practice: Origins, Effects and Development*, Oxford, UK: Elsevier Science.

Goffee, R. and Jones, G. (2005). Managing authenticity: the paradox of leadership. *Harvard Business Review*, 83 (12), 87–94.

Gubman, E. L. (1998). *The Talent Solution: Aligning Strategy and People to Achieve Extraordinary Results*. New York, NY: McGraw-Hill.

Guthridge, M. and Komm, A. B. (2008). Why multinationals struggle to manage talent. *McKinsey Quarterly*, 4 (5), 19–25.

Hind, P., Wilson, A., and Lenssen, G. (2009). Developing leaders for sustainable business. *Corporate Governance*, 9 (1), 7–20.

Iles, P., Chuai, X., and Preece, D. (2010). Talent management and HRM in multinational companies in Beijing: definitions, differences and drivers. *Journal of World Business*, 45 (2), 179–89.

Kakabadse, N. K., Kakabadse, A. P., and Lee-Davies, L. (2009). CSR leaders road-map. *Corporate Governance*, 9 (1), 50–7.

KPMG (2012). *Rethinking Human Resources in a Changing World*, London: KPMG International.

Lewis, R. E. and Heckman, R. J. (2006). Talent management: a critical review. *Human Resource Management Review*, 16, 139–54.

Li, S. and Scullion, H. (2006). Bridging the distance: managing cross border knowledge holders. *Asia Pacific Journal of Management*, 23, 71–92.

(2010). Developing the local competence of expatriate managers for emerging markets: a knowledge based approach. *Journal of World Business*, 45 (2), 190–6.

Mayrhofer, W., Reichel, A., and Sparrow, P. R. (2012). Alternative forms of international working. In G. Stahl, I. Björkman, and S. Morris (eds.) *Handbook of Research into International HRM*, 2nd edn. London: Edward Elgar, pp. 300–27.

McDonnell, A., Collings, D. G., and Burgess, J. (2012). Asia Pacific perspectives on talent management. *Asia Pacific Journal of Human Resources*, 50 (4), 391–8.

Michaels, E., Handfield-Jones, H., and Axelrod, B. (2001). *The War for Talent*. Boston, MA: Harvard Business School Press.

Schiemann, W. A. (2009). *Reinventing Talent Management: How to Maximise Performance in the New Marketplace*. Hoboken, NJ: Wiley.

Schuler, R. S., Jackson, S. E., and Tarique, I. (2011). Global talent management and global talent challenges: strategic opportunities for IHRM. *Journal of World Business*, 46, 506–16.

Scullion, H. and Collings, D. G. (eds.) (2011). *Global Talent Management*. London: Routledge.

Scullion, H. and Starkey, K. (2000). In search of the changing role of the corporate human resource function in the international firm. *International Journal of Human Resource Management*, 11 (6), 1061–81.

Scullion, H., Collings, D. G., and Caligiuri, P. (2010). Global talent management. *Journal of World Business*, 45 (2), 105–8.

Senge, P. M. (2008). *The Necessary Revolution: How Individuals and Organizations are Working Together to Create a Sustainable World*. New York, NY: Doubleday.

Silzer, R. and Dowell, B. E. (2010). Strategic talent management matters. In R. Silzer and B. E. Dowell (eds.) *Strategy-Driven Talent Management: A Leadership Imperative*. San Franciscio, CA: Jossey-Bass–Society for Industrial and Organizational Psychology, pp. 3–72.

Skuza, A., Scullion, H., and McDonnell, A. (2013). An analysis of the talent management challenges in a post-communist country: the case of Poland. *International Journal of Human Resource Management*, 24 (3), 453–70.

Solimano, A. (2010). *International Migration in the Age of Crises and Globalization: Historical and Recent Experiences*. Cambridge: Cambridge University Press.

Sparrow, P. R. (2007). Globalization of HR at function level: four UK-based case studies of the international recruitment and selection process. *International Journal of Human Resource Management*, 18 (5), 144–66.

(2012). Global knowledge management and international HRM. In G. Stahl, I. Björkman, and S. Morris (eds.) *Handbook Of Research into International HRM*, 2nd edn. London: Edward Elgar, pp. 117–41.

Sparrow, P. R., Brewster, C., and Harris, H. (2004). *Globalizing Human Resource Management*. London: Routledge.

Sparrow, P. R., Hird, M., and Balain, S. (2011). *Talent Management: Time to Question the Tablets of Stone?* Centre for Performance-led HR White Paper 11/01. Lancaster University Management School.

Stahl, G. K., Bjorkman, I., Farndale, E., *et al.* (2012). Six principles of effective global talent management. *MIT Sloan Management Review*, 53, 25–32.

Tarique, I. and Schuler, R. S. (2010). Global talent management: literature review, integrative framework, and suggestions for further research. *Journal of World Business*, 45 (2), 122–33.

Thunnissen, M., Boselie, P., and Fruytier, B. (2013). A review of talent management: 'infancy or adolescence'? *International Journal of Human Resource Management*, 24 (9), 1744–61.

Tung, R. and Lazarova, M. (2006). Brain drain versus brain gain: an exploratory study of ex-host country nationals in Central and Eastern Europe. *International Journal of Human Resource Management*, 17, 1853–72.

(2007). The human resource challenge to outward foreign investment aspirations from emerging countries: the case of China. *International Journal of Human Resource Management*, 18 (5), 868–89.

Vaiman, V. and Collings, D. G. (2013). Talent management: advancing the field. *International Journal of Human Resource Management*, 24 (9), 1737–43.

Vaiman, V., Scullion, H., and Collings, D. (2012). Talent management decision making. *Management Decision*, 50 (5), 925–41.

Valverde, M., Scullion, H., and Ryan, G. (2013). Talent management in Spanish medium-sized organizations. *International Journal of Human Resource Management*, 24 (9), 1832–52.

2 | Multiple lenses on talent management: definitions and contours of the field

PAUL SPARROW, HUGH SCULLION,
AND IBRAIZ TARIQUE

2.1 Introduction

As noted in the previous chapter, there have been a number of different philosophies that have come to dominate the field of talent management. Collings and Mellahi (2009) helpfully outlined these different philosophies as follows.

1. People approach: talent management as a categorization of people.
2. Practices approach: talent management as the presence of key HRM practices.
3. Position approach: talent management as the identification of pivotal positions.
4. Strategic-pools approach: talent management as internal talent pools and succession planning.

These are often presented as competing approaches to talent management, or definitions of it, alternative conceptualizations, and better or worse ways of doing it.

In this chapter we:

- use this way of categorizing approaches to talent management to organize our discussion about the nature of strategic talent management
- build on the categorization by showing how each philosophy has come about and evolved, its essence, and some of the assumptions it is based on
- lay out the different assumptions they make about organizational effectiveness, how they have shaped mainstream thinking, and the different strategies they argue are necessary to achieve it
- provide a range of critiques of talent practice, notably the people philosophy
- put the four philosophies into a framework to help think about, and position, the design of different organizational talent-management systems and determine when each should become most dominant.

In all of this, we ask the question "what makes someone talented" and outline four sources of capital that become important in answering this question. We therefore build the argument that:

- the four philosophies represent a range of dilemmas that any talent system has to deal with
- rather than being alternatives, in practice most organizations use various combinations of them
- however, the approaches need to be accommodated into the design of talent-management systems more sensibly
- talent management and knowledge management are becoming much more closely intertwined.

The chapter concludes by developing two significant implications for practice:

- organizations need to develop the capability to better align the design of their talent-management architecture with its underlying philosophies.
- we need to broaden out our assessment of talent.

The arguments in this chapter are intended, then, to set up the agenda for Part II of the book, which goes on to look at the changing intellectual boundaries that are coming to define the field of strategic talent management.

However, we begin by putting the four philosophies into a framework (see Figure 2.1) that can be used to think about, and position, the design of different organizational talent-management systems and determine when each should become most dominant. The reasons why we place each philosophy where we have on the figure are explained, and should become more apparent, later in the chapter when we review each talent philosophy. For now, however, we explain the framework.

Figure 2.1 has two axes. The first axis is whether the focus of the talent-management philosophy is on the management of certain segments of people (which we argue is the case with the people approach and the strategic-pools approach) or is more on the systems and practices that are used (which we argue is the case in the practices and positions approaches). This is a fairly easy categorization to make.

The second axis concerns the level of business-model change that is taking place in the organization. Where there is a very high level of

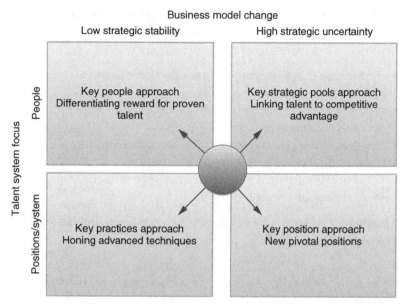

Figure 2.1 Matching different talent philosophies to the strategic context

business-model change then there is strategic uncertainty within the organization. It becomes important to analyse the business model and identify from it, from an organizational design perspective, which roles, positions, and jobs become central to the effective delivery of the strategy, almost regardless of the people in those jobs (the position approach). And, in analysing how competitive advantage is actually delivered through that business model, which parts of the organization and pools of talent will have the most bearing upon organizational effectiveness (the strategic-pools approach). If the level of flux in business models is relatively low – strategic stability – then it becomes easier to predict who will be successful and what constitutes being talented. The organizations can therefore pursue a people approach with a degree of validity and also, knowing what constitutes being talented, it becomes easier to hone and improve the specific practices that form part of the talent system (i.e., also pursue the practices approach). This level of business-model change (a construct from the field of strategy) then has very significant implications for the type of focus around talent management that is needed.

In Chapter 1 we argued that there has been increasing demand that we put the "strategy" back into talent management. If we are to incorporate the word "strategy" into the debate about talent management, we need to think much more fundamentally about what such a linkage entails. One way of doing this is to use the idea of business models, which pulls together a number of developments within the field of strategic management. There have been three main developments in this field: the advent of the competitive-positioning perspective; followed by the development of the resource-based view of the firm(see Chapters 3 and 4 for how this view should make us think about talent management); and then as a consequence of the advent of technological developments and the potential for radical changes to their strategic contribution, development of the concept of "business models." Organizations are using the language of business models to articulate what they consider is the dominant *performance logic* inherent in their strategy (Johnson, Melin, and Whittington, 2003). Through their strategy, they are continually seeking ways to exploit the knowledge that they (and their collective talent) have, and the upstream and downstream information that flows along their value chain. They are aware that they may be bypassed by existing intermediaries in that value chain, and so continually explore new business models and other improvements that might be made to the value system (that value may be economic or social). The term "business model" therefore applies to the framework and analysis of two key issues (Magretta, 2002; Yip, 2004; Schweizer, 2005; Shafer, Smith, and Linder, 2005; Chesbrough, 2007):

- how the organization creates value: by defining of a series of activities (from raw materials through to the final customer) that will yield a new product or service, and explaining how value is added throughout the various activities
- how the organization's strategy captures a portion of that value – by establishing how a unique resource, asset, or position within that series of strategic activities can help the organization enjoy a competitive advantage.

It is a *business performance logic*, or storyline, that can be used to weave together and demonstrate the importance of a range of core components. By modelling how performance is dependent on the management of all these components, brought together as part of a greater whole, organizations are better placed to derive value from their strategy. Talent is just one of the components, but a central one nonetheless, important for the execution of a strategy (Sparrow *et al.*, 2010). Business-model change has deep implications for the performance logic inside the organization, the sorts of insights that talent might be able to contribute, the nature of executive talent, the way employees must be managed, and with what talent of whatever level would be expected to engage with.

From the strategic HRM and organizational learning literatures, we know that during a process of business-model change, HR functions have to consider the significance and depth of knowledge change associated with the new model on the specification for talent. Kang, Morris, and Snell (2007) drew upon the earlier distinction made by Henderson and Clark (1990) between two different types of knowledge that are needed about how organizational performance is delivered within a business model. People talented for a particular business model know how to combine both: component knowledge (knowledge of the business model's parts rather than the whole); and architectural knowledge (a shared understanding of the interconnection of all the components, or how things must fit together, in order to deliver effective performance). The ability to bring together the known constituents or knowledge bases associated with a new business model is "mission critical" (organizational learning experts call this "architectural capability").

Business-model change, then, alters the strategic value that is attached to particular types of knowledge. It also changes the way that different types of knowledge have to relate to each other. Of course, knowledge represents the starting point, but once this knowledge has become internalized into an organization, and is supported by all of the supporting systems, structures, and processes, a deeper capability has been created.

By using the extent of business-model change – and strategic uncertainty – as a contingency to help think about the type of focus that the talent-management system should focus on, organizations can deal with the "talent for what?" question. While everyone has talents, and parts of the system may deal with this challenge, when it comes to the purpose of the organization, it becomes clearer what talents are supposed to be used for, and which talents are more appropriate than others.

But first we must understand the different contexts – or political spaces – that HR functions typically find themselves operating in through the design of their talent-management system.

2.2 The people approach: talent management as a categorization of people

We begin with the key-people approach. We have argued that this philosophy focuses on the people (not the practices) aspects of talent management, and is best suited when the level of business-model change is low, which means that it has been easier for people to demonstrate their superior performance and potential for a known business problem.

Is talent management really about the management of top elites, an important, but small, handful of key people? Certainly the Collins English Dictionary defines talent as "innate ability, aptitude, or faculty, especially when unspecified; above average ability." There are, then, employees with unique skill sets – skills that are rare and much sought after by competing organizations. These talented individuals are hard to find and therefore difficult to replace. They add a disproportionate amount of value to the organization compared to other employees. From a people perspective, a talent-management strategy starts with identifying these individual "star" performers, who are deemed a source of competitive advantage. The philosophy then advocates differentiating the management of these people using practices that are designed to attract, retain, and develop these high-performance and high-potential employees.

The people perspective on talent has been suggested by a number of writers, but the most famous – perhaps now infamous – exposition of the position was the book titled *The War for Talent* (Michaels, Handfield-Jones, and Axelrod, 2001). There were, however, three enabling concepts that preceded many of the ideas in that book.

2.2.1 The enabling concepts behind a people philosophy

The first core enabling concept underpinning a differentiated approach to talent management is what has become known as the 9-box model of performance–potential. It is very hard to find the original ownership of this model – it began to appear and be cut and pasted into consulting presentations and in designs for organizations' talent-management systems, so a number of people lay claim to it. Hird, Whelan, and Hammady (2010), however, traced the ideas back to an article by

Odiorne (1984) in which he recommended utilizing the Boston Consulting Group strategic portfolio matrix as the basis for constructing what he termed a "human resources portfolio." By the early 1990s, many HR functions were basing their high-potential identification and succession-management practices around frameworks that were derivatives of Odiorne's HR portfolio (Sparrow, Hird, and Balain, 2011) and this portfolio approach provided an influential framework for early talent-system architecture. Odiorne (1984) felt that potential was best seen as the likelihood of the job holder making a future contribution to the organization, and this was felt to be based on six factors: past performance; intelligence and aptitude; future availability to the organization; interests and desires; supply and demand factors; and biographical information.

Figure 2.2 summarizes the evolution of talent-management practice, from the original strategic product market portfolio, through the HR portfolio, to the now ubiquitous 9-box model. Note the subtle shifts in language in the lower quadrants: from "deadwood" (in Figure 2.2b) to "requires close scrutiny" (in Figure 2.2c)! However, the message was clear. Human resources were the function who categorized people, and people represented a strategic portfolio.

The second core enabling concept, dating back to the work of Shoshana Zuboff (1988), was the assumption that "informated" workplaces were changing the power of talent. She argued that technological innovations and information technology (IT), in creating more fluid, social, distributed, and less hierarchical work arrangements, were impacting the value of talent. In an informated workplace, individuals and groups could now create the meaning of the information they used. These shifts were upgrading the need for people who had the power to understand (intellective skills) business and social opportunities that now existed. Such high-value, difficult-to-replace technical talent was best seen as a strategic asset.

Finally, the third core-enabling concept, based on writing about the individualization of organizations and the importance of management competences, was the shift from a pay-for-the-job approach to a pay-for-the-person approach in selection systems (Lawler, 1994). A pay-for-the-job approach assumed that jobs could be designed, evaluated, and differentiated dependent on their size and complexity. Employees were fitted to the job (or fitted to the broader organization

(a)

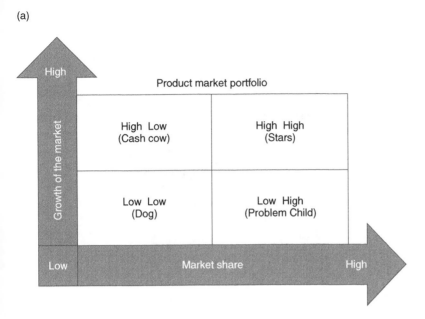

(b)

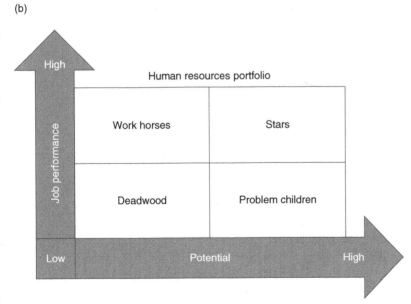

Figure 2.2 From (a) the BCG matrix, through (b) a human resources portfolio, to (c) the 9-box model of performance potential

(c)

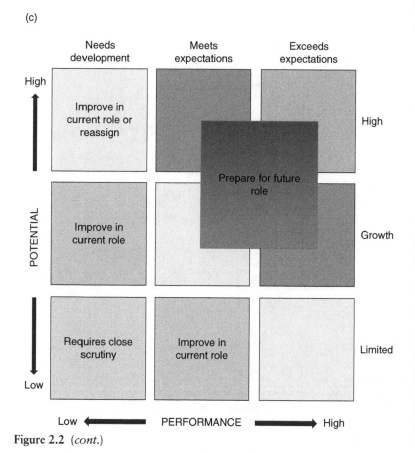

Figure 2.2 (*cont.*)

culture or values in which jobs sat) through selection. A pay-for-the-person approach argued that jobs were too flexible, uncertain, and unpredictable to be "sized" and it was more appropriate to design HR systems around highly skilled people, who would have the capabilities to design their own jobs in appropriate ways. However, for Lawler (2008), reflecting his organization effectiveness and design perspective, while star-talent management is necessary, it is not sufficient. Organizations have to seek a balance between sourcing great individual talent and melding individual talent into a collective organizational capability, and ensuring how their knowledge is turned into performance. This requires equal attention to the processes that reliably create talent.

2.2.2 The war for talent narrative

Building on these foundations, the next idea was that there was a *war for talent* and in order to win this, organizations needed not just to manage a portfolio of employees, but to concentrate effort on those most able to help the organization edge to victory. This was to stress two competitions – one between individual talent (an interpersonal talent-management focus) and one within the individual so that they could be of their best (an intrapersonal talent perspective). This was first expressed by Steven Hankin of McKinsey and Company in 1997, and further developed in a series of McKinsey articles by Elaine Chambers and colleagues (Chambers *et al.*, 1998), Beth Axelrod, Helen Handfield-Jones, and Ed Michaels (Axelrod, Handfield-Jones, and Michaels, 2002), and then Matthew Guthridge and colleagues (Gutheridge, Komm, and Lawson, 2006). It was argued that businesses were at a moment of dramatic change – an inflexion point – that required a significant shift in policy. Based on a survey of 6,000 managers in across 56 US organizations conducted in 2000 it was argued that organizations in the top 20% of self-identified talent-management practices outperformed their industry's mean return to shareholders by 22% (Axelrod, Handfield-Jones, and Welsh, 2001). For the majority of organizations the term talent management, and the consequent sets of activity, has its prime focus on unearthing those employees who qualify for the term "high potentials" and, if they do not exist internally, searching for such employees outside the organization.

In his book *Successful Talent Strategies*, Sears (2003) argued the McKinsey book on *The War for Talent* (Michaels, Handfield-Jones, and Axelrod, 2001) was describing a situation in which organizations were designing competitive HR strategies in the struggle of employers to land and "upskill" employees in a cut-throat free-agent employment market. Under this philosophy, rather than just being a desirable HR program, talent management is a leadership imperative – a cultural *mindset*. The whole HR system of an organization has to be aligned to such a performance-led talent strategy that makes it clear that only the very best are recruited, retained, and the rest are slowly exited from the system. Talent was defined as the sum of a person's abilities (gifts, skills, knowledge, experience, intelligence, judgment, attitude, character, and drive) and as a sharp strategic mind, leadership ability, emotional maturity, communication skills, the ability to attract and inspire other talented people, entrepreneurial instincts, functional skills, and the ability to deliver results (Michaels, Handfield-Jones, and Axelrod, 2001).

Under a people philosophy, all the HR systems – but particularly performance appraisal, rewards and incentives, work or job design – are designed around a pay-for-the-person as opposed to pay-for-the-job philosophy. Under a war-for-talent philosophy the employer brand is also positioned to attract these people – the stars – and then to exceed their expectations. Human resource management policy was also influenced by marketing thinking (see also Chapter 6) through the adoption of employee-value propositions (EVPs). In the same way that organizations asked why should you buy my product or service – they were encouraged to ask why would a highly talented person want to work in my organization? In answering this question, organizations used the resultant proposition to drive attraction and retention behavior, and to convey a clear statement of some of the more explicit obligations that the organization would commit to for talent.

Under this philosophy talent management is all about differentiation of employees – infamously into A, B, and C players. This means assessing the performance and potential of employees and pursuing an elite strategy, i.e., investing in the A players by giving them promotion, compensation, and development opportunities, affirming the potential of B players, and acting decisively (either quickly re-engaging or more likely removing) C players.

A number of consulting firms also now argue the need for workforce segmentation – to isolate particularly critical workforce segments based on a combination of their needs as consumers of the talent system – what critical talent cares about most – or based on some kind of strategic differentiation of their importance, such as their contribution to the revenue and their linkage to the value chain (O'Donnell, 2009; Watson Wyatt Worldwide, 2009). It is hard to see how the latter actually differs from the A, B, and C player mentality – though perhaps there is a bit more science behind the differentiation.

2.2.3 Critiques of the people perspective

The people perspective has attracted much criticism. Some of the criticism is directed at the nature of the philosophy and its underlying assumptions – that individual talent is one of the most significant sources of competitive advantage. Some of it simply concerns the level of balance between this approach and the other parts of a talent system. Some of it reflects ideological discomfort with a differentiated approach to talent. Some of it reflects an ideological – or cultural – discomfort with some of the practices that seem to have come hand in hand with the philosophy, for example the level of reward given to those differentiated by the system, i.e., the problem being the by-product, which is high or perceived over-inflated salaries.

The philosophy was famously attacked, many years before the global financial crisis legitimized some of the discomfort, by Pfeffer (2001), who argued that a mindset that emphasized a fight to source talented individuals was hazardous to the organization's health. We call this the locus of organizational effectiveness critique. It essentially argued that the approach assumed the wrong fulcrum for improving effectiveness (i.e., people, or stars, at the expense of systems). Anyway, it went on to say that given the way people behave in organizations, such a system would create a set of side effects that would nullify any gains.

The consultants at McKinsey were preaching at Enron what they believed about themselves. They were there looking for people who had the talent to think outside the box. It never occurred to them that, if everyone had to think out of the box, maybe it was the box that needed fixing. (Pfeffer, 2001)

Pfeffer's key objections were:

1. The star approach to talent shifts the emphasis onto individual performance at the expense of teamwork and gives rise to a system that can create disharmony between employees who otherwise need to work collaboratively. HR practices that go along with such a approach, for example individual-based performance-related pay, can make it hard for sharing of knowledge, ideas, and best practices.
2. Celebration of individual brilliance creates an elitist attitude marked by arrogance and can lead to a poor learning attitude, where those dubbed as "stars" have their way over an otherwise perfectly good idea but coming from a "B" or "C" player.
3. Most organizations that adopt the "A" player approach to talent management rely heavily on monetary incentives to attract and retain these key individuals, making this approach non-strategic and easily imitable.
4. Labelling (especially as a C player) can lead to a negative self-fulfilling prophecy. Lower expectations led to fewer resources

being available, demoralization, and thus poor performance; exactly the opposite becomes true for the "A" players.

5. The "star" perspective on talent suggests individual ability is a fixed invariant trait – a dangerous assumption and not supported by research on careers. Performance appraisals are susceptible to the horn and halo effect, with past performances biasing judgments of current performance and future potential.

A second critique can be called the "cognitive limits" problem. Work on the psychology of strategic management by cognitive psychologists, again preceding the global financial crisis asked "how could organizations with high profile and historically successful track records fall prey to catastrophic chains of events that led to their demise?" It was drawing attention to the natural limitations of strategic leaders having to operate in a hypercompetitive business system – the problems of strategic leadership in a world turned upside down.

[Strategic leaders] cannot hide behind economic rationality and analysis, and have to admit... they may be as lost as the rest of us, sailing and experimenting in uncharted waters, tentatively seeking answers to what are increasingly loaded questions, and understanding increasingly the limits to their power and the "downside" to their decisions... [strategic leadership] is inextricably linked with the management of strategic risk... This managerial role specification has given rise to concerns about the "cognitive limits" of managers. Are they capable of such skilful thought? (Sparrow, 2000: p. 17)

Strategic insight fails to materialize because of limitations in the mental models of strategic leaders, either because the organization proves incapable of implementing what they see to be important based on evidence or insights (called the knowing–doing problem) or because so-called talent do not act on the basis of good evidence (called the doing–knowing problem). The necessary insights are often unconscious, constrained by managerial beliefs and ideologies, and involve different ways of thinking about and conceptualizing competitive forces and business models that result in new and innovative offerings. The locus of strategy making invariably does not reside in the upper echelons of the organization, and implementation is everyone's business.

Research on strategic competence (Hodgkinson and Sparrow, 2002; Hodgkinson and Healey, 2008, 2011) saw it as concerning the ability of organizations (or more precisely their members) to acquire, store, recall, interpret, and act upon information of relevance to the longer term survival and well-being of the organization. The key message was that, in practice, being a strategically competent organization was a collective capability, beyond the limits of even the most talented individuals, that requires:

being agile, open to the environment, capable of picking up those weak signals indicative of the need for change, which are then selected, filtered, stored, recalled and interpreted in a fashion that enables the organization to respond as appropriate... Knowledge management is thus central to this process. (Hodgkinson and Sparrow, 2002: p. 3)

Along with the "cognitive limits" critique, has come a third critique that asks whether the creation of organizational capability requires more than just the performance of individual stars. These arguments are developed in both Chapter 3, which looks at how strategists see organizational capability, and Chapter 4, which looks at the role of expert talent. But for now we can signal that before the global financial crisis broke out, there was some cautionary research warning about the risks of over-emphasizing a star approach to talent management. Groysberg, Nanda, and Nohria (2004) studied 1,052 star stock analysts working for 78 investment banks from 1988 to 1996, and found that when star employees moved across to other organizations, they were seldom able to repeat their high performance. They cited a 2001 study of mutual fund managers by Baks (2003), which found that just 30% of a star's performance could be attributed to individual ability – 70% of it was due to resources and qualities specific to the organization such as reputation, information technology, leadership training, and team chemistry. Subsequent to the global financial crisis, academic research on CEO failures (Stein and Capape, 2009) similarly argued that a good part of individual performance is driven by good systems prevalent in the organization, rather than just due to individual brilliance. Talent declines as CEOs change organizations, indicating that performance is also due to the organization's resources, systems, processes, and networks of people.

Building then on such perspectives came a fourth key critique, noted also in Chapter 1, which we can call the egalitarian critique. There are many contrasts that might be drawn in terms of talent-management philosophies, but one of the most obvious ones is whether the practices that come along with the philosophy are associated with a view that talent management is best focused on the management of a small elite – those high-performance and high-potential individuals – or whether a more egalitarian, universal, and inclusive focus is also needed, one that looks at talent-management practice as it relates to the majority of employees (Collings and Mellahi, 2009; Schuler, Jackson, and Tarique, 2011; Scullion and Collings, 2011).

2.2.4 Summary: a false dichotomy?

Given the above, we would argue that putting to one side the problem of the level of reward given to talent (which is a separate issue to believing that some people can have a differential contribution to a strategy), an elite approach to talent management might form part of a talent system. But it can only really be valid where there is a low level of strategic uncertainty, i.e., where the strategy of the host firm is known, and any prior record of success might reasonably allow a separation of individual versus collective capability.

However, the elite–egalitarian distinction is a false dichotomy and debates about whether talent management should be defined in an elitist or an egalitarian way can sometimes be a product of the ideological preferences of the researcher (or pick up attitudes to the rewards issue). Most talent systems are not really either/or, but combine both approaches. This becomes evident when a more "problem-based" definition of talent management is taken. Consider Stahl *et al.*'s (2012) definition of talent management as an organization's ability to attract, select, develop, and retain key talented employees in a global context. What most organizations do to address this challenge is to bring to bear various HR strategies (components of practice) – some driven by an elite philosophy and others by an egalitarian one.

An egalitarian issue might be, for example, how do we source a plant with a sufficient level of skills (which in themselves might be skills at different levels of complexity from entry level to intermediate or advanced) in order that the plant achieve a sufficient level of productivity. There need be no ideological attachment to an egalitarian approach – it is just a matter of requisite practices. The answer might include building relationships with certain schools and universities, influencing the national educational syllabus to improve the supply of certain types of knowledge, releasing managerial time to work with organizations down the supply chain, building the brand of the organization among specific target skill groups, and so forth. The practices might be classed as egalitarian in that they can impact the whole workforce, but later on in the talent management life cycle, the individuals so managed might have moved into a career space managed by a more individualized, elite, and differentiated philosophy, because the problem faced by the organization is one dependent on the qualities and performance of a handful of people. The more wide-scale activities that relate to the workforce as a whole often, however, still come under the structural control of a resourcing director, while the more "internal career" and elitist sets of activities fall into the lap of the talent director.

2.3 The practices approach: talent management as the presence of key HRM practices

The second talent management philosophy is the practices approach. While the people approach argues that the differentiator for high-performing firms is *not* sophisticated HRM processes, but rather a fundamental belief held by leaders throughout the organization about the importance of individual talent and the creation of internal "talent markets," the practices approach acknowledges that there is a need for a dedicated set of advanced and sophisticated practices. For many organizations, talent management is seen as a collection of key activities, components, or practices, all of which need to be connected and integrated.

We argue that this philosophy is needed to counterbalance the attention on people, but that it too is more important where the level of business-model change is relatively stable. Hence, it becomes possible to capture effective performance and build it into the various key tools, such as the assessment centers. Prediction becomes more manageable rather than generic and speculative.

So, in addition to managing people, or broader populations, talent architectures need to bring to bear a suite of practices that enable this management to take place.

What might the practices really need to be? There are different prescriptions, and they are usually case-study based. Fernández-Aráoz, Graysberg, and Nohria (2011) found that only 15% of major organizations in North America and Asia, and 30% in Europe, believe they have enough qualified successors for qualified positions. Using firms with a reputation for sophisticated talent processes, such as GE, Unilever, PepsiCo, and Shell, they identified three important activities: the establishment of clear strategic priorities that shape the way high-potential leaders must be groomed, aligning the programmes with corporate strategy; careful selection of candidates and communication of who is in the pool to the rest of the organization through a combination of nominations and objective assessments; and the active management of the talent pool to ensure development, reward, and retention, by rotation through matched jobs.

Sparrow, Hird, and Balain (2011) used the example of the consumer multinational Diageo to exemplify this integration process. It considered that in order to build talent it needed: a sophisticated performance-development review process; assessment of both an individual's contribution to *organizational-level* capabilities (such as consumer insight, business-system transformation, and rapid capability development) coupled with more traditional individual leadership competences (such as living the values, emotional energy, ideas generation), embedded in a system and surrounding package of HR practices (including deployment-decision forums, high-potential review processes, external-resourcing strategies, reward and recognition policies driven by data from employee motivation surveys, talent benchmarking system based on 360-degree feedback and personal development plans, and a partnership approach with managers driven by personal coaching). The latter attention to partnership and within-the-person development (intrapersonal talent perspective) has its origins in the literature on giftedness and sporting achievement, and in stressing the optimization of an individual's performance (be-my-best) it highlights practices that are well beyond those traditionally associated with HRM – reflective coaching, avoidance of career and performance derailment, and so forth.

In summary, although there is no agreement about the exact bundle of differentiating practices that should be involved, the thinking behind a practices approach is similar to that seen in the high-performance work practices debates within HRM. Organizations need an additional, or a strategically integrated, set of practices to be able to say they are good at talent management. Typically, these key activities, or components, revolve around:

- identifying and recruiting talent (analysis of labor pools, benchmarking competitor strategies, decentralizing or centralizing recruitment strategies, co-ordinating preferred suppliers, establishing brand and reputation among key employee segments)

- attracting talent to the organization (creation of employee-value propositions, management of an employer brand)
- minimizing attrition through engagement and retention (effective onboarding, aligning rewards and recognition structures, improving line-management skills, and engagement with talent-retention initiatives)
- identifying key internal talent (systematic and effective approaches to affirm individuals with the status of talent, high-potential identification systems, identify the roles that are most talent dependent, and use of assessment instruments and frameworks)
- managing talent flows (developing effective succession systems, creating flexibility in internal mobility, career management and planning systems, succession management)
- developing employees (coaching and mentoring, flexible portfolios of development activities, learning opportunities and options for employees, team-learning processes, strategic and operational leadership-development programmes, coaching)
- delivering performance (organization talent-review processes, linking data on organizational performance to the selection of talent, stretching the performance of talented individuals, managing underperformance).

Organizations may then choose to build suites of sophisticated practices, activities, and processes. They may sharpen and align the focus of this suite of practices, and ensure that the activities build high-quality data. They may use this data to reduce risk, and ensure that it serves to help calibrate people across different parts of the organization and different geographies. These component practices have to be more than just a string of HR programs, practices, and processes. They need to form part of a broader system driven by the business strategy and must be managed as a core business process (Gubman and Green, 2007; Silzer and Dowell, 2010).

2.4 The position approach: talent management as the identification of pivotal positions

The third talent-management philosophy picks up on the Pfeffer (2001) critique of the people perspective. Huselid, Beatty, and Becker (2005) noted that while some HR professionals have ethical objections to classifying people as "A, B, or C," there might not be the same emotional reactivity to classifying positions – or segmenting jobs – within the organization. "A positions" have two major characteristics: a disproportionate role in an organization's ability in executing some part of its strategy, but wide variability in the quality of work displayed by the employees in that position. Although different ways of identifying key positions are used, for Huselid, Beatty, and Becker (2005):

- A positions are strategic, require autonomous decision-making, have performance-based compensation, create disproportionate value for the organization as compared to other positions, and the consequences of mistakes (in job design or in hiring the wrong employee) can have serious financial repercussions.
- B positions are largely support roles that may be strategic for the company but the skills required to perform them are common and there may be little variability in the performance of employees in these positions.
- C positions may be required for the company to function but are not strategic to its success and may easily be outsourced or even weeded out.

Organizations do not need A players throughout their operations; just in A positions. "A positions" can also be more enriched and give substantial job autonomy to the employees in those positions. By building an element of intrinsic reward into these positions for those who seek job enrichment at their workplace, the talent-management strategy can be less reliant on monetary rewards, making the strategy more acceptable to the wider organization.

For Collings and Mellahi (2009) too, strategic talent management must include activities and processes that involve the systematic identification of key positions that differentially contribute to the organization's sustainable competitive advantage. This must be accompanied by the development of a talent pool of high-potential and high-performance incumbents to fill these roles. There must also be an HR architecture that facilitates the filling of these positions with competent incumbents and differentiates their management to ensure their continued commitment to the organization.

By implication, in this perspective, talent management is no longer just linked to top-tier employees of the organization. These positions can be anywhere and talent management truly becomes a company-wide strategy. These positions do not just include those near the strategic core of the organization – they may be a key part of the operating core. Work on employee engagement with McDonalds, as predicted by the service-profit chain, showed that customer-facing crew members become the "A position" (Sparrow *et al.*, 2010). They also found that 59% of HR directors reported that the organizational capabilities featured in their planning processes were new to the strategy; 40% reported that there had been a shift in the jobs, roles, or skill groups that were consequently seen as critical to performance.

This approach then de-links the talent-management strategy from leadership development. It makes talent management more contextual and dependent on the business model.

We have two observations on this approach.

1. While it is always needed and invariably used as part of a talent system, it becomes of particular important when there is a high level of business-model change. When there is a high level of strategic uncertainty, and a new business model is in operation, the relative contribution of important roles to the success of the organization changes. The success (or failure) of the business model may become crucially dependent on the job design of a small number of mission-critical jobs – key positions.
2. However, the assessment of how "valuable" is a role is complex, and the value varies depending on the judgment made. Sparrow *et al.* (2010) use three judgments: value creation, value leverage, and value protection. The latter involves ensuring value created does not get lost and this requires the design and maintenance of effective governance, constructive surfacing of risks, protection of brand and reputation, and the ability to retain capabilities. Often it is only an accident that shows the true value of jobs. The strategic importance of jobs needs an assessment of their role in all three aspects of value.

This leads us into the fourth perspective on talent management, which we argue must also be given more attention during periods of significant business-model change.

2.5 The strategic-pools approach: talent management as internal talent pools, human capital, and human-resource planning

In a refinement of the positions perspective, Boudreau and Ramstad (2006, 2007) introduce the notion of "pivotal talent pools." These are groupings and clusters of talent (not just positions) where human-capital investments make the biggest difference to strategic success – because the improvements in capabilities brought about by investment will have the most significant impact on competitiveness. The approach is underwritten by both human-capital theory – which argues that the costs associated with the development and retention of talent should be viewed as investments on behalf of the firm – and expectancy theory – which argues that people can make choices about the investments they choose to make in themselves and so will make more investment if there are signals that they are in an area of especial importance to the organization. From this perspective, talent management requires differential investments in special groups of employees who have strategic importance to the organization – pivotal talent.

While the focus is still on pivotal groups of people in whom investments should be made to achieve greatest leverage, it is the effective use of *metrics* and a more open form of strategic thinking needed to identify these pools, that differentiates this approach from the last.

It is also driven by practices associated with human-capital management. These include human-capital (or workforce) analytics or accounting (HCA), which blends techniques such as forecasting principles and scenario planning to create forecasts of the current and future workforce, often looking at key roles under various business scenarios. This in turn is evolving toward strategic workforce planning (SWP), aimed at identifying the characteristics of human capital needed to achieve a strategic objective and then scaling the activities needed. Strategic workforce planning tends to use a combination of data and analytics to create insight into relative value of specific talent to the execution of an important strategy, and the necessary investments and actions needed to avoid any loss of value. These insights typically include:

- translating the organizational capabilities articulated in the strategy into specifications for talent
- using frameworks to segment the existing or target talent population in different ways (either on the basis of the centrality of the roles to the strategy, or through the application of marketing and consumer thinking and treating talent segments on the basis of their expectations of the organization)
- assessing the consequences or feasibility of the above for build-or-buy talent strategies.

The workforce plan in essence becomes the talent component to the business strategy. Strategic workforce planning approaches are generally seen as a subset of talent management, although in terms of the HRM structure and reporting relationships, this is not always the case.

This human-capital planning perspective is typically seen in the work of a number of writers such as Boudreau and colleagues (Boudreau and Ramstad, 2005, 2006, 2007; Boudreau, 2010; Boudreau and Jesuthasan, 2011), Ingham (2007), and Cappelli (2008). For Cappelli (2008), talent management is the process through which employers anticipate and meet their needs for human capital. The word capital reflects a concept from economics, which denotes potentially valuable assets (Nahapiet, 2011).

How do you create value from your human capital? For Boudreau and colleagues, HR functions have to reposition themselves so that they can better inform key business decisions. Many of these decisions either depend upon or have an impact on talent resources. Line managers therefore need to be provided with better frameworks, data, and HR analytics that will help inform their decision-making. Boudreau and Ramstad (2007) originally defined the goal of what they called a "talentship decision science" as being "to increase the success of the organization by improving decisions that depend on or impact talent resources" (p. 25).

This perspective argues that organizations draw their energy from people, their individual strengths, interests, and motivations. However, people and organizations must be better aligned with long-term business strategy in order to provide a basis for differentiation and competitive advantage. Human resources and business leaders are implored to broaden their traditional focus and develop frameworks to identify which decisions about human capital are most crucial, and then to connect these decisions logically to questions of organizational effectiveness. They apply the principles of decision sciences, such as finance and marketing, to the field of talent management in order to link superior human capital and talent, such as Zuboff's (1988) technological innovators, to sustainable competitive advantage.

As with the positions approach, pivotal talent pools might exist in undervalued parts of the organization. They use the examples of FedEx, where the top few critical components of its success are shipping time and efficiency, and Disney, for whom it is the visitor experience in the park. Rather than pilots, logistics designers, and senior managers having the greatest performance impact, some of the largest opportunities to improve on-time performance and customer satisfaction lie with couriers and dispatchers, whose quality contributes significantly to the effectiveness or ineffectiveness of the entire system.

Despite promoting a strategic-talent-pools perspective, they note that decisions around talent are rarely optimal (Boudreau, 2010; Boudreau and Jesuthasan, 2011).

• They are not based on such frameworks, but are still driven by the informed preferences, or intuitive instincts, that senior managers have of the visible talent within their organization.
• Even when informed by data provided by HR functions, they often lack a synthesis, provision of usable metrics and analysis, or come with important nuances explained (Vaiman, Scullion, and Collings, 2012).
• They are also bounded by the natural cognitive limits of managers who have neither the time, capability, or inclination to access data about all global talent – the inclination is to select those who are "good enough" based on previous experiences and beliefs about talent (Mäkela, Björkman, and Ehrnrooth, 2010).

For Cascio and Boudreau (2010, 2012) the answer to these problems is to use a risk-optimization, management, and mitigation framework to look at HR strategy, and strategic workforce planning. Human-capital strategies have to be built on the reduction of uncertainty, elimination of bad outcomes, and insurance against bad outcomes. While cautioning against the illusion of predictability, this might still include efforts at increased precision in predictions about future supply and demand for skills, or the application of quality-control tools to important HR processes (such as talent management) to achieve the same "low-defect" rigor seen in engineering and operations processes. Given the challenge of global-talent risks, and looming talent and skills scarcities that threaten the strategic initiatives of organizations, they argue that organizations *need* HR functions capable of creating talent strategies. However, such strategies require a move away from the traditional HR framing of the problem (which would be one of minimizing the risk of talent being unprepared for the future by developing generic competences applied across the board), into the development of appropriate business tools (Boudreau, 2010). These might, for example, include the use of portfolio analysis to enable choices about investments versus expected returns across several uncertain future scenarios.

A risk-aligned talent strategy would balance the risks in talent planning, with investments in talent for several future scenarios, according to their relative likelihood and risk. Governance of talent systems, and the management of risk, have become important considerations.

For Sparrow and Balain (2008), looking at organizations operating in environments where the business model was fluid and the successful technologies were as yet still to be demonstrated, part of this management of risk was seen by them taking different "talent options" out against the various projected developments of their business model. They were attempting to "future proof" their organization by attracting pools of talent associated with several alternative ways in which the organization might develop. The expense of having competing pools of talent was nothing compared to the cost of not having the winning pool.

Therefore, in situations of continuous business-model change, organizations need to adopt a risk-management approach, and this requires the development of the capability to take out positions or options on key talent (talent seen more in the context of expert talent discussed in Chapter 4).

2.6 Implications for practice: linking the capital that talent possess to the strategy

What does a more strategic lens on talent management suggest is important? In this section we summarize some of the implications for practice from our analysis of different talent-management philosophies. When we say that we need to link talent more *to* strategy, we actually mean that we need to link talent to the strategy *for* whatever the performance outcome of that strategy might be (a strategy for innovation, customer centricity, globalization) and we also need to embed that individual talent into the collective wisdom across talent, and into the broader capabilities that the organization has managed to build.

The field of talent management may appear to look very normative, but as this chapter has shown, this can be deceptive. Underneath the adoption of headline practices the reality of practice is often very messy, very nuanced. While some decisions within the scope of talent directors clearly can be much improved by adopting, for example, a decision-science perspective, as noted earlier, looking across the wide spectrum of issues that talent directors must advise on, we see talent management more as a craft, not a science, certainly when it comes to making the political decisions as to how best to design the whole system. The field is clearly very context dependent, as is the decision of when to favor one of the above philosophies over another. The fact that there are four different talent-management philosophies raises some important questions, and some important future research directions.

2.6.1 *Aligning talent-management system architecture*

The first implication for practice is that organizations need to better match the whole talent-management system architecture to the four philosophies that we have outlined in this chapter. Although, in Figure 2.1, we argue that there are certain strategic contexts when one approach becomes more important, or impactful, than another, we also argue that to a large extent, and at any one time, organizations will likely have elements of all four philosophies in place. The balance is also likely to be industry specific, and even within an organization, the balance may need to be different from business division to division. It is also the case that while organizations in practice may adopt multiple approaches, they do alter the design of their talent-management architecture, or the emphasis that it provides, from time to time. The factors that trigger switches in emphasis will be important for researchers to explore.

We do not see the four philosophies as necessarily being competing choices. Instead they represent four different dilemmas or judgments built into any talent system – four components of the talent-management architecture that can be given more or less weight within a system at any one time. How much attention do we give to the analysis and management of people, positions, practices, and strategic talent pools?

It is also tempting to argue that because each philosophy is based on different assumptions about organizational effectiveness (which they are), both practitioners and researchers must decide which philosophy to espouse, and build their talent-management architectures accordingly. It is certainly true that using certain combinations of the philosophies may be difficult to reconcile, or argue to a workforce when the assumptions are made transparent. Some of the philosophies may be more easily combined than others. In particular contexts, some of the critical roles in the organization may need to change, and an organization's talent-management architecture might therefore put an emphasis on this philosophy, but at the same time it may still adhere to a philosophy of focusing on the top tier of talent. Most talent systems can therefore attend to both the critical roles and critical people at certain points in time.

Other philosophies, however, do not really fit together very well, particularly when used as part of a talent ideology. The people approach, with its argument that talent management is not about sophisticated process but is about differentiation, for example, stands in stark contrast to the practices approach, which is about honed practices to a known recipe for talent. You cannot pursue both these philosophies without risking sending mixed messages to the line. Communicating why there is a changed focus from one philosophy to another is also important.

While there are no simple decision rules as to when to emphasize one approach over another, one key decision point is whether or not there is significant business-model change. Referring back to the relative focus that organizations might give to each of the four talent-management philosophies and approaches outlined in Figure 2.1, business model change often pulls the talent system in directions it has not previously gone – talent systems generally lag behind the strategy. Organizations can, however, be more proactive in the choices they make about the talent-management architecture, and push a new talent system into the organization.

A logical way to work around the approaches outlined in Figure 2.1 is to ask questions as follows. Is the business facing a high degree of business-model change and strategic uncertainty? If yes, then organizations should use the two philosophies to the right of the matrix. New talent systems have to learn how to cope with new business realities – and the practices should only be honed once the strategic talent pools and positions have surfaced. They should only consider a practice or people approach once the strategic capabilities the organization needs are clearer. In times of strategic uncertainty, organizations need to redefine the pivotal positions first (a position approach) and design the talent system around these. Then they also need to consider how to deal with the people challenges associated with the management of these positions (a strategic talent pools approach).

2.6.2 Broadening the data capture about talent: putting the strategy back into talent management

The second implication for practice then is that the language of risk management has rightly been given prominence again in talent thinking. Investing in talent creates opportunities, but it also contains risk, in that the investment in potential may never be delivered in end performance. As the credit crunch showed, those deemed talented may also risk the performance of the organization through their own performance. There is now an important overlap between talent management in the organization, and the broader knowledge management needed to build organizational capability. The bottom-line question is, how comfortable can organizations be about the knowledge claims made by its top talent? Storey and Salaman (2005) studied what happens in top teams as strategy develops. At senior levels of the organization, external talent is often brought in to inject a new knowledge system into the team's thinking. To judge whether they were "talented" or not, they looked at the "knowledge claims" made by directors at the strategic apex of organizations – the claims they make about what their organization needs to do, what it should be like to do these things, and why. These knowledge claims – or business knowledge – involve knowledge about the organization's purpose, products and or/services, environment, customers and competitors, structure, processes, and its people. Such insights into the business model may be shared among the senior team, or there may be competing variants around them. They emerge from the knowledge system that is in practice – and that is the constellation of the strategic diagnoses, values, guiding principles, and solutions that senior talent come up with. When talent is brought into the organization, these are unfettered by the knowledge constraints of the previous regime. In the search to confirm that the right candidate has been chosen, peers scramble to find confirmatory evidence of this sound judgment. In practice, most business models remain contested for a considerable time. Despite a common ability of CEOs to provide a narrative, knowledge of the strategy of the organization varies considerably across members of the executive teams, and there are differing and incomplete accounts of the business model. Knowing *about* the organization, in terms of the interpretations given to various forms of information, performance goals, appropriate metrics, and knowing *how* the design of the organization delivered this, is central to the execution of business models, but was always contested territory. Talent management is risk management.

This requires that a talent-management system be able to help the organization make two bellwether judgments about the knowledge possessed by talent (Sparrow, Hird, and Balain, 2011): is the individual capable of high-quality strategic thought; and does the "capital" that they possess enable them to make a potential contribution to value creation? To be able to arrive at a satisfactory answer to this question, leads to a second implication for practice. This is that organizations need to broaden the data that they capture about talent. For Sparrow, Hird, and Balain (2011) talent is typically forged uniquely within organizations, making export across organizations potentially more risky. When talent directors are asked to assess the relative balance of the important forms of capital that their talent systems are designed to create, each organization fosters a different combination. Talent are only really talent if they possess *all four* forms of capital below.

- The assessment of threshold skills and competences necessary to be deemed talented, typically called *human capital* and defined as "the knowledge, skills, competences and attributes embodied in individuals that facilitate the creation of personal, social and economic well-being (OECD, 2001: p.18).
- An understanding of the key components of the business model, how these components fit together, and with what organizational consequences (we suggest potentially called *business-model capital*). Intellectual capital remains a contested idea and conveys something that exists both in the collective of an organization and to a degree within individuals who form part of that capability. It is linked to a cluster of concepts including tacit knowing, working knowledge, and knowledge and the firm (O'Donnell, 2011). Drawing upon the strategy literature, however, individuals have mental models of the organization, its strategic context, and scope for agency (Hodgkinson and Sparrow, 2002; Pfeffer, 2005). This has particular value when applied to an understanding of an organization's business model. For us, business-model capital is an intellectual capability that enables insight into the dominant *performance logic* inherent in an organization's strategy (Johnson, Melin, and Whittington (2003), facilitating rapid diagnosis of competing business models (Sparrow *et al.*, 2010).

- The collective value of an individual's social networks and the inclinations that arise from these networks for members to do things for each other and for that individual, called *social capital*, defined as "the sum of the actual and potential resources embedded within, available through and derived from the network of relationships possessed by an individual or social unit" (Nahapiet and Ghoshal, 1998: p. 243).

- An assessment of being known in the network for getting things done and the capacity to effectively build constituent support and acquire legitimacy by using traditional forms of power. Shown to be important for example in the expatriate literature, this is called *political* (Harvey and Novicevic, 2004) or *reputational and representative capital*. The reputational dimension of political capital reflects the individual's standing in team members' eyes, whereas the representative dimension of political capital reflects the members' support for the individual (Harvey and Novicevic, 2009). Individuals without political capital cannot deliver on their talent.

These are not qualities that are easily discernable or assessed within talent, but efforts now need to be made in this direction. For Silzer and Dowell (2010), this effort is needed because organizational success or failure can ultimately be traced to the talent within that organization, in that this talent must:

make the right decisions regarding where to invest financial and human resources, how to innovate and compete, and how to energise and direct the organization to achieve the business strategy... it is the quality of talent throughout the organization that ultimately leads to the creation and effective execution of successful strategy... having the right people comes before having the right strategies. (Silzer and Dowell, 2010: p. 3)

They quip that while financial resources may be the lifeblood of an organization, it is an organization's human resources that are the brains.

Therefore organizations need to consider how to develop the necessary linkages between the capital that talent possess and the organizational strategy. Boswell and colleagues (Boswell, Wright, and Snell, 2000; Boswell and Boudreau, 2001; Boswell, 2006; Boswell, Bingham, and Colvin, 2006) drew upon the compensation literature to stress the notion of line of sight, and emphasize the alignment between an employee's knowledge and their behaviour – the ability to link an employee's understanding of the organization's goals with the actions and strategic priorities necessary to achieve those goals. For Buller and McEvoy (2012) this linkage required that HRM practices (such as talent-management practices, although they considered only four HR functions of recruitment and selection, performance appraisal, training and development, and compensation) create the necessary human and social capital in employees – and that social capital be used to improve human capital and vice versa. They noted that:

the specific HRM practices and their configuration are unique, complex and dynamic in each firm because each firm's environment and requisite strategy are also unique, complex and dynamic. This conclusion is not comforting to those who are intent on finding universal HRM best practices. (Buller and McEvoy, 2012: p. 53)

In the final analysis, and in reflecting the link back to strategy, it seems evident that talent management in today's organizations needs to be much more about the management of the collective wisdom of talent. It needs to focus less on just identifying and categorizing talent, and more on getting effective brokerage out of the talent data. It is less about talent management, and more about *the management of talent*. Effective talent management is about getting talent to talk to each other. Human resources functions need to proactively manage the talent data and treat talent systems as a "distributed capability system."

The opening two chapters of Part II of this book now pick up on this need to think more about the collective aspects of talent. Part II therefore starts to lay out the new intellectual boundaries for the field of talent management.

References

Axelrod, E. L., Handfield-Jones, H., and Welsh, T. A. (2001). The war for talent. Part 2. *McKinsey Quarterly*, 2 (5), 9–11.

Axelrod, E. L., Handfield-Jones, H., and Michaels, E. (2002). A new game plan for C players. *Harvard Business Review*, 80, 80–90.

Baks, K. P. (2003). On the performance of mutual fund managers. Working paper. Emory University, Atlanta.

Boswell, W. R. (2006). Aligning employees with the organization's strategic objectives: out of line of sight, out of mind. *International Journal of Human Resource Management*, 17 (9), 1489–511.

Boswell, W. R. and Boudreau, J. W. (2001). How leading companies create, measure and achieve strategic results through line of sight. *Management Decision*, 39 (10), 851–9.

Boswell, W. R., Wright, P. M., and Snell, S. A. (2000). Research update: employee alignment and the role of line of sight. *Human Resource Planning*, 23 (4), 46–9.

Boswell, W. R., Bingham, J. B., and Colvin, A. J. S. (2006). Aligning employees through line of sight. *Business Horizons*, 49, 499–509.

Boudreau, J. W. (2010). *Retooling HR: Using Proven Business Tools to Make Better Decisions About Talent.* Boston, MA: Harvard Business School Press.

Boudreau, J. W. and Jesuthasan, R. (2011). *Transformative HR: How Great Companies Use Evidence Based Change for Sustainable Advantage.* San Francisco, CA: Jossey-Bass.

Boudreau, J. W. and Ramstad, P. M. (2005). Talentship and the evolution of human resource management: from 'professional practices' to 'strategic talent decision science'. *Human Resource Planning*, 28 (2), 17–26.

(2006). Talentship and HR measurement and analysis: from ROI to strategic, human resource planning. *Human Resource Planning*, 29 (1), 25–33.

(2007). *Beyond HR: the New Science of Human Capital.* Boston, MA: Harvard Business School Press.

Buller, P. F. and McEvoy, G. M. (2012). Strategy, human resource management, and performance: sharpening line of sight. *Human Resource Management Review*, 22. 43–56.

Cappelli, P. (2008). *Talent on Demand: Managing Talent in an Age of Uncertainty.* Boston, MA: Harvard Business Press.

Cascio, W. F. and Boudreau, J. W. (2010). *Investing in People: Financial Impact of Human Resource Initiatives.* New York, NY: Financial Times Press.

(2012). *A Short Introduction to Strategic Human Resource Management.* Cambridge: Cambridge University Press.

Chambers, E. G., Foulon, M., Handfield-Jones, H., Hankin, S. M., and Michaels III, E. G. (1998). The war for talent. *The McKinsey Quarterly*, 3, 44–57.

Chesbrough, H. W. (2007). Why companies should have open business models. *Sloan Management Review*. 48 (2), 22–8.

Collings, D. G. and Mellahi, K. (2009). Strategic talent management: a review and research agenda. *Human Resource Management Review*, 19 (4), 304–13.

Fernández-Aráoz, C., Graysberg, B., and Nohria, N. (2011). How to hang on to your high potentials. *Harvard Business Review*, 69 (10): 69–83.

Groysberg, B., Nanda, A., and Nohria, N. (2004). The risky business of hiring stars. *Harvard Business Review*, 82, 92–101.

Gubman, E. L. and Green, S. (2007). *The Four Stages of Talent Management.* San Francisco, CA: Executive Networks.

Guthridge, M., Komm, A. B., and Lawson, E. (2006). The people problem in talent management. *McKinsey Quarterly*, 2 (1), 6–9.

Harvey, M. and Novicevic, M. M. (2004). The development of political skill and political capital by global leaders through global assignments. *International Journal of Human Resource Management*, 15 (7), 1173–88.

(2009). Mutual adjustment of expatriates and international team members: the role of political and social skill. In P. R. Sparrow (ed.) *Handbook of International Human Resource Management: Integrating People, Process and Context*. Chichester: Wiley, pp. 115–30.

Henderson, R. M. and Clark, K. B. (1990). Architectural innovation: the reconfiguration of existing product technologies and the failure of established firms. *Administrative Science Quarterly*, 35 (1), 9–30.

Hird, M., Whelan, J., and Hammady, S. (2010). BAE: using senior management assessment as part of a talent strategy. In P. R. Sparrow, M. Hird, and C. Cooper (eds.) *Leading HR*. London: Palgrave MacMillan, pp. 122–35.

Hodgkinson, G. P. and Healey, M. P. (2008). Cognition in organizations. *Annual Review of Psychology*, 59, 387–417.

(2011). Psychological foundations of dynamic capabilities: reflexion and reflection in strategic management. *Strategic Management Journal*, 32, 1500–16.

Hodgkinson, G. P. and Sparrow, P. R (2002). *The Competent Organization: a Psychological Analysis of the Strategic Management Process*. Buckingham: Open University Press.

Huselid, M. A., Beatty, R. W., and Becker, B. E. (2005). "A players" or "A positions?" The strategic logic of workforce management. *Harvard Business Review*, 83 (12), 110–17.

Ingham, J. (2007). *Strategic Human Capital Management: Creating Value Through People*. London: Butterworth-Heinemann.

Johnson, G., Melin, L., and Whittington, R. (2003). Micro strategy and strategizing: towards an activity-based view. *Journal of Management Studies*, 40 (1), 3–23.

Kang, S.-C., Morris, S., and Snell, S. A. (2007). Relational archetypes, organizational learning and value creation: extending the human resource architecture. *Academy of Management Review*, 32 (1), 236–56.

Lawler, E. E. (1994). From job based to competency-based organizations. *Journal of Organizational Behavior*, 15, 3–15.

(2008). *Talent: Making People your Competitive Advantage*. San Francisco, CA: Jossey-Bass.

Magretta, J. (2002). Why business models matter. *Harvard Business Review*, 80 (5), 86–93.

Mäkela, K., Björkman, I., and Ehrnrooth, M. (2010). How do MNCs establish their talent pools? Influences on individuals' likelihood of being labelled as talent. *Journal of World Business*, 45 (2), 134–42.

Michaels, E., Handfield-Jones, H., and Axelrod, B. (2001). *The War For Talent*. Boston, MA: Harvard Business School Press.

Nahapiet, J. (2011). A social perspective: exploring the links between human capital and social capital. In A. Burton-Jones and J.-C. Spender (eds.) *The Oxford Handbook Of Human Capital*. Oxford: Oxford University Press, pp. 71–95.

Nahapiet, J. and Ghoshal, S. (1998). Social capital, intellectual capital and the organizational advantage. *Academy of Management Review*, 23, 242–66.

O'Donnell, D. (2011). Understanding interdependencies between human capital and structural capital: some directions from Kantian pragmatism. In A. Burton-Jones and J.-C. Spender (eds.) *The Oxford Handbook of Human Capital*. Oxford: Oxford University Press, pp. 433–58.

O'Donnell, M. (2009). Talent management. Deloitte HR Professionals Services. www.deloitte.com/view/en_IE/ie/services/consulting/consulting-services/human-capital-advisory-services/987fa6c82-b10e110VgnVCM100000ba42f00aRCRD.htm.

Odiorne, G. S. (1984). *Human Resources Strategy: a Portfolio Approach*. San Francisco, CA: Jossey-Bass Inc.

OECD (Organization for Economic Co-operation and Development) (2001) *The Well-Being of Nations: The Role of Human and Social Capital*. Paris: OECD.

Pfeffer, J. (2001). Fighting the war for talent is hazardous to your organization's health. *Organizational Dynamics*, 29 (4), 248–59.
  (2005). Changing mental models: HR's most important task. *Human Resource Management*, 44 (2), 123–8.

Schuler, R. S., Jackson, S. E., and Tarique, I. (2011). Global talent management and global talent challenges: strategic opportunities for IHRM. *Journal of World Business*, 46, 506–16.

Schweizer, L. (2005). Concept and evolution of business models, *Journal of General Management*, 31 (2), 37–56.

Scullion, H. and Collings, D.G. (eds.) (2011). *Global Talent Management*. London: Routledge.

Sears, D. (2003). *Successful Talent Strategies: Achieving Superior Business Results through Market-focused Staffing*. New York, NY: American Management Association.

Shafer, S. M., Smith, H. J., and Linder, J. C. (2005). The power of business models. *Business Horizons*, 48, 199–207.

Silzer, R. and Dowell, B. E. (2010). Strategic talent management matters. In R. Silzer and B. E. Dowell (eds.) *Strategy-Driven Talent Management: a Leadership Imperative*. San Franciscio, CA: Jossey-Bass–Society for Industrial and Organizational Psychology, pp. 3–72.

Sparrow, P. R. (2000). Strategic management in a world turned upside down: the role of cognition, intuition and emotional intelligence. In P. C. Flood, T. Dromgoole, S. J. Carroll, and L. Gorman (eds.) *Managing Strategy Implementation*. Oxford: Blackwell Publishers.

Sparrow, P. R. and Balain, S. (2008). Talent proofing the organization. In C. L. Cooper and R. Burke (eds.) *The Peak Performing Organization*. London: Routledge, pp. 108–28.

Sparrow, P. R., Hird, M., Hesketh, A., and Cooper, C. L. (2010). *Leading HR*. London: Palgrave.

Sparrow, P. R., Hird, M., and Balain, S. (2011). *Talent Management: Time to Question the Tablets of Stone?* Centre for Performance-led HR White Paper 11/01. Lancaster University Management School.

Stahl, G. K., Bjorkman, I., Farndale, E., *et al.* (2012). Six principles of effective global talent management. *MIT Sloan Management Review*, 53, 25–32.

Stein, G. and Capape, J. (2009). *Factors of CEO failure: mapping the debate. IESE Business School Study-85*. Barcelona: IESE.

Storey, J. and Salaman, G. (2005). The knowledge work of general managers. *Journal of General Management*, 31 (2), 57–73.

Vaiman, V., Scullion, H., and Collings, D. (2012). Talent management decision making. *Management Decision*, 50 (5), 925–41.

Watson Wyatt Worldwide (2009). *5 Rules for Talent Management in the New Economy*. Watson Wyatt.com.

Yip, G. S. (2004). Using strategy to change your business model. *Business Strategy Review*, 15 (2), 17–24.

Zuboff, S. (1988). *In the Age of the Smart Machine: the Future of Work and Power*. New York: Basic Books.

PART II

Redefining the boundaries of strategic talent management

3 A resource-based view of talent management

CLIFF BOWMAN AND MARTIN HIRD

The opening chapter has introduced the field of talent management, its evolution, and the core practices it involves. In this chapter we take the resource-based view (RBV) of the firm and use it as a lens to explore and critique talent-management practices. We begin with a brief summary of the RBV and use this to highlight a number of implications for the talent debate. We then summarize some of the assumptions to identify nine tenets inherent in the talent perspective, and use ideas from an RBV perspective to challenge and critique this paradigm. This critique, we argue, should make us question the idea of "manageability" within the talent agenda. Many of the assumptions of a talent-management perspective are antithetical to the key principles and notions that underpin the RBV. We conclude by suggesting six developments to practice that should be made by adopting a more strategic RBV-influenced approach to talent management.

3.1 The RBV perspective

The RBV tries to explain how some firms are able to sustain competitive advantage, and as a consequence they can continually earn superior profits compared to rival firms (Rumelt, 1984; Wernerfelt, 1984; Barney, 1986, 1991; Dierickx and Cool, 1989; Conner, 1991; Kogut and Zander, 1992; Amit and Schoemaker, 1993; Peteraf, 1993; Teece, Pisano, and Shuen, 1997). The RBV locates these sources of advantage in the firm's special assets and capabilities. These assets and capabilities have qualities, referred to as "isolating mechanisms" (Rumelt, 1984), that make it difficult for rival firms to replicate them and compete with the firm that has built these qualities. These isolating mechanisms include situations where:

- it is hard or even impossible to relate the consequences or effects of a phenomenon to its initial states or causes, and decision makers find it hard to understand the relationship between organizational inputs and outputs, referred to as "causal ambiguity"

- the set of decisions one faces for any given circumstance is limited by the decisions one has made in the past, even though past circumstances may no longer be relevant (path dependency)
- interconnected social relationships and macro- and micro-factors of a social system create new properties (social complexity)
- knowledge is created that is difficult to capture, codify, or transfer, and people may not be aware of the knowledge they possess or how it can be valuable to others (tacit knowledge)
- complex synergies exist between assets, infrastructure, or capabilities.

The RBV emphasizes the unique nature of a specific firm's capabilities, and it recognizes that these special capabilities are "built" and are not "bought" (Rumelt, 1984). Firm advantages tend to emerge and evolve from complex processes of interaction, often over considerable time periods (years, not weeks). These capability-development processes are relatively unmanaged and emergent, particularly with respect to the development of tacit knowledge and embedded tacit routines involving many people in extended interactions. Luck or chance also plays a part, and given that firms interact with an external environment that is unpredictable, there is only a limited scope for deliberate interventions in creating unique sources of advantage.

The RBV also emphasizes differences between firms, particularly with respect to their histories. If a firm has a competitive advantage over rivals this is because of some valuable idiosyncrasies. These differences derive from employees and managers doing things in a different way to rival firms. Enduring sources of advantage consist in the skills of employees that are manifested in embedded collective routines that involve multiple actors and are embodied in the special know-how of a designer, or the client relationships a salesperson has developed over time.

For example, if the firm has cost advantages these may derive from the innovative way in which an engineer has redesigned the plant layout, or the efficient processes that the procurement team have developed. Where a firm has been able to identify and exploit a new market opportunity, this is likely to be the outcome of someone's entrepreneurial insight. Firm advantage derives from the collective efforts of many people, who interact with unique and valuable assets created through collective efforts in the past.

In terms of the talent-management debate, it is important to note that the emphasis in the RBV is on collective interactions, interconnections, and path dependence, *not particularly on the efforts of individuals.*

Sources of advantage are also usually difficult for competing firms to comprehend (they are "causally ambiguous"). But this causal ambiguity can also make it difficult for managers to fully understand quite how their firm sustains advantage. If the firm's value-creation processes are fully transparent, then they are likely to be readily imitated, unless they are protected by a barrier to imitation, such as a patent. This suggests that enduring sources of advantage are likely to be subtle and complex.

Hence, unless a manager has been deeply immersed in these value processes, he or she is likely to form only an abstract approximate understanding of them. The manager would perceive some general overview of the value processes, rather than have a detailed intuitive knowledge of them. Moreover, these enduring sources of advantage are likely to be dependent on activities that combine codified explicit knowledge with experience-driven tacit know-how, the latter being generally resistant to codification.

Thus the firm's sources of advantage derive from decisions and actions taken in the past that are different to rival firms. Firms that achieve enduring advantage develop firm-specific knowledge, which adds value to this firm, but it may not be as valuable to other firms.

Where firms face uncertain and dynamic environments it is likely to be difficult to specify exactly what capabilities the firm will need to succeed in the future. In these uncertain contexts firms need to encourage difference and diversity. Changing what is produced, how it is produced, and how these products are sold occurs through two key processes:

1. experience-based learning in the core
2. entrepreneurial insight.

Again, in terms of managing talent, neither of these processes is particularly amenable to deliberate, "managed" developmental interventions. They are more akin to complex emergent processes of variety creation (where new combinations of knowledge or the reuse of ideas create new sources of value) and environmental selection.

3.2 The talent-management perspective

The talent-management perspective (TMP) is typically manifested through a talent-management process that seeks to identify and nurture "high potential" employees, who will constitute the future senior management cadre. The key assumptions behind the creation of talent-management processes are as follows.

1. Firms create value and gain a competitive edge through the quality of their managerial talent.
2. Talented managers create value through their individual and group impact on the firm.
3. Talented managers are able to move from one part of the firm to another and apply their capabilities across a wide range of contexts.
4. High potentials can be identified reasonably early in their careers.
5. Talent can be identified and it can be developed.
6. High potentials possess generic capabilities that are valuable to many firms; therefore they need to be "engaged" and rewarded or they may leave.
7. Generic capabilities can be developed through generic high-potential development programmes.
8. The "engagement" of talent is reflected in their "effort."
9. Talented people should "rotate" through different positions; this aids their development.

3.3 Challenging the talent paradigm

We now take our RBV perspective and consider these nine tenets of talent management.

3.3.1 Firms create value and gain a competitive edge through the quality of their managerial talent

Why assume that the prime source of a firm's competitive advantage derives from its managers? The RBV informs us that, although a firm may have some uniquely capable individuals in leadership roles, the likelihood is that advantage derives from a combination of capabilities and assets, built up through time, that are embedded in complex social processes (Dierickx and Cool, 1989). The RBV also recognizes that luck plays a big role in explaining how some firms succeed (Barney, 1986).

3.3.2 Talented managers create value through their individual and group impact on the firm

The firm creates value through "team production" processes (Alchian and Demsetz, 1972). In team production it is not possible to isolate the value contribution of a team member. Therefore the best we can hope for is that talented managers have a positive impact on the firm, but this impact cannot be measured.

3.3.3 Talented managers are able to move from one part of the firm to another and apply their capabilities across a wide range of contexts

This implies that "talented managers" have generic skills and capabilities. The RBV alerts us to the importance of history, context, specificities, and idiosyncrasies that can be sources of advantage. If "talent" have generic skills that are equally valuable across the breadth of a firm's operations, then this strongly implies that these capabilities could have value in any rival firm. By definition, then, these generic skills cannot explain firm advantage.

If "generic talent" is introduced into an area of the firm's operations what will be the effects? If the manager's beliefs about managing are generic and widely applicable any decisions the manager introduces will interact with the existing firm practices. The outcomes might be to inadvertently or deliberately eliminate idiosyncratic practices. We might suppose that beliefs about "best practice," maybe learned from external sources, would form the basis of any generic managerial skill set. Spreading these practices may or may not be helpful to the firm. All we can be sure about is that introduced "best practices" will interact with established routines and the result will be neither the existing routines, nor best practices, but rather some unpredictable hybrid outcome.

As we write, Apple remains one of the most profitable companies in the world. If talent management is valuable then we would expect these practices to not only be adopted by Apple, but they would largely account for its success. However, Apple is notoriously disdainful of "general managers," they do not look to employ MBAs, and they have a firm belief in expertise not "management" (see the next chapter, Managing expert talent, by Greg Linden and David J. Teece). They recognize that expertise is built up through experience, therefore Apple expects people to remain in their specialist areas of expertise.

It is worth noting here that the belief in the value of general management may be a peculiarly Anglo-Saxon phenomenon. Our experience of working with many European firms is that they privilege deep expertise over "general management." Indeed, one of us was upbraided by a German engineer when we referred to him as a senior manager: "I am not a manager; I am the chief engineer!"

3.3.4 High potentials can be identified reasonably early in their careers

This practice relies on a set of beliefs about what "talent" constitutes that would be widely acknowledged, that these qualities are manifested in some way, and that they can be measured at an early stage in a person's career.

The danger here is that we restrict entry to the "talent pool" by applying a limited set of talent "signifiers." The earlier in one's career that talent spotting takes place, the less firm-specific (or more generic) any talent signifiers would have to be. This may well introduce an inadvertent "homogenizing" process into the firm. For example, early career talent signifiers will necessarily rely heavily on upbringing, schooling, degree qualifications, etc., rather than the individual's performance within the firm.

We know that for a firm to be resilient it needs to have a requisite amount of diversity in its employees and managers. The danger here is that by recruiting and developing employees to a particular template or set of beliefs about what "talent" looks like, we reduce the organization's diversity and resilience, thus restricting its capability to respond to unpredictable external events.

3.3.5 Talent can be identified, and it can be developed

To believe that talent can be developed requires us:

1. to understand what "talent" looks like
2. to understand how those qualities were created
3. to believe that these developmental processes can be deliberately managed.

A recent study of CEOs sought to identify how they acquire their strategic-leadership capabilities (Laljani, 2009). All had MBAs or had attended significant residential programs at leading business schools in Europe and the United States. However, not one CEO suggested that they had acquired their capabilities from attending business school. All of them cited just two developmental processes:

- stretch assignments
- mentoring.

These practices could form part of a development plan for an individual. However, in contrast to formalized training and education programs, mentoring or stretch assignments are complex processes that are difficult to manage and the outcomes are hard to predict. Indeed, the wrong assignment or mentor could prove to be quite damaging to an individual.

Successful individuals tend not to fit a template. People display immense diversity, and an individual is the product of a unique "development path." Nature, nurture, formative experiences, relationships, feedback, etc., combine to make us who we are. Any developmental intervention interacts with that individual's past experiences and personality, which is unique; therefore the outcomes of a deliberate attempt to shape development are not predictable. Testing and categorizing individuals, e.g., using a Myers–Briggs Type Indicator, might help talent managers cope with the presence of diversity, but the assumptions made about appropriate development interventions based on these classifications run the risk of being dangerous generalizations.

3.3.6 High potentials possess generic capabilities that are valuable to many firms; therefore they need to be "engaged" and rewarded or they may leave

We have already addressed the issue of generic capabilities. If there is in fact a set of generic managerial capabilities that could be of equal value in any firm, then those that possess them have a huge market for their talent. But the RBV would suggest that any assets or capabilities that can be easily acquired cannot be a source of firm advantage. Generic managerial talent would be an asset that can be "bought"; it does not have to be built (Rumelt, 1984).

If we can envisage a market for generic managerial talent, such as the market for footballers, then clearly there will be some individuals perceived to have more of these skills than others. These managers will be able to command a premium price for their talents. We have explained that it is not possible to identify the value contribution of a hired manager either before or after they have been hired. If we are paying a high price for their services this investment entails a significant risk, especially if we are not sure how their generic skill set will interact with the extant organization. Indeed it is possible that in the current inflated state of the "market for talent," managers may be able to capture any rents they generate for the firm, or, worse, they create less value than they capture through their remuneration packages.

But a more worrying issue is the nature of the manager's involvement with the firm that is implied by this practice. This practice assumes a "calculative involvement" (Etzioni, 1964) with the firm, that in turn raises a number of questions.

• Do we really want our "talent" continually comparing their reward packages with those supposedly available in other firms?
• Why should we look to encourage these attitudes?
• Why do talented people need to be continually bribed to turn up and do a decent job?
• Do we really want these people?

This assumption about calculative involvement is at odds with what we think we know about motivation. Pay is rarely something to motivate people; it's generally a source of dissatisfaction, if anything. We should value people who are fired up by the job they are doing, and by the challenges and contributions they can make, who enjoy working with others. We do not need people who are only interested in their relative pay.

From an RBV perspective, then, the most valuable individuals would be those with firm-specific know-how. These individuals are likely to have invested a good deal of their working life acquiring skills, and insights that really make a difference to the firm. They should be rewarded for their efforts, of course, but their firm-specific know-how has no market value, so there's no need to pay some notional market rate. Alternatively, where the individual has a generic managerial skill set, they may be mobile, but there are thousands of managers with the same skills, so again, no need to pay premium prices.

3.3.7 Generic capabilities can be developed through generic high-potential development programs

Any generic program must be designed to develop generic skills. But in our experience most formal development programs that high potentials attend focus essentially on imparting knowledge about business and management. While we would agree that this knowledge is useful, its impact on what managers *actually do* is limited. Managing is an activity, doing it well requires know-how, not just knowledge, and know-how is learned through experience, not from attending courses.

Given the uniqueness of each individual manager, the effect of the same diet of training on each person is unpredictable. It is therefore difficult to see talent development as a managed process given the uncertain effects of these developmental interventions.

3.3.8 The "engagement" of talent is reflected in their "effort"

The RBV alerts us to firm assets that are very difficult for rival firms to replicate. Easily replicable assets would be the codified systems that represent talent-management practices. These practices are described in books, so are widely available, and individual HR practitioners can take their understandings of these practices from firm to firm. In essence, employee engagement is about a quantifiable measure of an employee's positive or negative emotional attachment to their job, colleagues, and organization that decisively influences their willingness to learn and perform at work. At a higher level, meaningful employee engagement involves two radical changes to accepted employee–manager relations.

1. Employees play a major role in plotting the future tactics, strategy, and ways of working.
2. Consequentially, managers behave very differently to the generally accepted role norms.

The valuable and inimitable assets that some firms have are embedded in the culture of the firm: in the atmosphere, values, and "feel" of the organization. People like to work there, they like to interact with like-minded people, and maybe they get a buzz from the work the firm does. In most cases these differentiating cultural aspects are entirely unplanned, unmanaged, and emergent. Indeed, probably the quickest way to destroy these subtle sources of identification and motivation would be for management to seek to "manage" them.

3.3.9 Talented people should "rotate" through different positions: this aids their development

Given the path-dependent nature of firm advantage it is likely that the know-how that gives a firm competitive advantage has been accumulating over years. If much of this expertise is tacit know-how, not explicit and codified knowledge, then it resides with people. To build deep expertise and leverage it requires some stability in job roles. Every time you move someone into an unfamiliar role they have to start more or less from scratch. Their performance will not be good, but we also need to recognize the disruptive impact of their departure and arrival on the other team members. The RBV recognizes the value of emergent collective routines that have been evolved by a group through their interactions. Assuming most of these are beneficial to the firm, every move of a team member disrupts the team they leave, and the team they join.

3.4 How should we adapt talent-management practices in the light of the RBV?

Based on the above critique of the basic assumptions of the talent-management perspective, we draw two conclusions. The first is that any generic talent-management process is likely to be the wrong thing for a particular firm. This is because of the unique history, assets, and capabilities that the firm possesses and the unique environmental circumstances it faces. So we need approaches to the development of our people that fit the firm's peculiar context.

Assuming our interest in developing our staff is ultimately to bring about a positive impact on firm performance, the starting point for deciding how to set about development must be a sophisticated appreciation of what currently gives our firm competitive advantage, and some clear thinking about what capabilities we will need in the future. This would at least avoid the pitfall of importing some generic talent-development practices that do not fit our firm's context. The more dynamic and unpredictable the firm's future environment is, the more difficult it is to be able to predict the kind of know-how and capabilities we will need. Beliefs about the value of generic and general management capabilities are rooted in a view of organizations as stable, enduring hierarchies, that display Weberian qualities of bureaucracy such that any context-specific information is codified and accessible to whoever moves into the managerial role. Some organizations do enjoy relative stability, and it is possible to anticipate the skill set required for particular roles into the future, e.g., civil service, armed forces. But most firms face dynamic and turbulent environments. We cannot know with any confidence today what skills will be required tomorrow. What this indicates is we need to build in some resilience and flexibility, and we need to allow for more diversity in the population of future leaders.

The second conclusion we need to draw is that we should challenge the assumption that managerial talent is the source of firm advantage. In some cases the decisions of a manager, their ability to inspire their team, etc., are critical in delivering firm success. But what can be almost guaranteed is that the qualities that delivered these successes are anything but generic. They are aspects of personality, they are situation-specific and probably rely on some particular insights that this person can provide, which are in turn largely experience driven and tacit. So, by all means, think about who are and may be the future value-creating individuals, but make these judgments based on a thorough understanding of the firm's current and future sources of advantage, not on a set of generic criteria imported from outside the firm.

3.5 Implications for practice: how might we change talent practices?

Finally, we believe there are some important and constructive implications for practice. If we accept the precepts that underpin the RBV, then we can only conclude that the characteristics of contemporary talent systems are, in many ways, antithetical to the key principles and notions that underpin the RBV. It is our intention to explore in this final section where talent managers responsible for devising company talent systems might want to reflect about their current focus and learn from the research that has been undertaken into the success of firms, utilizing an RBV perspective. We identify *six* developments to practice that should be adopted.

First, there is a strong argument that before designing a talent system within a company the talent manager should recognize that the RBV supports the notion that competitive advantage for the firm may be buried deep in a culture that has developed over many years – this culture may be key to what we describe as "valuable idiosyncrasies," in addition to tacit knowledge and embedded collective routines. Talent managers would be strongly advised to understand the deep-lying culture, delve into its characteristics, test some hypotheses about what might constitute the company's characteristics of competitive advantage, before committing to any overall design, particularly in nominating the key criteria for identifying those elite "high potentials." Companies may find the problem of failing to effectively link the criteria for identifying talent with the firm's current and future sources of competitive advantage. This problem is a likely outcome if the firm has recruited a talent manager externally, who may possess little or no intuitive understanding of the key, competitive cultural characteristics.

Second, we have flagged earlier in the chapter that the emphasis in the RBV is on collective actions, interconnections, and path dependence, not on the efforts of individuals. This clearly brings into question the highly individualistic nature of talent systems with their emphasis on a small minority of high potentials. Talent systems are similar to many performance-management systems in that they rarely encompass team effort in their focus. The RBV, which highlights the problems of causal ambiguity, gives food to the thought that those apparently high-potential individuals may, in fact, be dependent upon their teams for their high performance rating. The learning is probably that when executive teams review individual talent ratings they should spend time evaluating the "context" in which the individual under scrutiny has been operating to allow a more informed view of who should take the credit – individual or team.

Third, talent systems were developed more formally within large companies from the late 1980s and early 1990s, and were mainly managed by HR functions. Talent systems were, in many ways, an evolution from two earlier HR activities – recruitment and career development. The role of talent manager (or head of talent/talent VP) evolved from that of heads of resourcing. These roles tended to focus upon senior employee role rotation, development of the senior cadre, identifying those members of the senior cadre (and just below) with the highest potential for senior/board roles, and often the exiting of managerial low performers. As talent-management activity was perceived as a high priority by senior teams the quest for "high potential" identification criteria became more intense. Initially criteria revolved around defining "performance" and separately "potential" often utilizing the so-called "9-box matrix." Recently more emphasis has been given to developing criteria, and how important each criterion factor was. One recent research project (Martin and Schmidt, 2010) claims that successful high potentials need to possess, to a degree, the following:

1. ability – intellectual, technical, and emotional
2. engagement – personal connection and commitment to the company
3. aspiration – the desire for recognition, advancement, and future rewards.

However, there may be a problem here. These universal high-potential criteria that underpin talent systems may not link at all to the RBV-type characteristics that have made a particular company successful. Talent managers need to be mindful of this possibility!

Fourth, in recent times a popular talent activity has been to "bench strength" executive talent within a particular company. The activity is focused upon attempting to compare the ability of members of the senior team, for instance the marketing director, with competitors operating in the same marketplace. If the exercise concludes that the senior team is not strong then the likely outcome is to resort to external search/recruitment. In terms of an RBV lens this may create problems. We have already established that sources of advantage are likely to be subtle and complex and to recruit external managers, not immersed in the firm's value processes and without experience-driven firm-specific tacit know-how, may be detrimental to retaining competitive advantage. We may be saying that if a firm does clearly possess competitive advantage, then a simplistic response to a bench strengthening exercise that appears to indicate team-member weaknesses may not yield the expected benefit. Careful thought may be required before exiting experienced team members.

Fifth, many talent systems have an in-built "reflex" to rotate high potentials through job roles at frequent intervals (every two to three years), particularly in an Anglo-Saxon management culture. In terms of the RBV these individuals may not develop the tacit knowledge and experience-driven insights that really create value. The message here is very simple: a longer job placement for any individual may reinforce overall competitive advantage. In practice, talent systems may need to reflect this requirement in their rules and procedures.

Sixth, and finally, as talent systems move further down the organizational hierarchy, with the aim of identifying talent at an earlier age, a process of selection occurs that can exclude individuals who do not possess all the formal high-potential criteria. However these "solid citizens" may be part of the bedrock of the know-how and experience that underpins competitive advantage. It is crucial to reward and recognize these individuals satisfactorily. Talent systems that are linked to reward systems that remunerate high potentials to a disproportionate degree may be damaging in the long term.

References

Alchian, A. and Demsetz, H. (1972). Production, information costs, and economic organization. *American Economic Review*, 62, 777–95.

Amit, R. and Schoemaker, P. J. H. (1993). Strategic assets and organizational rent. *Strategic Management Journal*, 14, 33–46.

Barney, J. B. (1986). Strategic factor markets: expectations, luck, and business strategy. *Management Science*, 32, 1231–41.

(1991). Firm resources and sustained competitive advantage. *Journal of Management*, 17, 99–120.

Conner, K. R. (1991). A historical comparison of resource-based theory and five schools of thought within industrial organization economics: do we have a new theory of the firm? *Journal of Management*, 17, 121–54.

Dierickx, I. and Cool, K. (1989). Asset stock accumulation and sustainability of competitive advantage. *Management Science*, 35, 1504–11.

Etzioni, A. (1964). *Modern Organizations*. Prentice Hall.

Kogut, B. and Zander, U. (1992). Knowledge of the firm, combinative capabilities, and the replication of technology. *Organization Science*, 3, 383–97.

Laljani, N. (2009). *Making Strategic Leaders*. Palgrave Macmillan.

Martin, J. and Schmidt, C. (2010). How to keep your top talent. *Harvard Business Review*, 88 (5), 54–61.

Peteraf, M. A. (1993). The cornerstones of competitive advantage: a resource-based view. *Strategic Management Journal*, 14, 179–91.

Rumelt, R. P. (1984). Towards a strategic theory of the firm. In R. Lamb (ed.), *Competitive Strategic Management*. Englewood Cliffs, NJ: Prentice Hall, pp. 556–70.

Teece, D. J., Pisano, G. P., and Shuen, A. (1997). Dynamic capabilities and strategic management. *Strategic Management Journal*, 18, 509–33.

Wernerfelt, B. (1984). A resource-based view of the firm. *Strategic Management Journal*, 5, 171–80.

4 | Managing expert talent

GREG LINDEN AND DAVID J. TEECE

4.1 Introduction

The previous chapter focused on using the resource-based view (RBV) of strategy to think about talent. One of the key critiques that it made of the talent management perspective was that it overplays the importance of general management and underplays the value of expert knowledge and is antithetical to the RBV that has come to dominate the field of strategy. The RBV is one of the foundational pillars of dynamic capabilities. This chapter builds on the previous arguments, and discusses the management of talent in terms of the dynamic capabilities framework.

In recent decades, expert talent has become more important than ever for the creation and management of technology in the global economy (Albert and Bradley, 1997; Reich, 2002). Many job categories are becoming so complex and interdependent that managing them in a traditional structured hierarchical format is no longer a realistic option. Some decomposition of processes into specialized functional tasks is still necessary, but deep hierarchies are too cumbersome and inflexible.

For some time now, it has been argued that managing expert talent, especially in the creative industries and in professional services, requires firms to implement a bundle of HR practices such as "rigorous recruitment and selection procedures, performance-contingent incentive compensation systems, management development and training activities linked to the needs of the business, and significant commitment to employee involvement" (Becker and Huselid, 1998: 55). While these processes are important, they must be enacted within a broader understanding of the firm's strategy, capabilities, and potential, which an understanding of the dynamic capabilities framework can provide.

The management of experts is also fundamentally different from the management style applicable to regular line employees, principally because it requires a much lighter touch. Top talent generally does not need to be told what to do, at least not by a manager with little familiarity with the expert's area of knowledge. In today's global business context, the business enterprise must accomplish the difficult but essential tasks of delivering intellectual stimulation to its experts, keeping them financially satisfied, fostering collegiality and collaboration among them, and allowing them the guided professional autonomy they seek (and that their work demands) while holding them accountable to the enterprise.

This is not to say that experts and highly credentialed professionals per se are what make a company great. In fact, if a company becomes too dependent on one or a handful of individuals, and especially if they are remunerated inappropriately, the morale of all employees can be undermined. And hiring more experts generally can't save a dysfunctional organization (Pfeffer, 2001). Likewise, experts won't salvage a flawed strategy (Huselid, Beatty, and Becker, 2005), although they may be able to help replace it with a better one.

In this chapter we argue that the competitive advantage of the enterprise in high-talent industries is more than ever rooted not only in the stock of experts it can access but also the organizational capabilities it can harness. Hence, competitive advantage by no means depends on experts alone. Their management must be part of the broader orchestration of the firm's resources as it exercises its dynamic capabilities in the service of a good strategy.

"Expert," as used here, refers to someone with a high level of specialized knowledge (human capital) derived from some mix of education and experience. Experts are also assumed to be strong on the complementary dimensions defined by Sparrow, Hird, and Balain (2011): business model capital (insight into the organization's value proposition for customers), social capital (the ability to tap into networks within and beyond the organization), and political capital (influence and prestige where needed). In other words, the experts here represent the successful product of the talent-management process discussed in the other chapters of this book.

Two categories of experts are introduced in this chapter:

- the literati and numerati
- entrepreneurial managers.

In this chapter, after briefly analyzing these two categories of top talent, we introduce the dynamic capabilities framework, which specifically addresses the responsiveness of organizations to changes in their environment. We argue that the quality of the management of a firm's experts (i.e., the quality of its management of talent) can make the difference between inertia and action for business enterprises facing particularly challenging competitive environments. The second half of the chapter addresses the key issues of managing a firm's experts in a way that maximizes their contribution to the firm's dynamic capabilities. Compared to the management methods used for most employees, experts must be allowed more autonomy, expert teams must be allowed more latitude, and expert incentives must allow for more differentiation among individuals.

4.2 Top talent

Society has always had a non-uniform distribution of productive talents, with some individuals being far more skilled and committed than others. The rise of "the expert" in the corporate world occurred in tandem with improvements in the US educational infrastructure in the early decades of the twentieth century (Galambos, 2010). Continual increases in the organizational and technical complexity of problems facing the business enterprise have heightened the need for experts.

Individual productivity in many fields is quite skewed. This was first observed by Alfred Lotka (1926) in a study of the authorship of articles in nineteenth-century physics journals. Lotka found that approximately 6% of publishing scientists produced half of all papers. Lotka's results are reasonably robust – they have been shown to hold for many disciplines in many different time periods.

Studies have found that the most productive and eminent scientists are strongly motivated. Almost all have good stamina in the sense that they work hard in the pursuit of long-run goals (Fox, 1983: 287).

4.2.1 Where experts come from

A firm's stock of experts will typically be a combination of those who came to the organization fully formed, so to speak, and those who have come up from within the organization. Their background may be theoretical/academic or practical/empirical.

Some avenues for securing the services of experts may be a better fit with the firm's capabilities than others (Chambers *et al.*, 1998). For example, hiring new graduates makes the most sense for a firm with an adequate training program. Gaining expert talent through the acquisition of small start-ups or other companies makes the most sense for a company that has integration routines in place. In medium- to large-sized organizations, good training and talent-management programs can help to ensure that high-potential employees are steered onto a management track and high-performing literati/numerati are appropriately tasked and rewarded.

External recruitment of top talent is challenging because of the need to compete for experts at market prices. External searches must be performed by experienced professionals and by a management team that is able to make accurate talent assessments, and who are in turn made accountable for their decisions. Individual hires must be assessed for compatibility with the prevailing corporate culture. If executed poorly, attempts to compete for "star" talent from external sources may produce a bad case of "winner's curse."

Every organization has a good chance of attracting/developing a percentage of top talent. Expert talent is highly mobile in most Western economies. The relative decline of corporate pension plans, the weakening of strong corporate cultures, and the erosion of loyalty toward employers have increased the opportunity for head-hunting highly skilled employees. However, these same factors also make it harder to retain experts, making it all the more critical that management addresses their needs while protecting the firm's profit margins. Research shows that those with the most training, education, and ability are the most likely to quit if dissatisfied (Sturman and Trevor, 2001).

Competition for high-end talent is also increasingly global. In the United States, immigrants have always been significant in the scientific and engineering workforce. In recent years, the foreign-born have also played a significant role in entrepreneurship. A survey by Duke University and the University of California (Duke Today, 2007) shows that one quarter of newly founded engineering technology firms in the United States in the decade 1995 to 2005 had at least one foreign-born founder. In Silicon Valley, the percentage was over 50%.

Needless to say, the recruitment of top talent can be fraught with hazards, as performance on one platform need not be a good indicator of performance on another (Groysberg, Nanda, and Nohria, 2004). The issue of "contextual talent" is analyzed below, under "4.4.4 Incentives and motivation."

4.2.2 Literati, numerati, and entrepreneurs

The two categories of expert considered in this chapter are the literati/ numerati and entrepreneurial managers. Entrepreneurial managers can be "members" of the numerati or literati, but it is by no means the case that they must be.

The literati and numerati are marked by high levels of education and/or experience (Teece, 2011). The literati tend to have both undergraduate and, usually, graduate degrees in arts and letters, economics, business, or law. The numerati are likewise highly educated, but in mathematics or statistics; the sciences, including computer science; information systems; engineering; or accounting and finance. In some fields, such as computer science, experience can substitute for an advanced degree. In other fields, such as medicine, both academic and practical (clinical) training are necessary for deep proficiency.

Both groups have significant analytical skills, but the literati tend to be more specialized at synthesis and the communication of ideas. The numerati excel at analysis, especially of large data sets.

A third type of expert is the entrepreneurial manager. As Baumol and Strom (2007: 233) note, "A close look at the extraordinary economic growth of the last two centuries, however, suggests that the market mechanism does not do its work without the input of individual actors – the entrepreneurs who bring cutting edge innovation to market." This holds as true for entrepreneurial managers within large firms as it does for the founders of start-up companies.

In fast-paced, globally competitive environments, consumer needs, technological opportunities, and competitor activity are constantly in flux. Opportunities open up for both newcomers and incumbents, putting the profit streams of incumbent enterprises at risk. As discussed by Teece, Pisano, and Shuen (1997), the path ahead for some emerging marketplace trajectories is easily recognized. In microelectronics this would include miniaturization leading to greater chip density. However, many emerging trajectories are hard to discern. For instance, it is not currently clear when, or even if, a new car battery technology will emerge that can make electric vehicles price- and performance-competitive with internal-combustion cars.

Entrepreneurial managers, like entrepreneurs, excel at the scanning, learning, creative, and interpretive activities needed to sense (and later seize) new technological and market opportunities. Investment in research is often a complement, but never a replacement, for such activities.

The ability to create and/or sense opportunities is clearly not uniformly distributed among individuals or enterprises. Opportunity discovery (or creation) requires specific knowledge, creative activity, the ability to understand user/customer decision making, and practical wisdom (Nonaka and Toyama, 2007). It involves interpreting information in whatever form it appears – a chart, a picture, a conversation at a trade show, news of scientific and technological breakthrough, or the angst expressed by a frustrated customer. One must accumulate and then filter information from professional and social contacts to create a conjecture or a hypothesis about the likely evolution of technologies, customer needs, and marketplace responses.

Once opportunities are glimpsed, entrepreneurs and managers must also devise a means for capturing value. Neither the identification nor even the creation of opportunities result spontaneously in capturing value. Indeed, many inventions go unexploited for extended periods. The pioneer may not turn out to be the winner (Teece, 1986, 2006).

When opportunities are first glimpsed, entrepreneurs and managers must decide which technologies to pursue and which market segments to target while continuing to interpret ongoing developments. They must also develop a forecast about how technologies will evolve and how – and how quickly – competitors, suppliers, and customers will respond. Competitors may or may not see the opportunity, and even if they do they may calibrate it differently. Their actions, along with those of customers, suppliers, standard-setting bodies, and governments can also change the nature of the opportunity and the manner in which competition will unfold.

On the basis of these conjectures, the entrepreneur/manager must move to seize the opportunity by designing and implementing a business model, preferably one that cannot readily be imitated. Getting the timing and the basic elements of the business model right is a critical part of the innovation process (Teece, 1986, 2010).

These functions of the entrepreneur are quite different from those of the ordinary manager. The managers of ordinary activities must oversee the ongoing efficiency of established processes. They need to ensure that schedules are met and contracts honored, that quality and productivity improve, and that the business model is constantly tuned. Although there are creative aspects to accomplishing these tasks, managing the operations of an ongoing business, especially in a relatively static environment, is comparatively straightforward. Great entrepreneurs need not be particularly adept at operations – but of course they do need to be supported by a strong operations team.

To summarize, entrepreneurial managers with responsibility for lines of business, departments, or the entire enterprise bear the primary responsibility for identifying and pursuing opportunities. The literati and numerati provide insight and analysis at each stage of the process.

But the ultimate determinants of success or failure are organizational. The best knowledge and leadership cannot transform a company or a marketplace if the company lacks the collective capabilities to carry out the underlying vision, and it is to the consideration of capabilities that we now turn.

4.3 Strategy, resources, and capabilities

In order to be fully effective, the activities and management of experts must be organized within an effective strategic-management framework. The activities of experts, somewhat more than of other employees, must be tightly linked to strategy development and execution. And strategy, as developed by entrepreneurial managers, must correctly take into account the available resources and capabilities of the organization (and of its experts), ensuring that any capability gaps are filled as needed.

One of the leading paradigms in the strategic-management field is the dynamic capabilities framework, which builds on the RBV of the firm. The resources framework has developed in the management literature, building on Penrose (1959), Rubin (1973), and others. In the 1980s, a number of strategic-management scholars, including Teece (1980, 1982, 1984), Rumelt (1984), and Wernerfelt (1984) began theorizing that a firm earns rents from leveraging its unique resources, which are difficult to monetize directly via transactions in intermediate markets.

This section begins by reviewing the concept of organizational resources, including ordinary capabilities. Then the dynamic-capabilities framework, which can inform the management of experts, is presented.

4.3.1 Resources and ordinary capabilities

Resources are firm-specific, mostly intangible, assets that are difficult, if not impossible, to imitate. Examples include intellectual property, process know-how, customer relationships, and the knowledge possessed by groups of especially skilled employees. They are typically not considered at all in the firm's financial statements, except perhaps in a balance sheet line item for "Goodwill" related to an acquired firm.

Resources – particularly intellectual capital – are idiosyncratic in nature, and are difficult to trade because their property rights are likely to have fuzzy boundaries and their value is context dependent. As a result, there is no well-developed market for most types of resources/ intellectual capital; in fact, they are typically not traded at all. They are also often quite difficult to transfer among firms simply from a management (let alone transactions) perspective.

The resource-based view of the firm was an important intellectual leap beyond the prevailing economic view that strategic success is obtained by efficiency and the creation of barriers to entry. Its stress on the fungible nature of assets accorded well with the understanding of many practitioners, especially in high-tech industries. They know that sustainable success comes from the laborious accumulation of technological assets and human resources, not from clever strategic positioning. But the resource-based approach failed to pursue the questions of how firms develop or acquire new competences and adapt when circumstances change. The dynamic capabilities approach deals directly with such questions.

Capabilities are a type of resource. It is perhaps easier to understand what dynamic capabilities are by juxtaposing them against the more familiar ordinary capabilities.

Ordinary capabilities undergird the firm's technical fitness, that is, how effectively the firm carries out its production and distribution functions, regardless of how highly the output is prized in the market (Teece, 2007). Technical fitness supports static efficiencies; it allows an organization to keep "earning its living by producing and selling the same product, on the same scale and to the same customer population over time" (Winter, 2003: 992). But, unless competition is very weak, ordinary capabilities are unlikely to support durable competitive advantage.

Ordinary capabilities derive from the presence of skills, facilities, and equipment; from the firm's processes and routines; and, potentially, from the networks in which the firm is embedded. There is a temptation to equate operational and ordinary capabilities; but they are not the same concept. Ordinary capabilities include administrative and governance capabilities, not just operational ones. These three elements must be practiced together. Operations need to be planned and coordinated in order for tasks to be performed appropriately.

An ordinary capability enables the firm to perform a definable task that can be measured against a target or an external "best practice" standard. Many best practices, however, diffuse rather quickly because they are often explicit.

As Bob Lutz (2011), the former vice-chairman at General Motors, observed about the auto industry:

> The operations portion of the automobile business has been thoroughly optimized over many decades, doesn't vary much from one automobile company to another, and can be managed with a focus on repetitive process. It is the "hard" part of the car business and requires little in the way of creativity, vision or imagination. Almost all car companies do this very well, and there is little or no competitive advantage to be gained by "trying even harder" in procurement, manufacturing or wholesale.

This statement is revealing because it indicates how ordinary capabilities are, to a large extent, imitable and hence likely to be widely distributed, at least in the developed economies. Ordinary capabilities that are less explicit and therefore capable of providing valuable differentiation from rivals (at least when the capabilities are strong) include how decisions are made, how customer needs are assessed, and how quality is maintained.

4.3.2 Dynamic capabilities

A firm's ordinary capabilities enable the production and sale of a defined (but static) set of products and services. But the presence of ordinary capabilities says nothing about whether the current production schedule is the right (or even a profitable) thing to do. The nature of such routine-based capabilities, and their underlying processes, is that they are not meant to change – at least not until they have to.

The change process is a key part of higher level competences called dynamic capabilities. Dynamic capabilities determine whether the enterprise is currently making good choices with respect to products and market segments, and whether its future plans are appropriately matched to changing consumer needs and technological and competitive opportunities (Teece, Pisano, and Shuen, 1997; Teece, 2009).

Dynamic capabilities are the firm's ability to integrate, build, and reconfigure internal – and, often, external – resources to address and shape rapidly changing business environments. Dynamic capabilities may sometimes be rooted in certain change routines (e.g., product development along a known trajectory) and analysis (e.g., of investment choices). However, they are more commonly also rooted in creative managerial and entrepreneurial acts (e.g., pioneering new markets).

Dynamic capabilities require the business enterprise (especially its top management) to develop conjectures, validate them, and realign assets and competences for new requirements. They reflect the speed and degree to which the firm's idiosyncratic resources can be profitably aligned and then, when needed, realigned to match the opportunities and requirements of the business environment.

Dynamic capabilities are also used to assess when and how the enterprise is to ally with other enterprises. The expansion of trade has enabled and required greater global specialization. To make the global system of vertical specialization and co-specialization (bilateral dependence) work, there is a need (indeed an enhanced need) for firms to jointly develop and align assets in order to deliver a joint "solution" that customers value.

Not infrequently, the innovating firm(s) will be required to create a market, such as when an entirely new product is offered to customers, or when new intermediate products must be traded. Dynamic capabilities, particularly the more entrepreneurial competences, are a critical input to these market-creating (and co-creating) processes.

Teece (2007) suggests that the dynamic capabilities necessary for continuous renewal can be divided into three clusters: (1) identification and assessment of an opportunity (*sensing*), (2) mobilization of resources to address an opportunity and to capture value from doing so (*seizing*), and (3) continued renewal (*transforming*).

Sensing is an entrepreneurial activity – whether conducted by a new or an existing firm – that involves the identification and conceptualization of opportunities both within and beyond prevailing technological paradigms. In some cases, as stressed by Kirzner (1973), the firm may have differential access to existing information relative to rivals. More often, though, it is a matter of the firm's managers and experts scanning, interpreting, and learning across the same technologies and markets that are visible to rival firms in an effort to discern the possibility of a new or better competitive position (March and Simon, 1958; Nelson and Winter, 1982).

The literature on entrepreneurship emphasizes that opportunity discovery and creation can originate from the cognitive and creative capacities of an individual. However, the discovery process can also be grounded in organizational routines, such as continuous research and development activity, external scanning for new technologies, and co-development activities with alliance partners.

As the global sources of invention and innovation become widely dispersed and technologies at the frontier increasingly complex, it is less likely that the enterprise can rely solely on internal R&D, even in very large firms. As a result, intangible assets that formerly needed to be built internally are outsourced, at least partially. Declines in the cost of computing and communications have facilitated collaboration with suppliers and other elements of the innovation ecosystem (Teece, 1989). The expansion of outsourcing and collaboration has increased the viability of an "open innovation" approach (Chesbrough, 2006). With open innovation, a firm identifies and exploits new technologies and creative capacities developed both inside and outside the boundaries of the firm.

In practice, management teams often find it difficult to look beyond a narrow search horizon tied to established competences. Henderson (1994) cites General Motors, Digital Equipment, and IBM as companies that faced major problems from becoming trapped in their deeply ingrained assumptions, information filters, and problem-solving strategies.

Seizing an opportunity requires investments in development via further creative and/or combinatorial activity that addresses the opportunity with new products, processes, or services. It may involve building a necessary new competence or identifying an appropriate external alliance that can secure access to one (Teece, 1986).

Transformation of the firm itself is the third group of capabilities required for creating (and capturing) value. Sensing and seizing delineate a path, but the firm still needs to periodically consider (and reconsider) its own "fit" to the opportunities it plans to exploit. Management must assess the coherence of the firm's business model, asset structure, and organizational routines with respect to its environment. Yet commitment to existing processes, assets, and problem definitions makes this extremely hard to do, especially in a firm that is currently performing satisfactorily.

Organizational innovation can allow the firm to escape unfavorable path dependencies. When such innovation is incremental, routines and structures can probably be adapted gradually. However, reconfiguring the firm is often costly in terms of both money and morale. Radical organizational innovation can potentially be accommodated by a "break out" unit where new capabilities are established before being introduced to the firm as a whole (Teece, 2000).

Entrepreneurial managers and key experts play a large role in sensing, seizing, and transforming, but the supporting routines and values must be deeply ingrained in the organization. Apple's former and now deceased CEO, Steve Jobs, was seen as critical to the company's success (based on Apple's declining performance after he was ousted as CEO in 1985, followed by the firm's stellar performance after his return in 1997).

Apple's success appears to have stemmed in part from Jobs' prioritization of possibilities based on his deep understanding of the market and an uncompromising insistence on ease of use and on appealing product designs. This approach can be routinized to some extent (the organization comes to know "what Steve likes") but Apple and its customers unquestionably benefited from the touch of a creative and brilliant conceiver of new (categories of) electronics products that appeal to consumers around the world.

There are, of course, risks in relying on a particular talented individual, especially if those talents don't translate into a set of replicable internal routines. Jobs himself was aware of this. In 2008, before his second medical leave, he established an internal business school at Apple in which academics were brought in to prepare cases about how key past decisions, such as the creation of the Apple Store, were reached (Lashinsky, 2011). By having executives teach these cases to the company's managers, Apple's high-level routines and top-management processes are propagated among its current and future leaders.

This example is by no means unique. IBM successfully routinized its selection, evaluation, and exploitation of "emerging business opportunities" in a process that has resulted in billions of dollars of additional revenue (O'Reilly, Harreld, and Tushman, 2009). Similarly, Cisco has routinized its selection and integration of acquisition targets (Mayer and Kenney, 2004).

An enterprise will be vulnerable if the sensing, creative, interpretive, and learning functions are left to the cognitive capacities of a few individuals. Many companies do become dependent on a key leader. Over time, however, a gifted individual's (or team's) talents, processes, and values can be embedded in corporate culture and organizational routines either formally, by the creation of systems, or informally, by repeated demonstration and communication.

4.4 Organizing and managing the literati/numerati

Although experts are required for some of the operational routines that constitute ordinary capabilities, they are especially vital contributors to a firm's dynamic capabilities. Bringing out their best in that regard requires a different management approach than is needed for operational excellence.

Many expert activities, such as developing new product lines, involve project work that requires cooperation/collaboration among the literati, the numerati, and entrepreneurs. An enterprise can hire the brightest, most creative people, but it is only through successfully fostering the sharing of information, collaboration, and the use of networks inside and outside the enterprise that their creative potential will be released (Subramaniam and Youndt, 2005).

To be effective, this collaborative model of knowledge generation must, in turn, be embedded in a knowledge-friendly enterprise. The literati and numerati are unlikely to be productive and satisfied in a traditional hierarchical organization, being compensated in traditional ways, and having compensation put at risk for events beyond their control. Dynamically competitive enterprises must understand the contextual value of talent, and must develop new ways of compensating exceptional talent.

Table 4.1 contrasts this knowledge model (right-hand column) with the characteristics of the archetypal industrial model that still characterize too many large organizations.

It is also important to recognize that not everything is appropriately organized in collaborative teams. Indeed, there is a great deal about traditional teams that involve hidden and unnecessary costs. When team requirements are too heavy, decision cycles lengthen, expenses mount, and the organization adopts an inward focus.

Put differently, one cannot simply assume that more is better when it comes to collaboration. Consensus and participatory leadership aren't

Table 4.1 *Contrasting management models of the business enterprise*

Organizational characteristics	Industrial model	Knowledge model (for literati and numerati)
Hierarchy	Deep	Shallow
Leadership	Centralized	Distributed
Work	Segmented	Collaborative
People viewed as	Cost	Asset
Basis of control	Authority	Influence and example
Assumptions about individuals	Opportunistic	Honorable
Financial incentives	Base salary + discretionary bonus	Metrics-based compensation; limited discretion

always a good thing, particularly when the issues are complex and there is considerable asymmetry in the distribution of talents in the team. The right voices need to be heard. Forced teaming often leads to excessive consensus building, slow decision making, and the wasting of time and money. While authentic dissent ought to be highly valued, unproductive collaboration can be more dangerous than missed opportunities for quality engagement and collaboration.

Project teams should be kept small, intimate, yet diverse. Project groups that complete their task or run into "blind alleys" should disband so that the mix of talents are ready to be reconfigured as needed to meet future demands. Assigning people to a project "because they're used to working together" is a path to failure.

This section presents the reasons for, and organizational implications of, light-touch management; the managerial aspects of teams, with an emphasis on the innovation process; and a special focus section on the top management team, where entrepreneurial managers should be well represented. A final section briefly discusses appropriate incentives for motivating and retaining top talent.

4.4.1 Light-touch management

With respect to the literati and numerati, strongly authoritarian management is likely to be dysfunctional. Rigidly bureaucratic corporate cultures around collaboration are likewise anathema.

Management of experts must have a light touch. Otherwise cooperative efforts will be suppressed, and creativity will be compromised. Management is seldom sufficiently informed to second guess the difficult and granular technical tradeoffs and judgments of the literati and numerati with respect to solving the problem at hand. Evaluations must be based more on results and less on the processes for reaching them.

The commonest purpose for hierarchy – to assign and oversee well-defined tasks – is simply not needed for many types of expert professional work. Experts tend to be substantially self-motivated and self-guided.

Accordingly, management of experts usually needs to be decentralized or "distributed." Traditional notions of management that rely heavily on hierarchy and decisions driven from the top are unlikely to work well when expert work is a large component of the firm's activities.

Of course, strong accountability is still required from the literati and the numerati. Autonomy and accountability go hand in hand; the more easily performance can be measured, the greater the autonomy that can safely be permitted.

Self-organized cooperative activity is frequently observed in science projects and in creative engineering projects. Richard Nelson (1962) studied the development of the transistor at Bell Labs and noted:

> the type of interaction we have noted in the transistor project requires that individuals be free to help each other as they see fit. If all allocation decisions were made by a centrally situated executive, the changing allocation of research effort called for as perceived alternatives and knowledge change would place an impossible information processing and decision making burden on top management. Clearly the research scientists must be given a great deal of freedom. (Nelson, 1962: 569)

Nelson likewise notes that teamwork in a creative context is likely to differ from traditional contexts. The development of the transistor did involve teamwork. But here is how Nelson describes what teamwork meant:

> it meant interaction and mutual stimulation and help... But several people outside the team also interacted in an important way...teamwork...did not mean a closely directed project...The project was marked by flexibility – by the ability to shift directions and by the rather rapid focusing of attention by

several people on problems and phenomena unearthed by others. (Nelson, 1962: 578)

and

the informality of the decision structure played a very important role in permitting speedy cooperative response to changing ideas and knowledge. Thus the transistor was a team invention, but not in the sense of the team which has grown fashionable in recent years. (Nelson, 1962: 579)

Fifty years later, the same lessons – particularly the importance of decentralization and flexibility – were being relearned. John Chambers, CEO of US network equipment company Cisco, remarked: "In 2001, we were like most high-tech companies – all decisions came to the top 10 people in the company, and we drove things back down from there" (Chambers quoted in McGirt, 2008: 93). Cisco instituted a more decentralized and collaborative management system, with a network of councils and boards entrusted and empowered to launch new businesses, and incentives to encourage executives to work together. Chambers claimed that "these boards and councils have been able to innovate with tremendous speed. Fifteen minutes and one week to get a [business] plan that used to take six months" (Chambers quoted in McGirt, 2008: 93). However, over time, the structure became sclerotic and, beginning in 2009, Cisco reduced the number of councils from 12 to 3, while dissolving the associated boards, in a renewed push to speed up decision making (Clark and Tibken, 2011).

The point here is a simple one: in fast-paced complex environments where there is heterogeneity in customer needs and the focus is on technological innovation, it is simply impossible to achieve the necessary flexibility and responsiveness with a command-and-control organizational structure. Moreover, with a highly talented workforce, excessive centralization can shut down local initiative.

The above admonitions are not meant to imply that top management should not guide and coordinate innovative activities. In fact, there are certain types of innovation – particularly "systemic" innovation (Teece, 1984) – where close coordination of different groups is required.

Managers of innovative enterprises must learn to lead without relying on the authority that comes from a position in an organizational chart or the 'C' designation in their title. This imposes new challenges for some companies and some individuals, but it is the way of the future in many contexts. The challenge is to connect individual initiatives to the overall corporate strategy without building an expensive and initiative-sapping hierarchy.

In some settings, it may even be desirable to invert the traditional hierarchy in order to create the organizational structures in which professionals can perform to their potential (Quinn, Anderson, and Finkelstein, 1996). With an inverted hierarchy, the job of the manager is to provide support by creating incentive alignment and ensuring resource availability. The experts may even take responsibility for determining executive wages.

In purely creative environments, it is indeed the highly skilled experts that, in effect, hire "bosses" rather than the other way around. The Hollywood agency model for creative talent was an early manifestation. As explained by Albert and Bradley (1997), the stars themselves, beginning with Newman, Streisand, and Poitier, broke away from the studios to create their own production company, First Artists. A key element of First Artists' strategy was to create a climate in which leading actors can control their professional environment and lives. The artists put a professional manager in place, but the manager's mandate was to effectuate the artists' view of how films should be produced. There have been many talent-based independent production companies founded since, with varying degrees of success.

University faculties have some similar attributes. The faculty arguably hires their Dean since the Dean generally serves at the sufferance of the faculty, at least in some of the major research universities such as the University of California, Berkeley. The university requires the discharge of teaching, research, and service obligations by faculty, but allows faculty members considerable discretion as to whether and when tasks (other than class meetings) are performed. Professional services organizations in the legal, medical, and other fields exhibit similar characteristics.

Implemented properly, the distributed-leadership approach is not an abdication of managerial responsibility. It is just the opposite. The executive leadership team sets strategy and goals and must retain credibility with its experts as well as being answerable to the board of directors and to other stakeholders.

While creative activities need to be organized in a distributed/ decentralized way, there are operational activities involving experts that should not be managed in this way. The accounting, finance, and treasury functions are obvious examples. As noted above, when the goal is to achieve systemic innovation, there may well be activities that require tight integration because the project/technology spans multiple lines of business, or because there are very significant sales benefits to be achieved from a coordinated approach.

4.4.2 Teams and innovation

Because of increased specialization, interaction among people from diverse disciplines or functional groups is almost always required to solve the complex problems that accompany the exercise of a firm's sensing, seizing, and transforming capabilities. The numerati and literati require considerable professional autonomy, but must nevertheless collaborate when collaboration yields benefits.

In principle, the outcome from a group such as a cross-functional team can exceed the capabilities of its best individual members (Larson, 2007). However, if not managed properly, the bringing together of specialists from different parts of the organization can impede innovation (Ancona and Caldwell, 1992).

At the same time, there are numerous ways that teams go astray, from unproductive conflict that leads to indecision to peer pressure that leads to a flawed conclusion. Team members may be undercommitted, too tied to their normal functions or disciplines, or unwilling to collaborate.

Groups that encourage expression of minority opinions make higher quality decisions (Maier, 1970; Nemeth, 2012). Avoiding conflict often results in low-quality decisions (Tjosvold, 1985). Emotional conflict, however, is more likely to have a negative effect than is substantive conflict over solutions to task-related problems (Pelled, Eisenhardt and Xin, 1999). Conflict is most likely to contribute to high-quality decisions when trust is high, i.e., when members don't suspect any one on the team of trying to score points at the others' expense (Dooley and Fryxell, 1999).

Group leaders can avoid suppressing healthy disagreement (based on the issues, not on the people, involved) by not expressing their positions too early in the process (Janis, 1972). Openness should be encouraged by not dismissing any idea too quickly.

Yet it is vital to have leadership, at the team level or higher, that knows which ideas can be rejected out of hand. A key role of entrepreneurial managers is, having enunciated a vision, to permit experimentation and search, then support promising paths and close down foolish ones.

Dougherty (1992) suggests that the interaction and collaboration necessary for innovation in cross-functional teams is best brought out by shared learning activities, such as focus groups and user visits. Shared activities also promote group cohesiveness, which has been shown to contribute to higher performance by R&D project teams (Keller, 1986).

An added wrinkle is that teams are increasingly spread across organizational boundaries and/or large distances. This is truer than ever for innovation, as large and small companies have begun to tap into pools of science and engineering talent in industrializing economies. Fortunately, the autonomy and trust that are appropriate for managing experts translate easily to the "virtual team" context, where continuous direct leadership may not be possible due to time zone differences. To overcome the social remoteness of distance, special measures, such as a project kick-off meeting that brings everyone to a single location for a few days, must be devised to at least partially formalize the process of fostering mutual support with a shared purpose (Siebdrat, Hoegl, and Ernst, 2009).

While physical distance forces the use of virtual teams, virtuality is actually a matter of degree since all teams, even those whose members are co-located, will employ some forms of computer-mediated communication. There is still much work to be done regarding the performance effect of virtual teams, but one consistent finding is that virtual teams require more time to complete tasks than face-to-face teams, so they may not be suitable for the most urgent projects (Martins, Gilson, and Maynard, 2004).

Whether team members are dispersed or co-located, their work must be tied to the overall strategy of the business (Wheelwright and Clark, 1992). Management of the team needs to tread the line between preventing the natural tension and creativity of innovation from descending into chaos and constraining the team by defining the goals and strategy linkage so narrowly that real innovation is impossible. Takeuchi and Nonaka (1986) call this "subtle control," which involves a monitoring function that leads to intervention (e.g., eliminating a team member) only when absolutely necessary.

In the case of teams engaged in innovation activities, perhaps the best interface between the team and upper management is a "heavyweight" project manager (Clark, Chew, and Fujimoto, 1987). The "heavyweight" has both credibility within the team and power/prestige in the organization as a whole. The latter is important for ensuring the team the necessary resources and room to maneuver, and is also important for gaining the project manager the respect and cooperation of the literati and/or numerati on the team.

In some special cases, when the stakes are high, the technical challenge great, or the deadlines too close, an organization may assemble a team consisting exclusively of its most able experts. The management requirements in this case are somewhat different from more traditional teams because experts' experts are typically used to being in the leadership position themselves. It may be helpful to provide some extra initial structure to foster collaboration, such as breaking into smaller groups or even pairs that can tackle segments of the overall challenge in parallel.

With these all-expert teams, the identity of the team leader is of even greater importance than in less intense settings. For all to succeed, there must be mutual respect between and among experts and the leader. In practice, this means that the team leader will need to be able to massage large egos without seeming patronizing.

The goal in such project groups, or "virtuoso teams" (Fischer and Boynton, 2005), is not accommodation and harmony; rather, the aim is to achieve excellence by unleashing individual creativity. A higher level of (topic-specific, non-personal) conflict is to be expected and bounded only by the common goal and deadline.

Table 4.2 summarizes some of the differences between traditional and virtuoso teams.

4.4.3 The top management team and leadership

A particular type of expert team is worthy of special attention. The top management team (TMT), meaning those who report directly to the CEO, tackles highly complex issues and bears responsibility for the future of the organization. Within the dynamic capabilities framework, the TMT bears the ultimate responsibility (individually and collectively) for deciding which opportunities are worth pursuing, for developing and promulgating a coherent vision and strategy, and for orchestrating the firm's resources accordingly. When the TMT performs poorly together, the result is likely to be organizational decline (Hambrick, 1994).

Top management team diversity, in terms of functional background, education, and company tenure, has been found by a study of the

Table 4.2 *Key differences between traditional teams and virtuoso teams*

Team characteristics	Traditional teams	Virtuoso teams
Membership	Members chosen based on who has available time	Members chosen based on expertise
Culture	Collective	Collective and individual
Focus	Tight project management. "On time and on budget" more important than content	Ideas, understanding, and breakthrough-thinking emphasized
Target	Conventional output	Breakthrough output
Intensity	High/medium	High
Stakes	Low/medium	High

Source: adapted from Fischer and Boynton (2005).

airline industry to lead to novel strategies, although action tended to be slower than for homogenous TMTs (Hambrick, Cho, and Chen, 1996). More importantly, the study found that heterogeneous TMTs were associated with better market share and profit outcomes.

A well-integrated TMT, in which members share openly and truly work together on strategic issues, has been shown to facilitate the pursuit of new concepts while not losing sight of current operations – so-called organizational ambidexterity (Lubatkin *et al.*, 2006). Ambidexterity, in turn, is a vital aspect of dynamic capabilities (O'Reilly and Tushman, 2008). Top management team integration is also associated with proactive strategy formation and agile implementation in fast-moving competitive settings (Chen, Lin, and Michel, 2010).

A well-functioning TMT is a resource that takes time to build. Studies have found that, contrary to conventional wisdom that suggests that lengthy CEO tenure leads to complacency, high CEO tenure is actually associated with better collaboration within the TMT, which in turn is associated with better firm performance (Simsek *et al.*, 2005). This CEO tenure effect appears to be independent of the length of time the TMT itself has been working together.

To manage the TMT, CEOs should be concerned with how the team works as a group, sharing information and solving problems, as much as with individual performance. Carmeli, Tishler, and Edmondson (2009) provide evidence that the extent to which a CEO encourages collaboration and open communication within the TMT contributes to the ability to learn from failures, which is in turn linked to the quality of strategic decisions. Norms that permit the airing of disagreements about the task at hand are beneficial for the critical evaluation of options (Jehn, 1995).

Carmeli, Schaubroeck, and Tishler (2011) found that participatory leadership, in which the CEO shares decision authority, improves the collaborative nature of the TMT and, more importantly, firm performance. When conflicts of interest arise between TMT members, the CEO must act as a facilitator for airing the differences and resolving them in the way that is best for the organization.

Bass (1985) identified two types of leadership, which have been adopted for numerous subsequent studies. *Transactional* leaders know how to motivate their employees to meet expectations and accomplish set tasks that fall within ordinary capabilities. *Transformational* leaders know how to inspire and challenge employees in ways that cause them to perform beyond expectations. According to Bass, transformational leadership "is more likely to emerge in times of distress and rapid change" (Bass, 1985: 39).

Naturally, these differences in leadership affect the functioning of the TMT and the organization. Ling *et al.* (2008) found that TMTs under transformational CEOs had more decentralized responsibilities, were more collaborative, and were more willing to tackle new growth opportunities. This result ties leadership style directly to the strategic transformation at the heart of dynamic capabilities.

4.4.4 Incentives and motivation

In today's global markets, unique skills and knowledge can command high returns. The compensation ranges for experts need to be less compressed than those for other employee categories, reflecting each individual's contribution. Yet incentives for motivating expert talent can be non-monetary as well as financial. Where experts are concerned, more money will generally not make up for an unsatisfactory work environment.

The salaries that top talent can command have risen because the creative, analytical, and "rainmaking" abilities of leading professionals can increasingly be leveraged across global markets. Skills that can help solve complex problems, help make critical decisions or resolve complex disputes, help save lives, help win business, and help design and develop new products and services, are vital to business success and are relatively scarce. In short, where the stakes are high and where top talent can make a difference, that talent can earn exceptional rewards.

Reich (2002: p. 107) and many others have observed that talented people can earn more today, relative to the median wage, than could talented and ambitious people in the industrial era. Larger and more open ("contestable") markets are one reason why dispersion in earnings has increased. For example, the outsourcing of components and low-end services to lower cost locations has disproportionately benefited skilled workers in the advanced economies of the United States, Western Europe, and Japan (Feenstra and Hanson, 1999).

Getting financial incentives right is fundamental. Suffice to note that there is ample evidence that pay for performance is associated with higher performance at both the individual (Jenkins *et al.*, 1998) and organizational levels (Gerhart, 2000). The resulting pay differentials are generally accepted by top talent – so long as they are truly capability/performance based.

Unfortunately, the more discretion that management has to set pay, the more energy and resources are likely to be wasted by people trying to capture more of the available resources (Milgrom and Roberts, 1987). This can best be avoided by setting quantifiable performance metrics as the basis for pay, but this is not always possible (Teece, 2003).

In setting pay levels, it is important to distinguish between intrinsic talent and contextual talent. Intrinsic talent is that talent which provides/commands full value on a stand-alone basis. In a professional services organization, for instance, this might represent the business that professionals can source based on their own wits and capabilities, i.e., independent of the brand or platform on which they stand.

Individual contextual value can exceed intrinsic value when the individual benefits from the other complementary assets (such as infrastructure and brand) that the organization provides. Contextual value may be very large, especially in circumstances where teams must be employed to get the job done, and when the firm's infrastructure and staffing play important support roles.

A firm may not need to pay as much for an expert whose "star" quality is so firm-specific that it would not transfer very well to other settings. An important exception is when the contextual skills and knowledge of the individual would be difficult and costly to replace if the expert departs.

Getting pay wrong can lead to a loss of competitiveness. In a professional services firm, where human capital is more important than any other inputs, it can lead to the departure of key experts, possibly benefitting rivals and beginning a negative feedback process in which reputation and quality decline (Teece, 2003).

For employee retention, compensation at competitive levels may be necessary but not sufficient. Prominent aspects of the job environment include the organization's culture, the quality of its management, the challenge of the work, and the autonomy afforded workers. Companies that rank higher on these and similar "quality of work life" measures outperform their peers in retention (Chambers *et al.*, 1998: 50).

In the case of employees with potential for management advancement, Martin and Schmidt (2010) recommend sharing future strategies interactively. By whatever means the strategies are communicated – a protected website, closed-door briefings, etc. – feedback from the employees should be welcomed. The collaborative atmosphere that makes for a successful TMT should pervade the avenues that lead there.

4.5 Conclusions

We conclude by noting that expert talent has become indispensable for solving problems, delivering service, designing products, and making quality decisions in today's hypercompetitive global economy. The imperatives for managing these valuable employees (and contractors) go beyond tying their actions to the firm's strategy. Their management must seek to maximize their contributions to the firm's dynamic capabilities. It is these dynamic capabilities that inform and shape strategy, ensuring that the chosen strategy incorporates and anticipates changes in the firm's business environment.

Traditional hierarchical approaches to managing the literati, the numerati, or entrepreneurial managers are unlikely to bring out their best, in the dynamic capabilities sense of forward-looking creativity that responds effectively to the business context. Narrow-band compensation systems are also unlikely to attract and retain the most skilled experts. Offering them challenging, creative opportunities can, in some cases, do more than extra money to increase their job satisfaction.

When experts are properly managed, their employment contributions will inform and help to realize the strategic goals identified through the exercise of a firm's dynamic capabilities. The ideal is to hire and/or train and promote the best people, provide them a transparent pay-for-performance package, find managers with sufficient skill and credibility to guide their work, then step back and let them work.

With respect to the subject of this volume, talent management, our view is that the handling of experts and their careers by HR systems must go beyond alignment with strategy, such as that advocated by Beatty, Huselid, and Schneier (2003). Talent management must also be conceived with a view to strengthening the firm's dynamic capabilities. Strategies may change, but the firm's capabilities for sensing, seizing, and transforming must be maintained.

A growing number of organizations are finding ways to break the shackles of rigid HR systems in order to create a space for experts to feel comfortable and to be productive. To do otherwise risks a downward spiral of lagging knowledge generation, erosion of expertise, and declining competitive advantage.

References

Albert, S. and Bradley, K. (1997). *Managing Knowledge: Experts, Agencies and Organizations*. Cambridge: Cambridge University Press.

Ancona, D. G. and Caldwell, D. F. (1992). Demography and design: predictors of new product team performance. *Organization Science*, 3 (3), 321–41.

Bass, B. M. (1985). Leadership: good, better, best. *Organizational Dynamics*, 13 (3), 26–40.

Baumol, W. J. and Strom, R. J. (2007). Entrepreneurship and economic growth. *Strategic Entrepreneurship Journal*, 1 (3–4), 233–7.

Beatty, R. W., Huselid, M. A., and Schneier, C. E. (2003). New HR metrics: scoring on the business scorecard. *Organizational Dynamics*, 32 (2), 107–21.

Becker, B. E. and Huselid, M. A. (1998). High performance work systems and firm performance, a synthesis of research and managerial implications. In G. Ferris (ed.) *Research in Personnel and Human Resource Management*. Greenwich, CT: JAI Press, pp. 53–101.

Carmeli, A., Tishler, A., and Edmondson, A. C. (2009). CEO relational leadership and strategic decision quality in top management teams: the role of team trust and learning from failure. *Strategic Organization*, 10 (1), 31–54.

Carmeli, A., Schaubroeck, J., and Tishler, A. (2011). How CEO empowering leadership shapes top management team processes: implications for firm performance. *Leadership Quarterly* 22 (2), 399–411.

Chambers, E. G., Foulon, M., Handfield-Jones, H., Hankin, S M., and Michaels, E. G. III (1998). The war for talent. *McKinsey Quarterly*, 3, 44–57.

Chen, M. J., Lin, H. C., and Michel, J. G. (2010). Navigating in a hyper-competitive environment: the roles of action aggressiveness and TMT integration. *Strategic Management Journal*, 31 (13), 1410–30.

Chesbrough, H. W. (2006). *Open Business Models*. Boston, MA: *Harvard Business School Press*.

Clark, D. and Tibken, S. (2011). Cisco to reduce its bureaucracy. WSJ.com (May 6). http://online.wsj.com/article/SB10001424052748703859304576304890449176956.html. [Accessed 7 Jan 2014].

Clark, K B., Chew, W. B., and Fujimoto, T. (1987). Product development in the world auto industry. *Brookings Papers on Economic Activity*, 3, 729–81.

Dooley, R. S. and Fryxell, G. E. (1999). Attaining decision quality and commitment from dissent: the moderating effects of loyalty and competence in strategic decision-making teams. *Academy of Management Journal*, 42 (4), 389–402.

Dougherty, D. (1992). Interpretative barriers to successful product innovation in large firms. *Organization Science*, 3 (2), 179–202.

Duke Today (2007) Skilled, educated immigrants contribute significantly to U.S. economy. Insight from study by Duke engineering students on formation of engineering and technology companies should inform national immigration debate January 3, 2007. http://m.today.duke.edu/2007/01/engineerstudy.html. [Accessed 7 Jan 2014].

Feenstra, R. C. and Hanson, G. H. (1999). The impact of outsourcing and high-technology capital on wages: estimates for the United States, 1979–1990. *Quarterly Journal of Economics*, 114 (3), 907–40.

Fischer, B. and Boynton, A. (2005). Virtuoso teams. *Harvard Business Review*, 83 (7), 116–23.

Fox, M. F. (1983). Publication productivity among scientists: a critical review. *Social Studies of Science*, 13 (2), 285–305.

Galambos, L. (2010). The role of professionals in the Chandler paradigm. *Industrial and Corporate Change*, 19 (2), 377–98.

Gerhart, B. (2000). Compensation, strategy, and organizational performance. In S. L. Rynes and B. Gerhart (eds.), *Compensation in Organizations*. San Francisco, CA: Jossey-Bass, 151–94.

Groysberg, B., Nanda, A., and Nohria, N. (2004). The risky business of hiring stars. *Harvard Business Review*, 82 (5), 92–100.

Hambrick, D. C. (1994). Top management groups: a conceptual integration and reconsideration of the "team" label. In B. M. Staw and L. L. Cummings (eds.), *Research in Organizational Behavior*. Greenwich, CT: JAI Press, pp. 171–214.

Hambrick, D. C., Cho, T. S., and Chen, M. J. (1996). The influence of top management team heterogeneity on firms' competitive moves. *Administrative Science Quarterly*, 41 (4), 659–84.

Henderson, R. M. (1994). Managing innovation in the information age. *Harvard Business Review*, 72 (1), 100–6.

Huselid, M. A., Beatty, R. W., and Becker, B. E. (2005). A players or A positions? *Harvard Business Review*, 83 (12), 110–17.

Janis, I. L. (1972). *Victims of Groupthink: a Psychological Study of Foreign-policy Decisions and Fiascoes*. Boston, MA: Houghton, Mifflin.

Jehn, K. A. (1995). A multimethod examination of the benefits and detriments of intragroup conflict. *Administrative Science Quarterly*, 40 (2), 256–82.

Jenkins, G. D, Jr., Mitra, A., Gupta, N., and Shaw, J. D. (1998). Are financial incentives related to performance? A meta-analytic review of empirical research. *Journal of Applied Psychology*, 83 (5), 777–87.

Keller, R. T. (1986). Predictors of the performance of project groups in R and D organizations. *Academy of Management Journal*, 29 (4), 715–26.

Kirzner, I. M. (1973). *Competition and Entrepreneurship*. Chicago: University of Chicago Press.

Larson, J. R., Jr. (2007). Deep diversity and strong synergy: modeling the impact of variability in members' problem-solving strategies on group problem-solving performance. *Small Group Research*, 38 (3), 413–36.

Lashinsky, A. (2011). How Apple works: inside the world's biggest startup. *Fortune* (online date August 25). http://tech.fortune.cnn.com/2011/08/25/how-apple-works-inside-the-worlds-biggest-startup [Accessed December 24, 2011]

Ling, Y., Simsek, Z., Lubatkin, M. H., and Veiga, J. F. (2008). Transformational leadership's role in promoting corporate entrepreneurship: examining the CEO-TMT interface. *Academy of Management Journal*, 51 (3), 557–76.

Lotka, A. J. (1926). The frequency distribution of scientific productivity. *Journal of the Washington Academy of Sciences*, 16 (12), 317–23.

Lubatkin, M. H., Simsek, Z., Ling, Y., and Veiga, J. F. (2006). Ambidexterity and performance in small-to medium-sized firms: the pivotal role of top management team behavioral integration. *Journal of Management*, 32 (5), 646–72.

Lutz, B. (2011). Life lessons from the car guy. *Wall Street Journal*, June 11, 2011.

Maier, N. R. F. (1970). *Problem Solving and Creativity in Individuals and Groups*. Belmont, CA: Brooks/Cole.

March, J. G. and Simon, H. A. (1958). *Organizations*. New York: Wiley

Martin, J. and Schmidt, C. (2010). How to keep your top talent. *Harvard Business Review*, 88 (5), 54–61.

Martins, L. L., Gilson, L. L., and Maynard, M. T. (2004). Virtual teams: what do we know and where do we go from here? *Journal of Management*, 30 (6), 805–35

Mayer, D. and Kenney, M. (2004). Economic action does not take place in a vacuum: understanding Cisco's acquisition and development strategy. *Industry and Innovation*, 11 (4), 299–325.

McGirt, E. (2008). Revolution in San Jose. *Fast Company*, 131, 90–3.

Milgrom, P. and Roberts, J. (1987). Bargaining cost, influence costs, and the organization of economic activity. In L. Putterman and R. S. Kroszner (eds.) *The Economic Nature of the Firm*. Cambridge: Cambridge University Press, pp. 162–74.

Nelson, R. (1962). The link between science and invention: the case of the transistor. NBER Chapters, In *The Rate and Direction of Inventive Activity: Economic and Social Factors*. National Bureau of Economic Research, Inc. pp. 549–84.

Nelson, R. R. and Winter, S. G. (1982). *An Evolutionary Theory of Economic Change*. Cambridge, MA: Harvard University Press.

Nemeth, C. J. (2012). Minority influence theory. In P. Van Lange, A. Kruglanski, and T. Higgins (eds.), *Handbook of Theories of Social Psychology, Volume Two*. New York, NY: Sage, pp. 362–78.

Nonaka, I. and Toyama, R. (2007). Strategy as distributed practical wisdom (phronesis). *Industrial and Corporate Change*, 16 (3), 371–94.

O'Reilly, C. A. and Tushman, M. L. (2008). Ambidexterity as a dynamic capability: resolving the innovator's dilemma. In Brief, A. P., Staw, B. M. (eds.), *Research in Organizational Behavior, Volume 28*. Oxford: Elsevier, pp. 185–206.

O'Reilly, C. A., Harreld, J. B., and Tushman, M. L. (2009). Organizational ambidexterity: IBM and emerging business opportunities. *California Management Review*, 51 (4), 75–99.

Pelled, L. H., Eisenhardt, K. M., and Xin, K. R. (1999). Exploring the black box: an analysis of work group diversity, conflict and performance. *Administrative Science Quarterly*, 44 (1), 1–28.

Penrose, E. G. (1959). *The Theory of the Growth of the Firm*. New York: Wiley.

Pfeffer, J. (2001). Fighting the war for talent is hazardous to your organization's health. *Organizational Dynamics*, 29 (4), 248–59.

Quinn, J. B., Anderson, P., and Finkelstein, S. (1996). Managing professional intellect: making the most of the best. *Harvard Business Review*, 74 (2), 71–80.

Reich, R. (2002). *The Future of Success: Working and Living in the New Economy*. New York: Vintage Books.

Rubin, P. H. (1973). The expansion of firms. *Journal of Political Economy*, 81 (4), 936–49.

Rumelt, R. P. (1984). Towards a strategic theory of the firm. In R. B. Lamb (ed.), *Competitive Strategic Management*. Englewood Cliffs, NJ: Prentice-Hall.

Siebdrat, F., Hoegl, M., and Ernst, H. (2009). How to manage virtual teams. *MIT Sloan Management Review*, 50 (4), 63–8.

Simsek, Z., Veiga, J. F., Lubatkin, M. H., and Dino, R. N. (2005). Modeling the multilevel determinants of top management team behavioral integration. *Academy of Management Journal*, 48 (1), 69–84.

Sparrow, P. R., Hird, M., and Balain, S. (2011). *Talent Management: Time to Question the Tablets of Stone?* Centre for Performance-led HR White Paper 11/01. Lancaster University Management School.

Sturman, M. C. and Trevor, C. O. (2001). The implications of linking the dynamic performance and turnover literatures. *Journal of Applied Psychology*, 86 (4), 684–96.

Subramaniam, M. and Youndt, M. A. (2005). The influence of intellectual capital on the types of innovative capabilities. *Academy of Management Journal*, 48 (3), 450–63.

Takeuchi, H. and Nonaka, I. (1986). The new product development game. *Harvard Business Review*, 64 (1), 137–46.

Teece, D. J. (1980). Economies of scope and the scope of the enterprise. *Journal of Economic Behavior and Organization*, 1 (3), 223–47.

(1982). Towards an economic theory of the multiproduct firm. *Journal of Economic Behavior and Organization*, 3 (1), 39–63.

(1984). Economic analysis and strategic management. *California Management Review*, 26 (3), 87–110.

(1986). Profiting from technological innovation. *Research Policy*, 15 (6), 285–305.

(1989). Inter-organizational requirements of the innovation process. *Managerial and Decision Economics*, 10 (Spring Special Issue), 35–42.

(2000). *Managing Intellectual Capital: Organizational, Strategic, and Policy Dimensions*. Oxford: Oxford University Press.

(2003). Expert talent and the design of (professional services) firms. *Industrial and Corporate Change*, 12 (4), 895–916.

(2006). Reflections on profiting from innovation. *Research Policy*, 35 (8), 1131–46.

(2007). Explicating dynamic capabilities: the nature and microfoundations of (sustainable) enterprise performance. *Strategic Management Journal*, 28 (13), 1319–50.

(2009). *Dynamic Capabilities and Strategic Management: Organizing for Innovation and Growth*. New York: Oxford University Press.

(2010). Business models, business strategy and innovation. *Long Range Planning*, 43 (2–3), 172–94.

(2011). Human capital, capabilities and the firm: literati, numerati, and entrepreneurs in the 21st-century enterprise. In Alan Burton-Jones and J.-C. Spender (eds.) *The Oxford Handbook of Human Capital*. Oxford: Oxford University Press, pp. 527–62.

Teece, D. J., Pisano, G., and Shuen, A. (1997). Dynamic capabilities and strategic management. *Strategic Management Journal*, 18 (7), 509–33.

Tjosvold, D. (1985). Implications of controversy research for management. *Journal of Management*, 11 (3), 21–37.

Wernerfelt, B. (1984). A resource-based view of the firm. *Strategic Management Journal*, 5 (2), 171–80.

Wheelwright, S. C. and Clark, K. B. (1992). *Revolutionizing Product Development: Quantum Leaps in Speed, Efficiency, and Quality*. New York, NY: Free Press.

Winter, S. G. (2003). Understanding dynamic capabilities. *Strategic Management Journal*, 24 (10), 991–5.

5 | A supply-chain approach to talent management

J. R. KELLER AND PETER CAPPELLI

5.1 Introduction

Talent management is the process through which employers anticipate and meet their needs for human capital. It is about getting the right people with the right skills into the right jobs at the right time. It is a lot to get right, and few organizations do. The difficulty in getting it right is a problem for firms insofar as talent-management decisions shape firm competencies and success. It is a problem for workers, because these decisions impact their careers. And it is ultimately a problem for society, because these decisions, in aggregate, ultimately affect economic growth and social stability.

If there is an upside to this problem, it is that we can easily identify its cause. The central new aspects of business are uncertainty and change, yet traditional workforce-planning models were based on predictability and stability, which allowed organizations to forecast demand with a relatively high degree of accuracy. The supply of talent was assumed to be under the organization's control, given the prevalence of internal labor markets and single-firm careers. As the external environment became more difficult to forecast and traditional internal labor markets began to disintegrate, the inability of these strategic workforce planning systems to account for uncertainty in demand and disruptions in supply led many organizations to abandon them altogether.

Talent management has, as a result, become little more than a guessing game for most organizations. Only 19% of companies responding to a Conference Board survey reported engaging in any sort of structured workforce planning in the mid 1990s. Moreover, of the respondents to a survey specifically targeting companies interested in talent management, more than half reported to relying on "ad-hoc" approaches. Put differently, over half of these organizations reported relying on "ad-hoc planning," which really means they engaged in no planning at all. Yet organizations consistently report that managing the supply and demand for talent, especially for skilled workers, remains a top concern (SHRM, 2002, 2004, 2006, 2008, 2011), with a 2010 global survey identifying managing talent, improving leadership development, and strategic workforce planning as the top three priorities for human resources professionals (Strack *et al.*, 2010).

What we need, then, is an approach to talent management that embraces planning in an environment characterized by uncertainty in supply and demand, one that acknowledges the inability to forecast away uncertainty and plan years into the future. Thankfully, the increasingly sophisticated literature on supply-chain management offers just such an approach. Supply-chain management is about delivering the right amount of product at the right price to meet demand at any given time – quite similar to the goal of the talent-management process. What supply-chain researchers have come to recognize – and account for theoretically and empirically – is that in reality, uncertainty in demand and disruptions in the supply chain make it all but impossible to achieve this goal with any regularity (Fisher and Rayman, 1996; Mabert and Venkataramanan, 1998). As a result, the supply-chain literature has taken a keen interest in understanding how organizations make sourcing decision under conditions of uncertainty (Fisher, 1997).

Adopting a supply-chain approach to talent management allows us to explore two pressing questions. First, how do organizations ensure a sufficient supply of human capital when both demand and supply are uncertain? Answering this question from a supply-chain perspective requires us to recognize that forecasting under conditions of uncertainty is incredibly difficult, almost inevitably leading to either an undersupply or oversupply of human capital. As a result, the focus shifts from meeting a point estimate of demand to minimizing the costs incurred as a result of these inevitable errors.

Second, what are the different human capital sourcing strategies available to firms, and when should each be used? Here, a supply-chain perspective is helpful because researchers are particularly interested in how firms combine internal and external sourcing in order to minimize the costs associated with undershooting or overshooting actual demand. The reliability and responsiveness of the available sourcing options, as well as whether those options are designed to mitigate potential disruptions to the supply chain or are more contingent in nature, emerge as key considerations.

5.2 A supply-chain perspective

We should be clear on what it means to adopt a supply-chain perspective. Operations researchers have offered various definitions of a supply chain, but generally agree that a supply chain consists of all parties involved, directly or indirectly, in transforming raw material into finished products and delivering them to customers (Mabert and Venkataramanan, 1998). The length and complexity of an organization's supply chain is a function of the goods it produces and the customers that it serves. Research on all varieties of supply-chain configurations has consistently shown that supply-chain efficiency, reliability, and responsiveness are key drivers of a firm's profitability (Hendricks and Singhal, 2005). Supply-chain management, in turn, is concerned with how to ensure the efficiency, reliability, and responsiveness of supply chains.

The ideal supply chain would deliver just the right amount of product at the right price to meet demand at any given time, equivalent to a just-in-time production strategy (Frazier, Spekman, and Oneal, 1988). Given that it takes time for raw materials to move through even the shortest supply chain, uncertainty in demand and disruptions in the supply chain are always potential problems. Recognizing this, operations researchers have developed theory and models enabling us to understand how to minimize the risks associated with making sourcing decisions under conditions of uncertainty (Fisher, 1997).

The sources of uncertainty in supply chains are less important to understand at this point than their effects. Uncertainty makes it difficult to forecast demand. Organizations should, and still do, generate point estimates of demand, but these forecasts inevitability contain some degree of error (Cappelli, 2009a). Even the most sophisticated forecasting models, which attempt to model or deal with uncertainty in some way, generate estimates with substantial variance (Fisher and Rayman, 1996). Further, disruptions in the supply chain make it difficult to meet demand forecasts, even if they are accurate (Tomlin, 2006). As a result, supply-chain theorists have de-emphasized the goal of meeting a point estimate of demand, characteristic of much of the literature on formal planning systems in organizations (e.g., Wood and LaForge, 1979; Kulda, 1980), instead advocating for the more realistic goal of minimizing the costs associated with undershooting or overshooting demand.

The choices an organization makes regarding how it sources its inputs is a key determinant of its ability to minimize these costs. Sourcing involves both the procurement of material on the market as well as internal product development (Mabert and Venkataramanan, 1998). Minimizing mismatch costs, therefore, involves strategic decisions regarding how to combine internal and external sourcing, or deciding which products and how much of those products should be made internally and what and how much should be outsourced.

This is precisely why we view a supply-chain perspective as a natural fit for advancing our understanding talent-management decisions. At its most basic level, talent management is a matter of anticipating the need for human capital and setting out a plan to meet it. Yet these decisions are made under conditions of increasing uncertainty, where the supply and demand for human capital are difficult to forecast with any degree of accuracy. Internal sourcing, transforming raw material into a finished product, is the equivalent of internal talent development, while external sourcing is the equivalent of external hiring (Cappelli, 2008). A supply-chain perspective directs our attention to understanding how firms combine internal and external sourcing – development and hiring – to meet estimated demand in a way that minimizes the mismatch costs associated with an oversupply or under-supply of human capital within the firm (Cappelli, 2008; Collings and Mellahi, 2009).

5.3 A brief history of approaches to talent management

It may surprise some readers that most firms are only just beginning to confront the challenge of combining internal and external sourcing to meeting their human capital needs. Rather, companies have generally adopted one of two approaches to talent management, depending on the prevailing external environment. The most common approach used today – and in several other periods throughout history – is reactive, with companies relying almost exclusively on external hiring to meet human capital needs as they arise. A second approach, rarely used today except in a few large firms, relies almost exclusively on internal development. Neither approach is likely to be particularly effective in today's competitive environment, where uncertainty in the demand for human capital is high and disruptions in the supply of human capital are frequent.

Talent management did not become a serious concern until companies grew complicated enough to have real management jobs to fill. Prior to the growth of the major railroads in the late nineteenth century, the typical firm had a simple structure where the owners were the managers (Chandler, 1977). And even then there was often little to manage, as organizations typically outsourced much of the work, from sales and distribution at companies such as DuPont (Zunz, 1990) to actual production tasks, which were often outsourced to contractors who found their own workers and managed them how they saw fit (Clawson, 1980: pp. 72–80).

Starting with the railroads, organizations began to expand to the point where the need for standardization and coordination became paramount, leading to the creation of what we would now call middle management jobs. These new positions were filled primarily through external hiring. Indeed, when the World War I Manpower Commission was established by the government to ensure that companies had the workers and skills needed to maintain wartime production, one of its specific goals was to reduce the ubiquitous pirating of workers by competitors. This also led to the rapid establishment of personnel departments to execute workforce planning practices throughout the 1920s (Jacoby, 1997). Yet these efforts were short lived, as the Great Depression eroded the need for managers (Melman, 1951) and with it the need for talent management. Talent development efforts remained stagnant throughout World War II, despite increases in demand, as most of the candidates who would have been hired into entry-level positions were serving in the military.

The lack of hiring and development from the Depression through World War II led to a serious shortage of talent across nearly all industries (Whitmore, 1952). Organizations responded just as they had at the beginning of the century – by raiding competitors for talent. A prominent retail executive noted that "to go to another store for assistant buyers, buyers, and other executives" was the approach "almost universally used" to meet their human capital needs (Carden, 1956 cited in Cappelli, 2009b). Yet external hiring proved insufficient in meeting the demand for talent, as pension plans with onerous vesting requirements, high marginal tax rates, and a lack of housing decreased the attractiveness of switching employers, even when competitors were able to offer higher salaries (Cappelli, 2010).

The difficulty in finding external talent led companies to the realization that they needed to develop talent internally. With precious little experience of doing so themselves, they turned to the military for help. Recognizing the need for a huge expansion of its officer ranks in a short period of time leading up to World War II, the Navy began what was arguably the first truly systematic effort at large-scale succession planning, resulting in the publication of "Personnel Administration at the Executive Level" in 1948, which the Industrial Relations faculty at Princeton (Princeton University, 1949) summarized as:

A principally graphic report of the composite practices of 53 companies in regard to executive inventory control. In these companies, reserves of trained executives are built up through five basic steps: (1) organization analysis, (2) selection, (3) evaluation, (4) development, and (5) inventory control.

Clearly borrowing language from the field of operations, this document was widely used by many companies as the basis for building their own talent-development programs (Business Week, 1949). These programs, in turn, served as the basis for the "organizational man" model of the 1950s in which expectations of lifetime employment and steady advancement opportunities emerged (Whyte, 1956). Companies began to rely almost exclusively on internal development. In 1943, the Conference Board could not find enough employers offering talent-development programs to study them, yet by 1955 they were present in 60% of companies with 10,000 or more employees. Newcomer's (1955) study of corporate executives found that 80% had been developed from within by 1950, compared to 50% in 1900.

Yet these efforts were also short lived, as changes in the way business operated in the early 1980s rendered the organizational-man approach to talent development obsolete. Firms in the United States experienced a sharp decline in the need for managerial talent following the 1981 recession and subsequent "re-engineerings" that led to flatter organizations, resulting in wholesale managerial layoffs (Cappelli, 1999: Chapter 4). Competition increased due to product market deregulation and internal competition (Useem, 1993) and consumer demands began to change more rapidly (Ghemawat, 1986), leading firms to move away from traditional employment systems (Stalk, 1988). This made it increasingly difficult for firms to forecast consumer demand and, as a result, to forecast their own human-capital needs. This, in turn, made firms reluctant to invest in the development of employees they may not need. The influence of financial markets also grew considerably during this time, encouraging firms to maintain more tentative employment ties (Davis, 2009: p. 28).

The peak of strategic workforce planning was probably a late-1960s model called MANPLAN, which attempted to model the movement of individuals within a career system by including individual behavior and psychological variables, supervisory practices, group norms, and labor market outcomes (Cappelli, 2008: p. 1). By 1984, only 9% of employers reported using elaborate statistical regression models to forecast talent needs and only 6% used sophisticated Markov-chain vacancy models (Cappelli, 2008). Even where they were used, formal planning systems seemed to have little effect on firm performance (Nkomo, 1987).

Not surprisingly, these changes led organizations to rely, yet again, on external hiring to meet their human-capital needs. This strategy worked well until the mid 1990s, when the excess talent available as a result of the earlier waves of restructurings began to dry up. Talent has become harder to find and more expensive as employers bid up salaries poaching from one and other. An ever-increasing amount of evidence suggests that external hires rarely work out as well as expected (Groysberg, Lee, and Nanda, 2008; Dokko, Wilk, and Rothbard, 2009; Bidwell, 2011).

If nothing else, this history reveals that – as the saying goes – history is bound to repeat itself. Over the past century, organizations have alternatively met their need for talent primarily through external hiring (late 1800s up to World War I), internal development (World War I until the Great Depression), external hiring again (post-World War II), internal development again (organizational-man model of the 1950s and 1960s), and back to external hiring today. Neither approach provides a sufficient means for meeting an organization's talent needs in an uncertain and rapidly changing environment. Recouping big investments in talent development can be difficult if human-capital needs change and if employees leave, both common occurrences. Relying solely on external hiring, on the other hand, leaves employers at the mercy of the labor market, resulting in talent shortfalls and other costs whenever labor markets tighten.

A key point of advancement in the field of supply-chain management came when scholars first recognized and began to account for the uncertainty that exists in managing the flow of products through the supply chain (Cohen and Lee, 1988; Mabert and Venkataramanan, 1998), resulting in the insight that strategically combining internal and external sourcing can help minimize the potential costs associated with operating under considerable uncertainty. In much the same way, recognizing uncertainty in both the demand for and supply of talent requires us to abandon talent-management approaches reliant on *either* external hiring or internal development and to instead consider how organizations can effectively *combine* hiring and development in order to meet their human-capital needs.

5.4 Minimizing mismatch costs in the human-capital supply chain

From a supply-chain perspective, the ideal talent-management system would provide just the right supply of human capital (i.e., employees) at a given point in the organization (i.e., in a job) at any given time, ostensibly a just-in-time human capital strategy. As with the production of goods and services, however, uncertainty in the demand and supply of human capital makes it all but impossible to achieve this goal with any regularity. Where does this uncertainty come from?

5.4.1 Sources of uncertainty

One source of supply-side uncertainty arises from the difficulty in predicting skills and competences needed in the future. If the skills and competences needed in the future change dramatically, a supply chain that looks robust now may look deficient in the future. A second source of supply-side uncertainty comes from the difficulty in predicting employee turnover. While organizations can use historic turnover rates to predict future exit rates, voluntary turnover is often driven by individual and environmental factors beyond the organization's control (Bretz, Boudreau, and Judge, 1994; Judge and Watanabe, 1995), introducing substantial error into these predictions. Additionally, firms have limited control over the future availability of skills and competences available on the labor market. Firms do exert indirect control over the future supply of such skills and competences, as when current demand influences the choice of college majors (Fiorito and Dauffenbach, 1982). Interestingly, however, a key concept in the supply-chain literature, the bullwhip effect, suggests that this is unlikely to be particularly effective in meeting future demand. The basic idea of the bullwhip effect is that small changes in demand toward the delivery end of the supply chain induce much larger fluctuations further down the supply chain (Lee, Padmanabhan, and Whang, 1997). Applied to the labor market more broadly, what often occurs is that when demand for a certain set of skills is high, students flock to majors in which they learn those skills. Given the time lag in acquiring those skills, however, by the time they reach the market there is often an oversupply of qualified candidates, which then decreases students enrolling on those majors, resulting in a subsequent shortage in the future, a cycle that can persist ad infinitum. Adding more difficulty is the fact that employers often signal to universities the skills they think they are going to need, but those needs are subject to changes on the demand side over which the organization often has little control.

Uncertainty on the demand side arises from changes in a firm's competitive environment. Industry deregulation, the rise of low-cost non-union competitors, increased global competition and the increasing influence of institutional investors and financial markets in general have all led to increased competition (Cappelli, 1995; Davis, 2009). Consumer demands have forced companies to shorten the development time on new products, quickly introduce updated models, increase product selection, and engage in mass customization (Fisher, 1997). Taken together, these changes have made it incredibly difficult to forecast demand for a firm's products and services, which in turn has made it difficult to forecast the human capital needed to produce and deliver those products and services. Linking back to the supply side, the rapidly changing technological landscape has further complicated firms' abilities to anticipate which skills and abilities they will need, and in which amounts, in order to meet future demand.

This combined uncertainty regarding the supply and demand of human capital has effectively eliminated most organizations' ability to accurately forecast their future human-capital needs and plan for the future. Historically, formal planning systems in general (Wood and LaForge, 1979; Kulda, 1980) and workforce planning systems in particular (Walker, 1980; DeVanna, Forbrum, and Tichy, 1981) have emphasized generating an exact forecast, or a point estimate of demand. Given what we know from the supply-chain literature – that meeting a point estimate of demand is essentially impossible – it is not entirely surprising that in reviewing a number of research studies,

Nkomo (1987) concluded that empirical results have failed to show a consistent link between strategic planning (including human-resource planning) and organizational performance. A more appealing theoretical approach is one that shifts the emphasis from meeting a target forecast to minimizing and dealing with the inevitable glitches that result in the inevitable undersupply or oversupply of human capital.

A supply-chain approach to talent management is appealing, then, precisely because it begins with the assumption that under conditions of uncertainty forecasts will be wrong and a firm's ability to exactly meet its need for talent at any given time is highly unlikely. We therefore need to consider the ways in which an organization can be wrong and the costs of being wrong.

5.4.2 Mismatch costs

There are two ways to be wrong. The first is having a surplus of talent on hand at a given time. The second is a talent shortage. In the language of supply-chain management, these problems of oversupply and undersupply collectively result in what are known as mismatch costs (Lee, 2002; Chopra and Sodhi, 2004). Mismatch costs are the costs of being wrong: the costs incurred when there is a mismatch between demand and supply. As Hendricks and Singhal (2005: 696) note, a long line of literature has discussed the negative economic consequences of mismatches, including their effect on revenues, costs, and asset utilizations, all of which "are likely to adversely affect the short and long-term profitability of the firm." Minimizing these mismatch costs thus becomes the central talent-management concern.

If the costs of oversupply and undersupply were always equal, the best strategy would, in fact, be to try to meet the point estimate of demand, similar to the prescriptions offered by earlier formal planning models. A key insight from the supply-chain field, however, is that the mismatch costs associated with oversupply and those associated with undersupply are rarely equal (Olivares, Terwiesch, and Cassorla, 2008); what really matters are the relative costs of oversupply and undersupply. Translated into the talent-management context, it is easy to imagine that the cost of having ten too many salespeople on the retail floor is likely to be quite different than the cost of having ten too few salespeople. It is therefore critical to assess the relative costs of each type of error; how does the cost of having an excess worker compare to the cost of a shortage of one worker? More generally, is it more or less costly to have too few as compared to too many workers?

The implications of this line of thinking are remarkably straightforward. Where the mismatch costs associated with an oversupply are higher, erring on the side of having fewer workers will minimize mismatch costs. In the talent-management context, oversupply costs include the investments in training that walk out of the door when employees leave due to a lack of advancement opportunities, the severance costs associated with terminating underutilized employees, and the pressure to restructure or "reduce fat" in order to lower short-term costs, among others. Where the mismatch costs associated with an undersupply are higher, erring on the side of having excess workers will minimize mismatch costs. Undersupply costs include the costs of outside hiring, lost productivity, or lost business opportunities due to worker shortages. And where the costs are roughly equal, then the best strategy is to try to meet the point estimate of demand.

The relative costs of each type of error are likely to vary not just across organizations, but also by job. For example, jobs vary in the extent to which they require firm-specific skills, as well as both the price and availability of external candidates in the labor market. In jobs that primarily require general skills, where those skills are readily available on the external market, and where the market rate is close to the internal wage, the costs of having too few workers are likely to be relatively low. In contrast, in jobs that require firm-specific skills, where those skills are more difficult to find externally and where search and compensation costs come at a premium, the costs of undersupply are likely to be quite high.

5.5 Sourcing strategies for minimizing mismatch costs

We now have an answer to the first question raised by adopting a supply-chain approach – how do firms ensure a sufficient supply of human capital when both demand and supply are both uncertain? Firms should seek to minimize mismatch costs by erring on the side of oversupply or undersupply, based on their relative costs.

The second question we must answer is, what are the different human-capital sourcing strategies available to firms, and when should each be used? This second question is closely related to the first, as the ability to minimize mismatch costs is a function of the array of available sourcing strategies and the risks associated with them (Swaminathan, Smith, and Sadeh, 1998). Clark (1989), for example, demonstrated the importance of considering the tradeoffs involved in choosing among internal versus external sourcing options. Key among these tradeoffs is the extent to which the available sourcing strategies ensure the reliability and responsiveness of the supply chain (Hendricks and Singhal, 2005).

5.5.1 Reliability and responsiveness

Reliability and responsiveness are key aspects of any supply chain's effectiveness (Beamon, 1999; Chen and Paulraj, 2004; Hendricks and Singhal, 2005). Reliability is the capacity to meet production requirements, including quantity, quality, timeliness, and availability. Not surprisingly, ensuring reliability is often quite expensive (Kim, 2011) and the costs of ensuring reliability are spread throughout the supply chain. Reliable suppliers can charge more because of the value they provide, incremental investments in product development can help to lower product failure rates (O'Conner, 2002), and investments in logistics can help to ensure timely delivery (Bodin, 1990). In the context of talent management, reliability translates into having the skills and capabilities on hand necessary to get jobs done. Ensuring such reliability often requires significant investments, such as maintaining a deep bench of talent and continuous investments in training and development.

Responsiveness is the capacity to adapt output or performance standards to changes in demand. Ensuring responsiveness can be equally costly. It is easier to sustain lower costs if volume and standards remain constant, but responsiveness requires flexibility, which in the modern economy translates to shorter lead times, essentially the ability to produce new products and newer versions of existing products, and the ability to increase or decrease production levels all at a moment's notice (Fisher, 1997). The necessary investments in technology and equipment needed to ensure such flexibility can quickly add up, especially when combined with the costs of using the market to address shortages in raw materials. In the context of talent management, responsiveness translates to the ability to quickly adjust human-capital levels to changing levels in demand as well as the ability to access and deploy new capabilities as needed. The costs of ensuring such responsiveness often include substantial investments in HR information systems (Dulebohn and Johnson, 2012) in addition to paying market premiums for instant access to qualified workers (Bidwell, 2011).

5.5.2 Risk and uncertainty

Problems of reliability and responsiveness are often related to labor (Cappelli, 2011a). Labor unrest, talent shortages, and retention challenges, such as the loss of a key employee, are threats to reliability that companies across the globe face to differing degrees. Contract terms, location, and transportation costs all have the ability to constrain firms' responsiveness. These problems are not necessarily routine, but they can be anticipated and, as a result, managed (Cappelli, 2011a: p. 312).

Knight (1921) was the first to distinguish risk from uncertainty. Risk relates to events that may be rare but that can be anticipated with some accuracy. Uncertainty relates to events that are largely unknown and extremely difficult to estimate. We can only manage problems when we have some ability to anticipate and predict the chance of the problems occurring. As a result, risk can be managed.

To this point, we have emphasized the role of uncertainty in generating mismatch costs. Problems of reliability and responsiveness, however, are much more like risk than uncertainty in that we can anticipate how they may unfold and, because they occur often enough, we have some reasonable sense of the likelihood that they will happen. We think about managing those problems under the general heading of risk management. The problem we face in making sourcing decisions is to choose the arrangement that does the best job of minimizing both mismatch costs and the risks of reliability and responsiveness (Cappelli, 2011a).

5.5.3 Mitigation and contingency strategies

Reliability and responsiveness problems arise from supply-chain disruptions (Hendricks and Singhal, 2005; Tomlin, 2006; Yu, Zeng, and Zhao, 2009), which include any event hindering the production and delivery of goods produced through the supply chain. Disruptive events range from small to large. In the manufacturing context, a small disruption may be the breakdown of a machine requiring repair, resulting in a temporary slowdown of the production process. Large-scale disruptive events may include the shutdown of a major supplier or a natural disaster such as an earthquake shutting down production entirely (see Tomlin, 2006; Yu, Zeng, and Zhao, 2009 for more examples). Sourcing disruptions have been shown to have significant and long-lasting consequences on organizational performance. Analyzing disruptions in the supply chains of 885 publicly traded firms, Hendricks and Singhal (2005) found that firms experiencing disruptions, regardless of their cause, had negatively affected operating income, return on sales, and return on assets. Further, the average firm was unable to recover quickly, with the negative effects persisting over a two-year follow-up period.

In considering disruptions in the human-resource supply chain, it is helpful to think about the stock and flow of human capital within an organization (Größler and Zock, 2010). An organization's stock of human capital refers to the employees occupying each job at a given point in time, whereas the flow refers to the movement of individuals into, through and out of the organization. In a perfectly efficient supply chain, the flow of materials through the supply chain will ensure that the stock will always meet demand at any given point in time; in other words, the human-resource supply chain will always deliver the right amount of employees (with the right amount of skills) to each job. Setting aside the difficultly in predicting demand, several types of disruptions may occur. A small disruption may be a key employee going on maternity leave, while a large disruption might be a competitor hiring away an entire team of key employees (Groysberg, 2010). Both of these disruptions will result in an undersupply of human capital.

Disruptions can also result in oversupply of human capital. While manufacturing supply chains generally strive to eliminate losses (i.e., Brewer and Speh, 2000), organizations tend to expect some level of employee turnover, and often encourage turnover as a way to rid themselves of low performers and access new knowledge (March, 1991). Organizations often make hiring decisions at lower levels based on the expectation that some percentage of these workers will exit over a given time period. When such exits fail to occur, the firm is faced with an oversupply of talent. Similarly, when employees at higher levels fail to exit at the expected rate, as we see now with older employees staying in the workforce longer due to the recent market downturn (Conference Board, 2011), this creates bottlenecks that impede the advancement of qualified workers, increasing their likelihood of exit and the costs associated with those exits.

Supply-chain disruptions, whether those affecting manufacturing or human-resource supply chains, can be managed because they are events that we have some ability to anticipate, and thus we are able to predict the chance of the problems occurring. They represent risk. And supply-chain research has categorized possible solutions as falling into two distinct groups. Mitigation tactics involve the firm taking some action in advance of potential problems. Contingency tactics involve the firm taking action only when a problem actually occurs (Tomlin, 2006: 640).

These two sets of solutions differ in important ways. Mitigation strategies tend to handle problems more effectively, but involve more upfront costs; the firm incurs the costs regardless of whether a disruption actually occurs. Contingency strategies tend to be less effective, but no costs are incurred unless or until a disruption actually takes place.

A useful way to conceptualize these different approaches is to think of mitigation strategies as the equivalent of preventative medicine, and contingent strategies as the equivalent of emergency-room medicine (Cappelli, 2011b: p. 312). Carrying the medical analogy through, we see that sensible strategies for risk management rely on a mix of the two approaches depending on the problem. We might change our diet to help prevent a heart attack – a mitigation strategy – because it is much more effective than seeking treatment once a heart attack occurs. Rather than wear football pads at all times to prevent broken bones, we go to the emergency room when a break occurs – a contingency strategy.

5.5.4 A typology of sourcing strategies

Combining the two dimensions of supply-chain effectiveness (reliability and responsiveness) with the two approaches to dealing with supply-chain disruptions (mitigation and contingency) reveals four distinct sourcing strategies (Table 5.1). Which strategy to pursue depends on its value, which is equivalent to the losses it prevents, or the extent to which it minimizes the mismatch costs resulting from an oversupply or undersupply of human capital. That value is further enhanced when supported by a set of complementary organizational capabilities.

Table 5.1 *A typology of sourcing strategies*

	Mitigation	Contingency
Reliability	*Inventory* Complementary capabilities: Knowledge-sharing infrastructure, analytics (causal modelling, forecasting, simulations), employee engagement and reward systems, training and development	*Just-in-time back-up* Complementary capabilities: External-market awareness, rapid talent acquisition (including assessment and onboarding); benchmarking, supplier collaboration
Responsiveness	*Internal capacity* Complementary capabilities: Knowledge-sharing infrastructure, analytics, training and development, learning orientation, collaborative structure	*Outsourcing* Complementary capabilities: Supplier collaboration, contract negotiation, performance monitoring

Building an inventory: a mitigation response to ensuring reliability
Inventory responses are the most common mitigation strategies for ensuring reliability. The basic idea is simple. Carrying excess inventory provides a buffer against disruptions in supply. Carrying excess raw materials, for example, gives the organization time to find a new supplier if an existing supplier were to go out of business. More generally, the creation of inventories helps to avoid the effects of machine breakdowns, quality problems, and schedule disruptions in other links of the supply chain (Flynn and Flynn, 1999: 1024). In these ways, stockpiling inventory helps to minimize problems of reliability throughout the supply chain.

And while the general consensus is that inventories should be minimized in an effort to increase a supply chain's efficiency (Gunasekaran, Patel, and McGaughey, 2004), studies have consistently shown that firms often make a strategic choice to hold larger inventories in order to protect against potential disruptions, particularly against unreliable suppliers (Mabert and Venkataramanan, 1998).

In the talent-management context, the most common inventory strategy involves carrying a deep bench of internal talent. The firm bears these costs upfront, and they are often significant. The most straightforward costs include the salary and benefits paid to underused employees, but training and developments costs are often quite significant. A firm has to continually invest in its employees to ensure they are ready to maintain an expected level of performance when an opportunity opens.

A second, though less used, inventory strategy is maintaining a supply of internal temps who can step in to fill shortfalls when they arise. Substitute teachers are an example of such workers. They are employed by school districts to replace full-time teachers on an as-needed basis for reasons such as a personal illness, personal emergencies, attendance at workshops, and the like. Substitutes often receive health and retirement benefits in addition to participating in formal training programs funded by the school districts in order to ensure that they are able to provide a consistent level of instruction (Ostapczuk, 1994) – all cost the districts incur regardless of the how frequently the substitutes are actually needed.

Given the significant upfront costs necessary to maintain a human-capital inventory when the need for such an inventory may never materialize, an inventory strategy is likely to be most effective for those jobs and organizations where the costs of undersupply are greater than the costs of oversupply.

Building internal capacity: a mitigation response to ensuring responsiveness

Developing internal capacity is the most common mitigation strategy for ensuring responsiveness. Responsiveness problems can arise from unexpected changes in demand or disruptions in supply, with the primary issue being the ability to increase production levels in the face of increasing demand or maintain production levels in the presence of disruptions in supply. Both are typically met by investing in internal capacity in an effort to provide the flexibility necessary to deal with such problems should they occur. In a manufacturing context, for example, one such strategy might include building a distribution center larger than initially needed in the event demand will increase in the future. Another might include investing in an additional assembly line, which can be used when the original line is down for maintenance or can be used simultaneously with the original line should demand increase.

In the talent-management context, investments in internal capacity include building recruiting and development capabilities that allow the firm to quickly hire and train workers to meet spikes in demand. They might also include investments in scheduling technologies allowing the firm to seamlessly schedule part-time workers during periods of peak demand, such as when retailers hire seasonal workers during the holidays. Continued investments in training and development, above that necessary for the current job, help ensure ready access to new skills and capabilities should they be needed. A simple example is offering tuition reimbursement for high-potential junior employees to develop managerial skills through an MBA program.

While helping to ensure responsiveness, all of these strategies involve significant upfront costs, investments that provide a positive return only if demand increases or there is a disruption in supply. Given the upfront costs involved, internal-capacity strategies are likely to be most effective for those jobs and organizations where the costs of under-supply are greater than the costs of oversupply.

It is worth noting that because both reliability and responsiveness are key aspects of any supply chain's effectiveness (e.g. Hendricks and Singhal, 2005), mitigation strategies to ensure reliability may overlap with strategies to ensure responsiveness. For example, while maintaining a ready supply of substitute teachers best represents an inventory strategy to ensure reliability, school districts also routinely invest in automated systems which allow them to keep track of available substitute teachers, send out alerts when a need arises, and coordinate the placement and scheduling of such teachers across multiple schools. These investments are akin to ensuring responsiveness by building the internal capacity necessary to meet fluctuations in the supply of and demand for substitute teachers.

Just-in-time back up: a contingency response to ensuring reliability

Just-in-time (JIT) back-up responses are the most common contingency strategies for ensuring reliability. They represent the opposite of an inventory strategy; the firm carries no excess inventory, instead meeting potential shortfalls by turning to external suppliers. In reviewing the vast literature on JIT supplier relationships, Frazier, Spekman, and O'Neal (1988: 53) emphasize that the distinguishing feature of such relationships is the emphasis on reliability, noting that "exactness is a critical consideration because the JIT exchange, in its extreme form, does not tolerate variances," with variance the antithesis to reliability. Finding a reliable supplier at the last minute, of course, can be quite costly. The tradeoff is that the firm only has to pay this market premium if and when a shortfall actually occurs.

In the talent-management context, there is a variety of JIT back-up options. Hiring externally is a common tactic for making up for skill shortfalls. However, the lack of information on external hires makes it difficult to ensure reliability, and overcoming this obstacle can be costly. For example, Bidwell (2011) has shown that employers tend to seek out external candidates possessing more observable signals of quality, such as education and years of experience, for which they pay a substantial salary premium compared to similarly qualified internal candidates. And at higher levels, companies are increasingly using search firms to fill key positions, also a costly proposition, as the typical fee runs upwards of 30% of the first-year base salary.

A more temporary option is using staffing agencies to provide workers who possess the necessary skills and capabilities needed to reliably perform the required tasks. If a worker underperforms, the firm can simply request they be replaced by the agency. This can also be an expensive way to ensure reliability, as the total costs for agency temporary employees, including agency mark-ups, often exceed those of comparable permanent employees (Barley and Kunda, 2004; Peck, Theodore, and Ward, 2005).

Whatever form they take, JIT back-up strategies can be costly. Yet these costs are only realized if and when a shortfall actually occurs. As a result they are likely to be most effective where the costs of oversupply are greater than the costs of undersupply.

Outsourcing: a contingency response to ensuring responsiveness

Outsourcing is the most common contingency strategy for ensuring responsiveness. Rather than invest in the internal flexibility necessary to adapt to changes in demand and disruptions in supply, such changes are met by contracting with third parties to perform the work. Such tactics are similar to the JIT back-up strategy, but differ in that they focus more on outsourcing the unexpected work to vendors.

This distinction is clearer in the context of talent management, where the most common strategy is engaging a professional services firm to provide expertise on a limited basis. For example, a firm may be required to provide the government with an environmental study in order to obtain a permit for the construction of a new store. A smaller retail chain or one that expands infrequently may not have the capability to perform such an analysis. Rather than hire a geologist, civil engineer, and environmental engineer, they instead contract with a consulting firm with the expertise and capacity to perform a thorough analysis in a timely manner.

Like JIT back-up plan strategies, such strategies involve no upfront costs, but the costs of enacting such strategies when needed can quickly escalate based on level of demand, availability of third parties able to meet such demands, and amount of customization required. As a result, outsourcing strategies are likely to be most effective where the costs of oversupply are greater than the costs of undersupply.

Outsourcing is primarily about responsiveness, but can become a source of reliability if the relationship moves beyond a simple market exchange and toward a relational exchange, such as when the firm and vendor engage in repeated exchanges for similar services. Over time, such repeated exchanges have been shown to become more oriented to the prevention of defects, ensuring reliability (Frazier, Spekman, and O'Neal, 1988).

Organizational capabilities

The ability to capture the full benefit of these sourcing strategies will be greatest when supported by a complementary set of organizational capabilities. We highlight those capabilities most likely to unlock the value of each strategy, recognizing that this list is far from comprehensive and many capabilities may complement all strategies. For example, while we focus on how a knowledge-sharing infrastructure complements mitigation strategies, it may also support contingency strategies, as when organizations use vendor-management systems to centrally manage requests for temporary agency workers.

The successful execution of both the inventory and internal capacity mitigation strategies rely on a technological infrastructure able to facilitate knowledge sharing throughout the organization (Gold, Malhotra, and Segars, 2001). A centralized human resource information system (HRIS) containing detailed data on employee skills and performance and accessible to decision-makers throughout the organization is an important first step. However, for such systems to ensure reliable performance and responsiveness to changes, they must be embedded within an organization's overall decision-support system, used to aid in data-driven decision making both within and outside of the HR function (see e.g., Dulebohn and Johnson, 2012). Analytic capabilities are critical to enabling the development of metrics to assess the efficiency, value, and strategic impact of the human-capital supply chain and communicating those findings to business leaders in a language they understand (Boudreau and Ramstad, 2007; Dulebohn and Johnson, 2012). Those same analytic capabilities allow the organization to unlock the value of HRIS data by developing causal models, identifying leading indicators to forecast business and staffing requirements, and running sophisticated workforce optimization simulations in an effort to redeploy existing talent and develop the right mix of new skills internally (Größler and Zock, 2010; Harris, Craig, and Light, 2010).

Finding different ways to engage and reward underused employees is critical in executing an inventory approach, because the benefits of maintaining a deep bench of internal talent disappear if skilled employees leave before they are needed. These efforts can be supported by the same training and development capabilities necessary to execute an internal-capacity approach, which can also be supported by a culture embracing employee interaction and ongoing learning, both of which facilitate the development of new skills. Organizational structure can also help build internal capacity, as modular or project-based teams facilitate knowledge sharing and skill development across the human-capital supply chain (Gold, Malhotra, and Segars, 2001).

A JIT contingency strategy is supported by strong capabilities around the talent-acquisition process. In order to hire quickly and effectively, an organization must be aware of the location and availability of different skill sets on the external market at all times, have processes in place to quickly and accurately assess potential new hires, and have an onboarding process in place enabling them to begin contributing almost immediately. Benchmarking is also a critical capability, allowing the organization to evaluate its stock of human capital against the skills available in the market and to allocate the budget necessary to ensure that external offers will be competitive when they are extended. Developing collaborative relationships with staffing agencies can help maximize the value from such transactions by ensuring that the agency has access to a ready supply of workers meeting the specific needs of the organization as well as by providing the organization with valuable information on external labor market conditions (Dyer, 1997; Bidwell and Fernandez-Mateo, 2008).

Collaboration is similarly important in executing an outsourcing strategy, especially in cases where an organization routinely engages the same vendor for similar work. The capability to structure and negotiate contract terms and monitor the work of external partners is also critical. Negotiating and including performance standards in sourcing contracts and developing metrics to monitor performance against those standards allows an organization to identify its best and worst performing suppliers, enabling it to shift sourcing requests away from poor performing suppliers while developing long-term relationships with its best suppliers (Gunasekaran *et al.*, 2001, 2004; Harris, Craig, and Light, 2010).

5.6 Theory and empirics

The preceding pages provide an outline of the conceptual foundations of a supply-chain approach to talent management. While practitioner-oriented literature has been quick to embrace these concepts (e.g., Bourdreau and Ramstad, 2007; Giehll and Moss, 2009; Wright *et al.*, 2011; Hoffman, Lesser, and Ringo, 2012), empirical research in strategic human resources and related fields has been much more cautious in embracing such an approach. We suspect this is in large part due to two factors. First, no one has yet to clearly articulate its theoretic appeal. Second, the empirical challenges appear to be somewhat daunting. We attempt to address these issues below.

5.6.1 Theoretic appeal

Perhaps the most appealing aspect of a supply-chain approach is that it identifies a primary mechanism through which human-resource management affects firm performance. As convincingly argued by others, the key challenge facing researchers in the field of strategic human-resources management is demonstrating a causal link between human-resource management and firm performance (Lengnick-Hall *et al.*, 2009; Huselid and Becker, 2011). While studies have shown that human-resource systems can have a significant positive effect on firm performance (e.g. Combs *et al.*, 2006), the mechanisms by which human resources drive firm performance are less clear. As Ketchen and Hult (2007: 574) note, strategic supply-chain management involves managing the supply chain in a way that delivers products to customers and "enhance[s] key outcomes that drive firm performance." The supply-chain approach outlined above suggests that human resources can affect firm performance through minimizing mismatch costs.

Empirical work in the supply-chain literature has begun to demonstrate the negative economic consequences of high mismatch costs on firm performance (e.g. Hendricks and Singhal, 2005). Another way to interpret these findings is that lowering mismatch costs improves performance. Mismatch costs are a proximate measure of performance, what Becker and Huselid (2006: 907) refer to as an intermediate outcome with "a theoretically clear line of sight to the ultimate strategic (financial) outcomes." Such intermediate outcomes enable us to extend theory by probing the proverbial "black box" between human-resource systems and firm performance. Moreover, mismatch costs are a particular appealing intermediate outcome because they represent a financial measure and thus have a clear strategic significance.

A focus on mismatch costs also has the potential to advance our understanding of differential human-resource architectures within firms (Becker and Huselid, 2006). The key idea behind such an approach is that some employees (Lepak and Snell, 1999) and jobs (Kaplan and Norton, 2004; Huselid, Beatty, and Becker, 2005) create more value than others and thus should be managed differently. As noted above, the relative costs of oversupply and undersupply are likely to vary across jobs, suggesting the optimal strategies used to minimize these costs are contingent, at least to some extent, on the nature of the mismatch costs. Scholars have also struggled in figuring out how to identify strategic jobs. To the degree that higher mismatch costs indicate the strategic value of a job, estimating mismatch costs may provide a useful means for identifying strategic jobs (Huselid and Becker, 2011).

At its core, the supply-chain research we draw on is about decision making under conditions of uncertainty. It may be even more accurate to say that it is about managing risk through decision making. We think it is fair to say that human-resource scholars are well aware of the role of uncertainty in human-resource decisions. For example, the vast literature on personnel selection boils down to finding more effective ways to reduce uncertainty in the hiring process (see Sackett and Lievens, 2008 for an excellent review of the more recent literature). Yet uncertainty is rarely dealt with explicitly, in large part because we talk about uncertainty instead of risk (Knight, 1921). The concept of risk is more appealing (and we think more accurate) because it suggests something that can be managed. And we are able to forecast and predict most outcomes and their associated error rates. Indeed, the most influential recent work in the supply-chain field has been conducted by scholars who embrace the concept of risk and explicitly consider it in both their theories and models (see Chopra and Sodhi, 2004 for a straightforward discussion of risk in supply chains). We will concede that those models get complicated very quickly (something we address below), but they also provide a guide for more fully integrating risk into our theories and models.

An addition benefit, admittedly somewhat more empirical than theoretical in nature, is that adopting a supply-chain approach opens the possibility of using supply-chain management performance measures (Boudreau and Ramstad, 2001; Größler and Zock, 2010). Human-resource scholars have long called for better human-resource measures, measures that can be communicated throughout the organization to inform strategy making (Boudreau and Ramstad, 2003, 2006). The most widely used supply-chain outcome measures are particularly appealing because they tend to reflect intermediate outcomes with clear causal lines to organizational performance (Brewer and Speh, 2000; Gunasekaran, Patel, and Tirtiroglu, 2001). Gunasekaran and colleagues (2004) lump these performance measures into four categories, those related to planning, sourcing, assembling, and delivery.

We offer a few suggestions on how some of these commonly used measures might be translated to a human-resources context. One planning measure shown to be a source of competitive advantage is order lead time (Christopher, 1992), which refers to time that elapses between receipt of an order and delivery (Gunasekaran, Patel, and Tirtiroglu, 2001). Reductions in the time it takes to fill a vacancy or fill a newly created position are roughly equivalent to reductions in lead time. Supplier pricing against market is a commonly used sourcing metric that suggests the need to compare the prices paid for external hires and to third-party vendors against market benchmarks. Capacity utilization (Slack *et al.*, 1995), an assembly measure, might be adapted to measure the utilization of recruiting and training capabilities. Number of faultless notes invoiced is used to determine whether perfect delivery has taken place or not, and to identify areas of discrepancy so improvements can be made (Gunasekaran, Patel, and

McGaughey, 2004: 337). Quality-of-hire metrics would be appear to be a similarly useful measure, as would performance variation among incumbents in a given job, with higher variation suggesting some employees lack critical skills (Huselid, Beatty, and Becker, 2005).

5.6.2 Empirical challenges

In the abstract, calculating mismatch costs is a straightforward exercise. The first step involves calculating the cost per excess worker (oversupply cost) and cost per worker shortage (undersupply cost). The second step involves calculating the number of excess workers (quantity of oversupply) or the actual shortage (quantity of undersupply). The mismatch cost equals the cost multiplied by the quantity. Given differences in jobs, the best estimates are likely to be calculated at the job level, which can then be aggregated at multiple levels (e.g., team, department, organization).

Of the two, oversupply costs initially appear to be the easiest to calculate. Given compensation and benefit data on job incumbents, a conservative estimate of the cost per excess worker in a given job can be calculated as the average annual cost per worker, the annual cost of the lowest paid worker (likely to be a lower bound), or the annual cost of the highest paid worker (likely to be an upper bound). These are only conservative estimates, however, because they do not include training and development costs invested in the excess worker, nor does it include estimates of turnover costs associated with losing a worker who may leave because of the lack of advancement opportunities associated with an oversupply of internal candidates. Estimating undersupply costs is likely to be even more difficult, as it involves projecting missed opportunities due to a lack of workers. In manufacturing roles, such a calculation may be relatively straightforward in terms of revenues lost per missing worker, but such a calculation would not account for additional costs such as damage to the firm's reputation, the loss of future opportunities stemming from the inability to meet demand in a given period, or even the search costs associated with quickly filling a vacant job. In more knowledge-intensive jobs and industries, estimating the costs of opportunities the firm was unable to pursue, for example, is even more problematic.

We do, however, sense that there are ways to overcome these issues. Our optimism comes, not surprisingly, from the supply-chain literature, where early researchers interested in these issues faced similar challenges. Our (admittedly incomplete) review of the supply literature suggests that partnering with organizations as a form of participatory action research (Whyte, 1990) is key.

One of the seminal articles in the field involved a long-term collaboration between the two researchers and an organization struggling with supply-chain issues (Fisher and Raman, 1996). Using both historic and real-time data provided by the organization, the researchers developed a decision model in which they were able to use parameters derived from the firm's own data. Based on a model using the same data available to the firm, they then executed their model in parallel with the firm's actual decision-making process in 1992–1993 and found that their model enabled the organization to cut the cost of both overproduction and underproduction in half, resulting in a significant increase in profits (Fisher, 1997). Moreover, a review of the recent supply-chain literature by Hendricks and Singhal (2005) reveals that empirical work quantifying the impact of supply-chain management practices on operating performance took off only after scholars became proficient in developing mathematical models of supply-chain issues, many of which resulted from close collaboration with the firms they were studying.

Adopting a similar approach, Größler and Zock (2010), partnered with a German service provider interested in overhauling their human-resource planning process. Using a combination of interviews and historical employment data from the firm, they were able to conduct a scenario analysis using a simulation model to estimate staff availability in various jobs under different sets of assumptions. An enterprising researcher willing to partner with an organization in a similar fashion would likely have the access to decision makers and historical data needed estimate job-level mismatch costs. The availability of simulation software packages would allow for estimating such costs under a variety of assumptions, which could then be tested using data from subsequent periods. Given the complexity of many supply-chain models, we see promise in future interdisciplinary collaborations, with human-resource researchers interested in applying a supply-chain logic to talent-management issues partnering with supply-chain researchers interested in exploring the wider applicability of their models.

A slightly different strategy would be to partner with human-capital consulting firms, many of which have already developed proprietary tools for estimating similar measures using data from their clients' HRIS. While their measures are likely subject to a number of short-comings, they may offer a good starting point given that they are actually used by firms to make critical human-capital decisions. And while mismatch costs may be somewhat specific to firms and jobs, accumulating enough data on enough jobs in enough firms (a potential benefit of working with a consulting firm) should allow us to get a sense of the average mismatch costs (or the variables needed to estimate them) and apply them more widely. Doing so will allow us to subject our conceptual framework to empirical testing, such as exploring whether, as predicted, firms use different sourcing strategies based on the relative costs of undersupply and oversupply, and whether job and sourcing strategy fit leads to lower mismatch costs and improved organizational performance.

5.7 Conclusions

We are encouraged by the growing interest in integrating research on human-resource management and supply chains (Fisher *et al.*, 2010). The majority of recent work has explored how the strategic management of human resources can support or improve the functioning of organizational supply chains. Studies in this tradition tend to focus either on the functioning of internal supply chains (e.g., Snell *et al.*, 2000; Gowen and Tallon, 2003; Koulikoff-Souviron and Harrison, 2010) or the links between firms in the supply chain (Scarbrough, 2000; Jin, Hopkins, and Wittmer, 2010). A second stream of research explores how the logic of supply-chain management can improve talent management within organizations (e.g., Cappelli, 2008, 2009a; Größler and Zock, 2010). We believe this second approach, while less developed, provides fertile ground for future talent-management research. In an effort to provide a foundation for future research in this direction, we have used this chapter to outline the conceptual building blocks of a supply-chain perspective, its theoretical appeal, and to address how to overcome potential empirical challenges.

As a brief summary, minimizing the mismatch costs associated with the oversupply or undersupply of human capital is the central concern of a supply-chain approach to talent management. Because the costs of oversupply and undersupply are rarely equal, firms are able to choose among a variety of sourcing strategies in order to minimize their mismatch costs. Mitigation strategies are most effective when the costs of undersupply are greater than the costs of oversupply, as they often involve significant upfront costs. Inventory responses ensure reliability, while internal capacity responses ensure responsiveness. Contingency strategies are most effective when the costs of oversupply are greater than the costs of undersupply, as they lack upfront costs but can quickly get costly if they need to be used. Just-in-time back-up responses ensure reliability, while outsourcing responses ensure responsiveness.

We hope that our readers see promise in a supply-chain approach to talent management, recognize its theoretical appeal, and are emboldened to tackle the empirical challenges we have identified and those we have undoubtedly overlooked.

References

Barley, S. R. and Kunda, G. (2004). *Gurus, Hired Guns, and Warm Bodies: Itinerant Experts in a Knowledge Economy.* Princeton University Press.

Beamon, B. M. (1999). Measuring supply chain performance. *International Journal of Operations and Production Management*, 19 (3), 275–92.

Becker, B. E. and Huselid, M. A. (2006). Strategic human resources management: where do we go from here? *Journal of Management*, 32 (6), 898–925.

Bidwell, M. J. (2011). Paying more to get less: specific skills, incomplete information and the effects of external hiring. *Administrative Science Quarterly*, 56 (3), 369–407.

Bidwell, M. J. and Fernandez-Mateo, I. (2008). Three's a crowd? Understanding triadic employment relationships. In P. Cappelli (ed.), *Employment Relationships: New Models of White-collar Work.* Cambridge: Cambridge University Press.

Bodin, L. D. (1990). Twenty years of routing and scheduling. *Operations Research*, 38 (4), 571–9.

Boudreau, J. W. and Ramstad, P. M. (2001). Beyond cost-per-hire and time to fill: Supply-chain measurement for staffing (CAHRS Working Paper #01–16). Ithaca, NY: Cornell University, School of Industrial and Labor Relations, Center for Advanced Human Resource Studies. http://digital-commons.ilr.cornell.edu/cahrswp/79.

(2003). Strategic HRM measurement in the 21st century: from justifying HR to strategic talent leadership. In M. Goldsmith, R. P. Gandossy, and M. S. Efron (eds.), *HRM in the 21st Century*. New York, NY: John Wiley and Sons, pp. 79–90.

(2006). Talentship and HR measurement and analysis: from ROI to strategic organizational change. *Human Resource Planning*, 29 (1), 25–33.

(2007). *Beyond HR: The New Science of Human Capital.* Cambridge, MA: Harvard Business School Publishing Corporation.

Bretz, R. D., Boudreau, J. W., and Judge, T. A. (1994). Job search behavior of employed managers. *Personnel Psychology*, 47 (2), 275–301.

Brewer, P. C. and Speh, T. W. (2000). Using the balanced scorecard to measure supply chain performance. *Journal of Business Logistics*, 21 (1), 75–94.

Business Week (1949). Multiple management: top executive seedbed. *Business Week*, June, 82–3.

Cappelli, P. (1995). Rethinking employment. *British Journal of Industrial Relations*, 33 (4), 563–602.

(1999). *The New Deal at Work: Managing the Market-driven Workforce.* Boston, MA: Harvard Business School Press.

(2008). *Talent on Demand: Managing Talent in an Age of Uncertainty.* Cambridge, MA: Harvard Business School Press.

(2009a). A supply chain approach to workforce planning. *Organizational Dynamics*, 38 (1), 8–15.

(2009b). What's old is new again: managerial "talent" in an historical context. *Research in Personnel and Human Resources Management*, 28, 179–218.

(2010). The rise and decline of managerial development. *Industrial and Corporate Change*, 19 (2), 509–48.

(2011a). HR sourcing decisions and risk management. *Organizational Dynamics*, 40 (4), 310–16.

(2011b). Managing talent in a changing landscape. In K. Oakes and P. Galagan (eds.), *The Executive Guide to Integrated Talent Management.* American Society for Training and Development, pp. 13–22.

Carden, C. J. (1956). Executive training. *Journal of Retailing*, 22, 1–4.

Chandler, A. D. J. (1977). *The Visible Hand: the Managerial Revolution in American Business.* Cambridge, MA: Belknap Press.

Chen, I. J. and Paulraj, A. (2004). Towards a theory of supply chain management: the constructs and measurements. *Journal of Operations Management*, 22 (2), 119–50.

Chopra, S. and Sodhi, N. S. (2004). Managing risk to avoid supply-chain breakdown. *MIT Sloan Management Review*, 46 (1), 53–62.

Christopher, M. (1992). *Logistics and Supply Chain Management.* London: Pitman Publishing.

Clark, K. B. (1989). Project scope and project performance: the effect of parts strategy and supplier involvement on product development. *Management Science*, 35 (10), 1247–63.

Clawson, D. (1980). *Bureaucracy and the Labor Process: the Transformation of U.S. Industry 1860–1920*. New York: Monthly Review Press.

Cohen, M. A. and Lee, H. L. (1988). Strategic analysis of integrated production-distribution systems: models and methods. *Operations Research*, 36 (2), 216–28.

Collings, D. G. and Mellahi, K. (2009). Strategic talent management: a review and research agenda. *Human Resource Management Review*, 19 (4), 304–13.

Combs, J., Liu, Y., Hall, A., and Ketchen, D. (2006). How much do high-performance work practices matter? A meta-analysis of their effects on organizational performance. *Personnel Psychology*, 59 (3), 501–28.

Conference Board (2011). More U.S. workers are delaying retirement. No. 350 May 2011. The Conference Board Inc.

Davis, G. F. (2009). The rise and fall of finance and the end of the society of organizations. *Academy of Management Perspectives*, 23 (3), 27–44.

DeVanna, M. A., Forbrum, C., and Tichy, N. (1981). Human resource management: a strategic perspective. *Organization Dynamics*, 23, 34–47.

Dokko, G., Wilk, S. L., and Rothbard, N. P. (2009). Unpacking prior experience: how career history affects job performance. *Organization Science*, 20 (1), 51–68.

Dulebohn, J. H. and Johnson, R. D. (2012). Human resource metrics and decision support: a classification framework. *Human Resource Management Review*, 23 (1), 71–83.

Dyer, J. H. (1997). Effective interfirm collaboration: how firms minimize transaction costs and maximize transaction value. *Strategic Management Journal*, 18 (7), 535–56.

Fiorito, J. and Dauffenbach, R. C. (1982). Market and nonmarket influences on curriculum choice by college students. *Industrial and Labor Relations Review*, 36 (1), 88–101.

Fisher, M. L. (1997). What is the right supply chain for your product? *Harvard Business Review*, 75, 105–16.

Fisher, M. and Rayman, A. (1996). Reducing the cost of demand uncertainty through accurate response to early sales. *Operations Research*, 44 (1), 87–99.

Fisher, S. L., Graham, M. E., Vachon, S., and Vereecke, A. (2010). Don't miss the boat: research on HRM and supply chains. *Human Resource Management*, 49 (5), 813–28.

Flynn, B. B. and Flynn, E. J. (1999). Information-processing alternatives for coping with manufacturing environment complexity. *Decision Sciences*, 30 (4), 1021–52.

Frazier, G. L., Spekman, R. E., and O'Neal, C. R. (1988). Just-in-time exchange relationships in industrial markets. *Journal of Marketing*, 52 (4), 52–67.

Ghemawat, P. (1986). Sustainable advantage. *Harvard Business Review*, 64 (5), 53–8.

Giehll, T. and Moss, S. (2009). *Human Capital Supply Chains*. Minneapolis, MN: Mill City Press.

Gold, A. H., Malhotra, A., and Segars, A. H. (2001). Knowledge management: an organizational capabilities perspective. *Journal of Management Information Systems*, 18 (1), 185–214.

Gowen, C. R. and Tallon, W. J. (2003). Enhancing supply chain practices through human resource management. *Journal of Management Development*, 22 (1/2), 32–44.

Groysberg, B. (2010). *Chasing Stars: the Myth of Talent and the Portability of Performance*. Princeton, NJ: Princeton University Press.

Groysberg, B., Lee, L. E., and Nanda, A. (2008). Can they take it with them? The portability of star knowledge workers' performance. *Management Science*, 54 (7), 1213–30.

Größler, A. and Zock, A. (2010). Supporting long-term workforce planning with a dynamic aging chain model: a case study from the service industry. *Human Resource Management*, 49 (5), 829–48.

Gunasekaran, A., Patel, C., and Tirtiroglu, E. (2001). Performance measures and metrics in a supply chain environment. *International Journal of Operations and Production Management*, 21 (1/2), 71–87.

Gunasekaran, A., Patel, C., and McGaughey, R. E. (2004). A framework for supply chain performance measurement. *International Journal of Production Economics*, 87 (3), 333–47.

Harris, J. G., Craig, E., and Light, D. A. (2010). *The New Generation of Human Capital Analytics*. Accenture Institute for High Performance.

Hendricks, K. B. and Singhal, V. R. (2005). Association between supply chain glitches and operating performance. *Management Science*, 51 (5), 695–711.

Hoffman, C., Lesser, E., and Ringo, T. (2012). *Calculating Success: How the New Workplace Analytics will Revitalize your Organization*. Cambridge, MA: Harvard Business School Publishing Corporation.

Huselid, M. A. and Becker, B. E. (2011). Bridging micro and macro domains: workforce differentiation and strategic human resource management. *Journal of Management*, 37 (2), 395–403.

Huselid, M. A., Beatty, R. W., and Becker, B. E. (2005). "A Players" or "A Positions"? The strategic logic of workforce management. *Harvard Business Review*, 83 (12), 110–17.

Jacoby, S. M. (1997). Are career jobs headed for extinction? *California Management Review*, 42 (1), 123–45.

Jin, Y., Hopkins, M. M., and Wittmer, J. L. S. (2010). Linking human capital to competitive advantages: flexibility in a manufacturing firm's supply chain. *Human Resource Management*, 49 (5), 939–63.

Judge, T. A. and Watanabe, S. (1995). Is the past prologue? A test of Ghiselli's hobo syndrome. *Journal of Management*, 21 (2), 211–29.

Kaplan, R. S. and Norton, D. P. (2004). Measuring the strategic readiness of intangible assets. *Harvard Business Review*, 82 (2), 52–63.

Ketchen, D. J. and Hult, T. M. (2007). Bridging organization theory and supply chain management: the case of best value supply chains. *Journal of Operations Management*, 25 (2), 573–80.

Kim, S. (2011). Strategic reliability investments in multi-indenture supply chains. Working paper. Yale School of Management

Knight, F. (1921). *Risk, Uncertainty and Profit*. Boston, MA: Hart, Schaffner and Marx.

Koulikoff-Souviron, M. and Harrison, A. (2010). Evolving HR practices in a strategic intra-firm supply chain. *Human Resource Management*, 49 (5), 913–38.

Kulda, R. J. (1980). The effects of strategic planning on common stock returns. *Academy of Management Journal*, 23 (1), 5–20.

Lee, H. L. (2002). Aligning supply chain strategies with product uncertainties. *California Management Review*, 44 (3), 105–19.

Lee, H. L., Padmanabhan, V., and Whang, S. (1997). Information distortion in a supply chain: the bullwhip effect. *Management Science*, 43 (4), 546–58.

Lengnick-Hall, M. L., Lengnick-Hall, C. A., Andrade, L. S., and Drake, B. (2009). Strategic human resource management: the evolution of the field. *Human Resource Management Review*, 19 (2), 64–85.

Lepak, D. P. and Snell, S. A. (1999). The human resource architecture: toward a theory of human capital allocation and development. *Academy of Management Review*, 24 (1), 31–48.

Mabert, V. A. and Venkataramanan, M. A. (1998). Special research focus on supply chain linkages: challenges for design and management in the 21st century. *Decision Sciences*, 29 (3), 537–52.

March, J. G. (1991). Exploration and exploitation in organizational learning. *Organization Science*, 2 (1), 71–87.

Melman, S. (1951). The rise of administrative overhead in the manufacturing industries of the United States, 1890–1947. *Oxford Economic Papers*, 3 (1), 62–112.

Newcomer, M. (1955). *The Big Business Executive: the Factors that Made him, 1900–1950*. New York, NY: Columbia University Press.

Nkomo, S. M. (1987). Human resource planning and organization performance: an exploratory analysis. *Strategic Management Journal*, 8, 387–92.

O'Conner, P.D.T. (2002). *Practical reliability engineering* (4th ed.). West Sussex, England: John Wiley and Sons.

Olivares, M., Terwiesch, C., and Cassorla, L. (2008). Structural estimation of the news vendor model: an application to reserving operating room time. *Management Science*, 54 (1), 41–55.

Ostapczuk, E. D. (1994). *What Makes Effective Secondary Education Substitute Teachers? Literature Review*. Washington, DC.

Peck, J., Theodore, N., and Ward, K. (2005). Constructing markets for temporary labour: employment liberalization and the internationalization of the staffing industry. *Global Networks*, 5 (1), 3–26.

Princeton University (1949). *Selected References on the Selection and Development of Executives*. Industrial Relations Section, Princeton University.

Sackett, P. R. and Lievens, F. (2008). Personnel selection. *Annual Review of Psychology*, 59, 419–50.

Scarbrough, H. (2000). The HR implications of supply chain relationships. *Human Resource Management Journal*, 10 (1), 5–17.

Slack, N., Chambers, S., Harland, C., Harrison, A., and Johnston, R. (1995). *Operations Management*. London: Pitman Publishing.

Snell, S. A., Lepak, D. P., Dean, J. W., and Youndt, M. A. (2000). Selection and training for integrated manufacturing: the moderating effects of job characteristics. *Journal of Management Studies*, 37 (3), 445–66.

Society for Human Resource Management. (2002, 2004, 2006, 2008, 2011). *SHRM Workplace Forecast*.

Stalk, G. J. (1988). Time: the next source of competitive advantage. *Harvard Business Review*, 66, 41–51.

Strack, R., Caye, J.-M., Lassen, S., *et al.* (2010). *Creating People Advantage 2010: How Companies can Adapt their HR Practices for Volatile Times*. Boston Consulting Group and World Federation of People Management Associations.

Swaminathan, J. M., Smith, S. F., and Sadeh, N. M. (1998). Modeling supply chain dynamics: a multiagent approach. *Decision Sciences*, 29 (3), 607–32.

Tomlin, B. (2006). On the value of mitigation and contingency strategies for managing supply chain disruption risks. *Management Science*, 52 (5), 639–57.

Useem, M. (1993). Management commitment and company policies on education and training. *Human Resource Management*, 32 (4), 411–34.

Walker, J. W. (1980). *Human Resource Planning*. New York: Mcgraw-Hill.

Whitmore, E. (1952). The executive manpower shortage – and what can be done about it? *American Business*, 22 (8–9), 9.

Whyte, W. F. (ed.). (1990). *Participatory Action Research*. Thousand Oaks, CA: Sage Publications.

Whyte, W. H. (1956). *The Organizational Man*. New York: Simon and Schuster.

Wood, D. R. and LaForge, R. L. (1979). The impact of comprehensive planning on financial performance. *Academy of Management Journal*, 22 (3), 516–26.

Wright, P. M., Boudreau, J., Pace, D., Sartain, L., McKinnon, P., and Antoine, R. (eds.) (2011). *The Chief HR Officer: Defining the New Role of Human Resource Leaders*. San Fransisco, CA: Jossey-Bass.

Yu, H., Zeng, A. Z., and Zhao, L. (2009). Single or dual sourcing: decision-making in the presence of supply chain disruption risks. *International Journal of Management Science*, 37 (4), 788–800.

Zunz, O. (1990). *Making America Corporate*. Chicago: University Of Chicago Press.

6 | Employer branding and career theory: new directions for research

GRAEME MARTIN AND JEAN-LUC CERDIN

6.1 Introduction

In this chapter, our aim is to combine insights from employer branding and career management to explain some of the issues facing the talent- and reputation-management agendas in organizations. More specifically, our objectives are:

1. to propose a revised model of employer branding and its links to talent management and organizational reputations, which are key elements in effective career management
2. to analyze links between employer branding and career management
3. to reflect on some of the problems raised by the interdisciplinary nature of employer branding in practice and the consequent implications for careers.

Previous research into employer branding and organizational reputations by one of the authors (e.g., Martin and Beaumont, 2003; Martin and Hetrick, 2009; Martin, Gollan, and Grigg, 2011) has led us to accept a working definition of an employer brand as:

a generalised recognition for being known among key stakeholders for providing a high quality employment experience, and a distinctive organizational identity which employees value, engage with and feel confident and happy to promote to others. (Martin, Gollan, and Grigg, 2011)

We argued that employer branding referred to the process by which branding, marketing, communications, and HR concepts and techniques were applied externally and internally to attract, engage, and retain potential and existing employees. Until the onset of the global financial crisis (GFC) experienced by many advanced economies, most practitioner-oriented work in the field has focused on talent attraction because of longstanding labor market conditions in developed and developing countries. Thus employer branding became associated with the external application of marketing and communications tools (e.g., recruitment advertising, publicity, events, and the new social media) to attract potential employees, though this external branding of the organization always recognized a need for employees to identify with and "live the brand" because of the discretion they could exercise over how they impacted customers and potential employees (Barrow and Mosley, 2005). With the onset of recession in many countries following the GFC and sovereign debt crises, employer branding has turned inwards on the organization itself to focus on engagement (CIPD, 2009; Sparrow and Balain, 2009; Sparrow *et al.*, 2010), a key element of which is the opportunity for employees to further their individual and organizational career aspirations.

While the importance of talent attraction and engagement of employees make employer branding a serious contender for inclusion in any list of high-performance work practices (HPWPs), we have also proposed that employer branding plays a strategic role in "future proofing" corporate reputations (CIPD, 2010; Martin, Gollan, and Grigg, 2011). This corporate-reputation agenda has been defined in terms of reconciling organizational needs to create strategic value by being simultaneously *different* from competitors but remaining *socially legitimate* by securing general recognition, approval, and esteem for providing high-quality goods and services (Deephouse and Carter, 2005; Rindova *et al.*, 2005; Highhouse, Brooks, and Gregarus, 2009; Bergh *et al.*, 2010). Yet, despite career theorists having shown that both organizational differentiation and legitimacy are shaped by how firms and individuals manage diverse career orientations and personal reputations (Zinko *et al.*, 2007), to date the notion of career has been neglected in discussions of employer branding and indeed the marketing and communications literature as it affects reputations. We attempt to fill this gap in this chapter by providing guidance for future research and practice for HR, careers, marketing, and communications specialists.

6.2 Modelling the links between employer branding and careers

Employer branding has been an important part of HR strategy and practice in global organizations for more than a decade (Schultz *et al.*, 2002; Martin and Beaumont, 2003; Backhaus and Tikoo, 2004; Martin and Hetrick, 2009), arguably because it is not seen as an HR initiative alone. Marketing and communications specialists have tended to dominate the conversation over both theory and practice (Martin and Beaumont, 2003; Backhaus and Tikoo, 2004), although organization studies has begun to take an interest in this growing phenomenon (Schultz *et al.*, 2002). Indeed, Martin, Gollan, and Grigg (2011) claim that "employer branding may even be synonymous with HRM itself rather than just another 'tool in its the box'" because it is key to building and sustaining corporate reputations, an issue that is increasingly important for global organizations' performance (Martin and Hetrick, 2006; Hatch and Schultz, 2008; Highhouse, Brooks, and Gregarus, 2009). In this context employer branding has been linked with a trend toward "corporateness," a term coined by Balmer and Geyser (2003) to describe a developing interest in corporate-level integration and identity management. However, the focus on its corporate nature has resulted in tensions between brand *differentiation*, which is concerned to mark the organization in question as being different from others, and organizational *legitimacy*, which is concerned with being seen as respectable and securing the approval of others – in short being the same as others (Highhouse, Brooks, and Gregarus, 2009; Martin 2009a, 2009b).

To address these issues, one of the present authors (Martin and Groen in't Woud, 2011) developed a theoretical framework of the employer-branding process, incorporating insights from signalling theory and from research into different foci of employee engagement comprising *work engagement* and *organizational engagement* (Beijer, Farndale, and van Veldhoven, 2009). More recently we have incorporated a third foci into the engagement dimension of the framework – engagement with each other – based on the powerful notion of relational coordination (Gittell, Seidner, and Wimbush, 2010). We argued then that signalling theory and engagement were essential to understanding and measuring the impact of employer-branding and talent-management practices in organizations, and this argument applies in equal measure to the relationship between employer branding and careers, the focus of this chapter.

6.2.1 Signalling theory and its application to employer branding

Signalling theory has been used to explain how leadership communications and actions, and bundles of HPWPs including employer branding, are used as organizational signals that are sent externally and internally to create impressions of quality and prominence, which are two key elements in managing employer reputations (Suazo, Martínez, and Sandoval, 2009; Boyd, Bergh, and Ketchen Jr, 2010; Celani and Singh, 2011; Martin and Groen-in't Woud, 2011). The impact of leadership behaviors and HPWPs on employer branding, employee engagement, and, we argue, employee careers, is shaped by the way these signals are sensed and enacted by employees (Weick, 2001).

The emergence of signalling theory resulted from the study of information economics under conditions in which buyers and sellers dealt with asymmetric information while interacting in the market (Spence, 1974). In his original formulation, Spence (1973) modelled the signalling function of education on labor markets. He argued, potential employers and job candidates face asymmetry of information where employers lack information about the quality of candidates, therefore candidates signal their quality and reduce information asymmetries by gaining educational qualifications, a proxy for career aspirations. This signal was considered reliable because lower quality candidates were unable to endure the rigors of higher education. The key point of Spence's model was that it contradicted prevailing human-capital theory because he played down education's role in escalating worker productivity but, instead, stressed that education was a means to communicate the characteristics of candidates that were otherwise unobservable to firms (Weiss, 1995).

At the heart of signalling theory is the notion of *honesty* of signals as interpreted by receivers, the *cost* of sending honest communications, and the possibility of *faking* honesty (Martin and Groen-in't Woud, 2011). At a basic level, honesty refers to providing employees with little more than the required information, such as cues about instrumental rewards that they can expect when joining the organization. From the perspective of HRM, however, honesty refers to symbolic and cultural cues that employees can expect from good employers, which include deeply held cultural values, beliefs and assumptions of the organization, and the meanings they expect to obtain from working for their organization (Davies and Chun, 2008). Thus, for example, firms that signal job security and opportunities for career development are key elements in the psychological contracts with staff, and that organizations characterized by a caring ethical climate can expect high-trust responses (Simha and Cullen, 2012).

Communications theorists believe that receivers' perception of honesty of signals is dependent on them being seen as novel, credible, trustworthy, and sustainable (Van Riel, 2003). The existence of such attributes will lead employees to accept cultural and symbolic cues that organizations attempt to signal (Martin and Groen-in't Woud, 2011). Credibility, trustworthiness, and sustainability are essential for the creation of sense of legitimacy, respectability, approval, prominence, and prestige, whereas novelty is important for making the signals distinctive from others. Thus, they believe that such criteria form key elements in internal and external stakeholders' sensemaking of organizations' legitimacy claims to positive corporate reputations (Highhouse, Brooks, and Gregarus, 2009; Martin, Gollan, and Grigg, 2011).

In signalling theory, honesty is not only concerned with the content of the signal, but is also concerned with the source of signals, and the structures, processes, and channels used for its conveyance. Thus, for example, research into the misuse of personal charisma to achieve leaders' personal goals at the expense of employees' interests has been shown to be destructive in leading to a low-trust dynamic as perceived by employees (Krasikova, Green, and LeBreton, 2013). Such breaches of trust, particularly in financial services, have caused organizations to focus more than ever on the perceived honesty of CEOs, in making appointments to senior positions, and in how they organize and communicate with external and internal stakeholders (Chartered Insurance Institute, 2012). Evidence also suggests that instead of trusting official communications, employees refer to other sources such as social media channels including employee blogs and social networking websites for honesty in the signalling process (Martin and Hetrick, 2009). Finally, the costs of sending honest signals are not only financial ones but are also linked to their strategic impact, strength, and consistency over time; whereas weak or inconsistent signals are often perceived by employees as dishonest. Consequently, organizations frequently engage in high-cost signalling, in the forms of high-cost promotional work, sophisticated public-relations campaigns, or in engaging in corporate-citizenship activities, to communicate messages they hope will be seen not only as honest in the short term but also in the long term to create reputational capital, which may subsequently be drawn on to reduce future signalling costs. One of the reasons used by HR and corporate communications staff for engaging in competitions run by media such as *Business Week*, the *Financial Times* and the Best Place to Work Institute is the long-term advantage they gain from investing in honest messages. Nevertheless, honest signals do not need to be costly, especially if there is a natural convergence of interests between the signaller and receiver (Cronk, 2005). This point can be illustrated by the extent to which bonus payments to key employees in the investment-banking sector have become ingrained in the culture of the global financial-services industry. Bonuses, while imposing short-term financial costs on many profitable banks, have not traditionally invoked strategic costs and handicaps precisely because they are an industry-wide norm; if you like, they are the necessary "table stakes." However, governments in a number of countries are now attempting to impose strategic, reputational costs on the banking sector by fuelling public outcry over excessive bonuses for "fat cats" in addition to financial costs through windfall taxes.

6.2.2 Engagement theory

We have also woven into our model three, connected levels of engagement, which we argue have a major impact on the degree to which employees perceive the honesty of employer-brand signals.

1. *Work engagement* – this is a well-researched and empirically verified concept (Bakker and Schaufeli, 2008; Salanova and Schaufeli, 2008).
2. *Engagement with each other* – especially in interdependent work groups, which draws on the notion of relational coordination, a construct that was been found to have a significant impact on performance outcomes in a range of industries (Gittell, Seidner, and Wimbush, 2010).
3. *Organizational engagement* – initially developed by consultants but is now being treated in academic literature as an important driver of organizational performance (Edwards and Peccei, 2007; Macey and Schneider, 2008; Beijer, Farndale, and van Veldhoven, 2009; Martin, Pate, and Bell, 2009).

Distinguishing among these three levels of engagement and showing how they are linked is an important step forward in making the overall concept of engagement a more useful concept to academics and practitioners. They are also helpful in mapping out the potential link between employer branding and careers, and the problems in thinking about careers in individualistic terms.

Taking the first level, that of work engagement, studies are increasingly based on a *demand–resources model of work engagement*

(Schaufeli and Bakker, 2004). This model has identified three forms of engagement that people have with their work. These are the levels of *vigor* employees invest in doing the job, their levels of *absorption* or immersion and attachment to their work, and their *dedication* to their work. Work engagement has been shown to predict valuable outcomes such as positive evaluations of organizations, lower job turnover, and higher levels of individual and unit performance. These forms of engagement are thought to be positively associated with key job resources and challenging work. However, they are also but negatively associated with hindrance demands, which can lead to over-engagement or employee burnout. High levels of work engagement also tend to be associated with "cosmopolitan" career orientations, which typically refer to the external career orientation of professionals such as academics, health care professionals, and research and development staff as distinct from the "local" or internal career orientations of occupational groups such as managers (Gouldner, 1957).

Taking the second level, that of engagement with each other, relationships among employees at a group or team level have also been found to be a key feature in leading to effective organizational performance. This has traditionally been theorized in terms of social capital and networking among employees to facilitate group and organizational learning (Levin and Cross, 2004). More recently, Gittell, Sneider, and Wimbush (2010) have developed a theory of relational coordination to explain the impact of effective coordination among task-interdependent groups on achieving soft and hard desirable organizational outcomes. They define relational coordination as "a mutually reinforcing process of interaction between communication and relationships carried out for the purpose of task integration" (p. 3), which involves groups engaging in frequent and high-quality communications, sharing goals and knowledge, and showing mutual respect for each other. While these authors restrict their analysis to the coordination of "highly interdependent, uncertain, and time-constrained work," we argue that the concept of relational coordination is relevant to most forms of work in modern organizations. It also provides a much-needed theoretical link and level of analysis between the individualistic notion of work engagement and organizational engagement, especially for talent-management and career-management scholars who are interested in why recruiting "stars" can often lead to failure (Groysberg, Sant, and Abrahams, 2008).

Taking the third level, that of organizational engagement, recent academic work has sought to define organizational engagement in terms of emotions and attitudes (state engagement) and behavior engagement (the traditional interest of management consultants). Key components of these different types of engagement with the organization include organizational satisfaction and commitment, vigor and absorption displayed toward an organization, and positive organizational citizenship behaviors (Macey and Schneider, 2008; Beijer, Farndale, and van Veldhoven, 2009). To these we would add employee identification with an organization, drawing on the well-established concept of organizational identification (Douglas Pugh and Deitz, 2008). This idea has been developed further by Edwards and Peccei (2007) and Edwards (2009), who have proposed a three-factor explanation of employee identification with their organizations. The first factor refers to how employees self-categorize their personal identities. As noted earlier, employees differ in their career orientations and the extent to which their employing organization helps define their identities. The second refers to their sense of attachment and belonging to their organizations, often related to how long they have worked in it. The third refers to the extent to which employees share the goals and values of the organization and incorporate them into their own goals, values, and beliefs. In these studies, high levels of organizational identification were shown to predict all categories of workers' helping behaviors, turnover intentions, and feelings of being involved in the organization.

In summary, we argue that a more complete understanding of employee engagement needs to take into account the different levels at which employees seek to engage with their organizations – at the level of their work, with each other in work groups, and with the mission, goals, and values of the organization or corporation – and how these interconnect. We also need to understand more fully the drivers of these different levels of engagement, which inevitably include the career orientations or career "anchors" that employees bring to an organization.

6.3 Modelling employer branding and its links with careers

Our revised model is set out in Figure 6.1, and in the first part of this chapter we explain these *signal design, signal evaluation,* and *outcomes* stages of the model in some detail. Following a well-established logic of model building in business and management described by

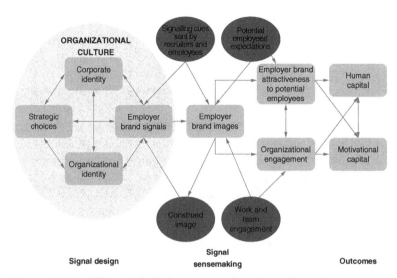

Figure 6.1 Modelling the links between employer branding and careers

Whetten (2002), in which he argues that what needs to be explained should come before the explanation, we begin our discussion with the intended outcomes of employer branding.

6.3.1 The outcomes of employer branding

The intended outcomes of employer branding as one of a range of high-performance work practices in organizations can be defined as human capital and motivational capital (Jiang *et al.*, 2012). Human capital can be defined as the stocks and flows of knowledge, skills, and abilities in and through organizations while motivational capital refers to the direction, intensity, and duration of employees' effort. High levels of human and motivational capital have been found to be strongly and positively related to important proximal outcomes such as operational effectiveness and efficiency, and to distal outcomes such as financial performance, including measures such as Tobin's Q (Jiang *et al.*, 2012).

6.3.2 Designing employer-brand signals: the interactions among organizational culture, corporate identity, organizational identity, and strategic choices on branding

The first stage of the model comprises five interacting factors: the existing *organizational culture* shaping and being shaped by a collective sense of *organizational identity, strategic choices* on the customer-facing brand, and a *corporate identity* to produce an *employer-brand image*. It is these conscious and unconscious signals that create employer-brand images among prospective employees and existing employees.

We begin by discussing *organizational identity, culture,* and *strategic choice*. Identity has become a core but contested concept in management research over the last decade (Hatch and Schultz, 2004; Oliver and Roos, 2007). For our purposes in developing this model we use a definition of organizational identity as the collective answer by employees and managers to the "Who are we?" question, revealed in the organization's shared knowledge, beliefs, language, and behaviors (Whetten and Mackey, 2002). This organizational self-concept is not just a collection of individual identities but has been described as having a metaphorical life of its own, independent of those who are currently employed in a corporation. In other words, it is a "social fact," capable of having an impact on an organization's ability to attract and retain resources, cause individuals to identify with its values, handle critical incidents, including brand advocacy, and prevent organizations from fragmenting (Oliver and Roos, 2007). In contrast, the marketing-related concept of corporate identity has been depicted as an organization's projected image of "who we want to be," expressed not only in the form of tangible logos, architecture, and public pronouncements, but also in its communication of mission, strategies, and values (Balmer and Geyser, 2003). In relation to employment, this notion is often described as the employee value proposition (EVP) or employment proposition (Martin and Hetrick, 2009).

Both of these drivers of employer brands are essentially products of the more deep-seated root metaphor of organizational culture, for our purposes best described by Schein's (2004) classic definition as the often-hidden values, assumptions, and beliefs of organizations that shape external adaptation and internal integration. This adaptation–integration definition highlights the two faces of organizational culture – the customer- and employee-facing functions – so linking the disciplines of marketing and HR in particularly useful ways. Hatch and Schultz (2004) make a strong case for organizational identity being the link between organizational culture and its image with outsiders. Culture shapes how organizational members define themselves collectively and through time, employees and managers self-consciously reflect on cultural values and assumptions to develop a collective sense of "we." In turn, organizational identity reflects back on culture.

Both organizational and corporate identity, however, are also a consequence of strategic choices by key decision makers. They include the clarity of strategic objectives, especially in firms characterized by unrelated diversification, perhaps across international boundaries, and the feasibility of developing standardized customer- or employee-facing branding (CIPD, 2007; Martin and Hetrick, 2009), and, in an international context, choices over how to segment markets.

The next factor is *employer and employee authorship of the employer-brand signals*. These cultural, identity, and strategic drivers shape the intended design of *employer-brand signals*, which comprise the signals senior managers intend to communicate to existing and potential employees about the package of extrinsic functional and economic benefits and intrinsic psychological benefits on offer, including the offer on careers in the organization (Martin and Hetrick, 2009). As we noted earlier, however, it is not just the communications content of a message that comprises the signal but the cues associated with bundles of HR practices put into place to reinforce the signals. These include the use of bonuses to reinforce the importance of key outcomes, workplace architecture to signal, for example, the importance of team working, and career development opportunities to signify the intention of fulfilling a relational psychological contract. This "autobiographical account" signals to employees the company's intentions, so forming employees' and potential employees' expectations of the psychological contract "deal" on offer (Rousseau, 1995; Conway and Briner, 2005). However, just as strategy and autobiographies can be intended/official and unintended/unofficial (Mintzberg, 1994), so too are employer-brand signals. As a number of authors have noted (Dowling, 2001; Miles and Mangold, 2004; Knox and Freeman, 2006), often the most powerful source of signals about the employer brand are the messages employees communicate to outsiders and new recruits about the "reality" of working in the organization, and their views of the honesty of the signals, including the material, symbolic, and cultural signals (Dowling, 2001; Highhouse, Brooks, and Gregarus, 2009). Miles and Mangold (2005) suggest that the failure of employees to understand and/or treat as honest the intended signals of employers' internal branding is one of the main points of fracture in this design phase of the employer-brand promise or employment proposition (Whetten and Mackey, 2002; Martin and Hetrick, 2006). As noted earlier, signalling theory predicts that dishonest signals are relatively easy to send but can incur enormous future costs in the evolution of any organization, especially in impacting organizational trust. Moreover, honest signals are typically costly in terms of the amount of senior management commitment needed to make them credible and authentic, and in removing barriers to change such as unnecessary organizational politics and bureaucracy, "turf wars," perceptions of procedural injustice, bullying or incompetent line managers – all factors that inhibit employee engagement with their work and their organizations (Rich, LePine, and Crawford, 2010).

Researchers have also identified *construed identity* as an important influence on employer-brand signals. This notion refers to how employees view external stakeholders' perceptions of their organization, including family, friends, employees of other organizations, the press, and other media. Press influence in shaping the reception of employer signals is one of the main rationales underlying the establishment of corporate communications departments in institutions as diverse as financial services, universities, and healthcare, and for developing "employer of choice" award schemes such as the those produced by national media such as *Business Week* and the *Financial Times* (Van Riel, 2003; Joo and McLean, 2006). These communications and awards schemes raise the costs of signalling initially but, as noted earlier, are deemed by participating organizations to reduce them in the longer run because of the reputational capital they create.

6.3.3 The evaluation of the employer-brand signals by employees and potential applicants

The first factor here is *employer-brand reputations as biographies*. If the employer-brand signal is self-authored, employer-brand images refer to receivers' perceptions of honesty, credibility, consistency, and strength of these signals. In earlier work we have likened these to the multiple *biographical accounts* of what an employer brand holds in terms of meaning for potential and new employees who, along with others, begin to write different stories about the signals. In doing so, they form themselves into distinct segments of interest and lifestyles. This notion mirrors debates in the literature on psychological contracting (Martin and Beaumont, 2003; Conway and Briner, 2005), whereby employee psychological contracts are sometimes defined in terms of their expectations arising from perceived promises or obligations on behalf of employers (the employer-brand image), what value employees place on these promises, obligations, or employment propositions, and the extent to which they perceive employers to have delivered on the psychological contract deal, including the career deal (Martin and Hetrick, 2006). The critical point here is that just as psychological contracts are essentially individual phenomenon, so too are the signals received and the biographies written about an organization. In the literature on reputation management, images are seen as plural (Dowling, 2001); different groups of people are likely to expect and attribute different values to particular employer-brand signal cues and view them differently in signal strength, honesty, credibility, and benefit.

The second factor is the *instrumental and symbolic aims of employer branding*. In discussing meaning, a further important feature of shaping the reception of employer-brand signals is that they are intended to fulfil two levels of expectations, needs, and meaning – the *instrumental* and *symbolic* levels – both of which have been identified as forming employees' views of their psychological contract (Conway and Briner, 2005) and the honesty with which signals are treated. These distinctions also parallel developments in the branding literature (Lievens and Highhouse, 2003; Holt, 2007; Lievens, Van Hoye, and Anseel, 2007). Instrumental needs and expectations of employees refer to the objective, physical, and tangible attributes that an organization may possess (Lievens, 2007; Lievens, Van Hoye, and Anseel, 2007). Most importantly in this case, these include the ability to provide opportunities for career advancement and job security, both of which are key elements of high-performance work systems. Symbolic needs broadly translate into perceptions and emotions about the abstract and intangible image of the organization, for example, employees' feelings of pride in the organization, the extent to which it gives them a sense of purpose, beliefs about its technical competence, and honesty in dealing with clients and employees, the extent to which it is an exciting or innovative place to work, and the extent to which it is seen as chic, stylish, and/or as aggressively masculine or competitive (Lievens, Van Hoye, and Schreurs, 2005; Davies and Chun, 2008). Distinguishing between instrumental needs and symbolic meaning mirrors recent trends in branding models. These models have moved away from a focus on so-called *mind-share approaches*, which refers to a brand's capabilities to occupy a central, focused appeal to individuals (through specific employee-value propositions on rewards, career development, etc.) to an *emotional* level, in which the brand interacts and builds relationships with people (Holt, 2007).

6.4 Employer branding and global careers

The perception of employer-brand signals is rendered more complex in a global context. Potential international employees can construe signals from an organization differently, depending on their country of origin or adoption. Although not without their critics, national cultural dimensions can be useful in predicting individuals' values, attitudes, and behaviors (e.g., Hofstede, 2001). Certain of these dimensions are particularly relevant when focusing on the employer branding and careers. Future orientation is one such dimension, which is defined as "the degree to which individuals in organizations or societies engage in future-oriented behaviors such as planning, investing in the future, and delaying individual or collective gratification" (House and Javidan, 2004: p. 12). Individuals from highly future-oriented cultures tend to place strong priority on long-term success, while those from national cultures characterized by low future-orientation would focus on the time at hand, with a hedonistic approach to life (e.g., Ashkanasy *et al.*, 2004). As a result, potential candidates from highly future-oriented cultures would put more emphasis on and be more convinced by an employment proposition centered on a career-advancement perspective than those from low future-orientated cultures. The latter are more likely to be attracted to an employment proposition that focuses on immediate reward, probably in terms of compensation.

At a micro-level, individuals from the same national culture might exhibit different preferences and cultural tendencies. Their responses to employer-brand signals and an employment proposition could be affected by several other factors. Potential employees may perceive the organization's personality (Slaughter *et al.*, 2004) differently according to their own personality or their values. Individual characteristics such as personal values might have an impact on their attitude and behaviour (e.g., Schwartz, 1992). Values matter, regardless of whether individuals respond favorably to the employment proposition in terms of career. Indeed, it is the congruence between individual values and organizational values that often determines an organization's attract-iveness (e.g. Judge and Bretz, 1992; Judge and Cable 1997).

This focus on values is associated with the person–organization fit theory (e.g., Kristof, 1996), which posits that the individual seeks that kind of environment that can enable the pursuit of a career in alignment with his or her values. Also, an organization's attractiveness will depend on the potential fit that individuals perceive between what they are and what the organization can offer them in terms of career. Regarding the aforementioned importance of values, we have already referred to Schein's (1990) concept of career anchors, which vary depending on individuals' values and interests and can impact the levels of engagement they seek with organizations. These anchors constitute the non-negotiable elements in a person's career choice. They vary within a society, and different individuals are likely to seek different careers according to their career anchors. Cerdin and Bird (2008) have proposed that career anchors can lead to different international careers. They show that the very meaning of career and career success may be different depending on the national cultural context (see also Briscoe, Hall, and Mayrhofer, 2011). So, when an organization seeks to develop an overall employer brand, it is important to know which career anchors are likely to "pull" recruits in and which are likely to "push" them away because of a lack of perceived compatibility in terms of career orientation. In the international context, the internationalism anchor appears as a particularly interesting new development in career-anchor theory. Identified by Suutari and Taka (2004) and recently operationalized (Cerdin, 2007) and validated (Lazarova, Cerdin, and Liao, forthcoming), it describes a career orientation where working in an international environment is key to individual career choices. Organizations can easily gauge to what extent potential appli-cants drawn to an organization display this anchor.

Finally, some individuals seek boundaryless careers (Arthur and Rousseau, 1996), which are oriented learning-related careers. These are more diverse than a traditional career inside an organization. Individuals consider their own careers to be less dependent on the organizations (Baruch, 2003) than on their own efforts and desired personal identities, which is typically the case for professionals in areas such as medicine, the law, academia, and engineering. Increasingly such "idiosyncratic" careers, built around individuals, are becoming the norm in knowledge-intensive organizations and present particularly difficult problems for firms seeking the use the organization as a brand and source of identification.

6.5 An illustrative case study

In this last section, before presenting our conclusions, we wish to reflect on some of the problems raised by the interdisciplinary nature of employer branding in practice and the consequent implications for careers. To do so, we have drawn on a case study of a multinational company, AERO, which is a leader in its industry sector. The case data are based on a professional master's thesis (Truffier, 2010) supervised by one of the authors of this chapter. The two key points that the case illustrates are: (1) the interdisciplinary nature of employer branding and the concept of career; and (2) the consequent problems of who owns employer branding and how this might impact careers.

AERO is a multinational company that owns several brands, each of them having a strong individual identity. For this MNE, being known as a good employer is a top priority as it not only competes for top-tier engineers within its own industry but also with the banking sector for managers and administrators. AERO is known for offering very attractive career paths and salaries in all companies in which it operates.

However, the HR function faces some difficulties in tackling employer branding in a global environment. These stem from the acknowledgement that HR communications, corporate communication, and corporate social responsibility all contribute to the employer-branding process. In other words, the notion of a brand has multiple meanings (Martin and Hetrick, 2006) and is interdisciplinary in nature.

AERO's corporate brand is strong in its two European countries of origin, but has a rather negative image outside those countries, partly because it operates in a hostile environment characterized by very strong global competition in a domain linked to the military and aeronautics sectors. This differential image represents a problem for HR management because they are responsible for developing a global workforce outside Europe. Thus senior management see improving the reputation of the company as a top priority particularly for strategic countries and regions such as India, China, the United States, and the Middle East.

When employer branding was first introduced into AERO, it was housed in the Talent and Executive Management department, and was subsequently integrated into the Competency Development/Strategy and Employment Operations department. Later on, several departments, such as Recruitment, Shared Services for Operations, and the Strategy and Employment department became involved in managing the employer brand. So even within HR, responsibility for employer branding was passed around and so failed to create a sense of ownership. At the time of writing the case, the employer-brand definition was a result of a joint effort between HR Marketing, which is responsible for initial recruitment and sourcing activities, the Marketing of Services department, which supports the employer-branding strategy through the definition of the brand, and taking charge of market research, planning, budgeting and controlling, and, finally Corporate Communication.

In addition, HR professionals and operations are involved in addressing applicants' interests and questions, especially during careers fairs. The company has also developed a graduate program managed by the Recruitment Center. However, AERO carries out separate procedures for potential candidates and current employees.

Thus, although the HR function recognizes a need to involve other departments, namely Communication and Marketing, it finds it difficult to communicate its needs to these departments.

By its very nature, employer branding is complex and interdisciplinary, requiring a common effort across various departments. So determining who is in charge is not always straightforward, which can strongly affect the output. Beyond the struggle for power, the interest of each department may vary according to their disciplinary background. Firstly, on the one hand, the Communication department is sometimes seen to put too much emphasis on a message portraying a desired corporate identity, without regularly ensuring that this signal corresponds to the lived experience of employees in the organization. On the other hand, HR seeks to implement realistic job previews (Wanous, 1980) to avoid new entrants experiencing unrealistic "surprises" when they get to work. This conflict becomes even more acute when communicating at the international level on the basis of messages formulated and shaped for the national level. Secondly, the Marketing department tends to view employees as individual "consumers," while HRM policy has to deal with aggregate grades and types, for example, over pay and conditions, and aggregated career-management paths. Thirdly, there is a risk that Marketing may wish to turn HRM policy too much on recruiting in the outside world without focusing enough on current employees' careers and engagement issues.

So, while HRM may claim to own employer branding and career management, it must also rely on, and work with, other departments who have different frames of reference, values, and interests. In our opinion, a significant area for future research lies in how such multidisciplinarity works in practice and whether it can produce a satisfactory interdisciplinary solution to effective employer branding and career management. Such research is especially needed in global companies, given the added complexity of national institutions and cultures.

6.6 Conclusions

In this chapter we have attempted to combine insights from employer branding and career management to explain some of the issues facing the talent and reputation management agendas in organizations. We have proposed a new model of employer branding based on concepts from signalling theory, reputation management, and strategic human resources management (SHRM), which should help researchers and practitioners think more systematically about the key variables, linkages, and processes. Our outcome measures are derived from recent research into SHRM – motivational and human capital. However, a further direction in which research might fruitfully take is to define more specifically the notion of reputational capital as an outcome. Although there are useful consultancy approaches to this notion, most notably work carried out by the Reputation Institute, we believe that more work is needed in this area, especially from a qualitative perspective. We have also attempted to analyze some of the links between employer branding and career management, especially in how they may be influenced by different levels of employee engagement within a firm. Again, this area needs further research. How different levels of employee engagement are interconnected and might be mutually constitutive is a topic that could form the basis for further research, especially in the context of career theory and the problems of idiosyncratic or boundaryless careers. Finally, we have also attempted to reflect on some of problems raised by the interdisciplinary nature of employer branding in our case illustration, and the multidisciplinary nature of the production of an employer brand. Again, we believe this is an area for further research. For example, is interdisciplinarity in management ever possible, given the tendency to professionalize different management functions and to instil professional difference values, frames of reference, and cognitions?

Two final pleas regarding research in this field: the first relates to the dark side of employer branding; the second relates to the dominant variance-theory approach to studying it. Some of our recent work with PhD students in this field has led us to focus on the contributions of critical-management theory and process theory. Firstly, nearly all research and practice in this area is approached from a functionalist perspective, which assumes a unitary frame of reference and a need for greater integration in organizations (Burrell and Morgan, 1979). How realistic these basic assumptions are is open to question in many organizations. Thus we believe that more work in this field is necessary to take a more critical perspective on employer branding and career management, focusing on questions such as: can employer branding ever deliver integration in organizations, especially in global companies or ones in which professionals dominate decision making, such as in healthcare. Secondly, process theory (Langley *et al.*, 2013) is a much more appropriate way of addressing questions connected with "how" and "why" employer branding works in practice, especially in the context of individual and organizational careers. While our framework attempts to map out connections, it is not a process model as such. Again, this is an area for further research.

These suggestions for further research have important implications for practice. One of the authors regularly acts as a judge on submissions by major companies to a prestigious award for employer branding in the UK. With few exceptions, the quality of these presentations and the thinking underlying them would benefit from considering the issues raised in this chapter. Most of these presentations amount to little more than exercises in undifferentiated HR rhetoric that appear to have very little chance of being regarded as authentic by employees on the ground. Understanding the complexity of employer branding as is relates to careers, especially from a more critical and processual perspective, might produce sharper thinking that will gain HR a more secure "seat at the top table" instead of the wobbly "three-legged stool" it sits on at present.

References

Arthur, M. B. and Rousseau, D. M. (1996). *The Boundaryless Career: A New Employment Principle for a New Organizational Era*. New York: Oxford University Press.

Ashkanasy, N., Gupta, V., Mayfield, M. S., and Trevor-Roberts, E. (2004). Future orientation. In R. J. House, P. J. Hanges, M. Javidan, P. W. Dorfman, and V. Gupta (eds.), *Culture, Leadership and Organizations: The GLOBE Study of 60 Societies*. London: Sage Publications. pp. 282–331.

Backhaus, K. and Tikoo, S. (2004). Conceptualizing and researching employer branding. *Career Development International*, 9 (5), 501–17.

Bakker, A. B. and Schaufeli, W. B. (2008). Positive organizational behaviour: engaged employees in flourishing organizations. *Journal of Organizational Behavior*, 29, 147–54.

Balmer, J. M. T. and Geyser, S. A. (2003). *Revealing the Corporation: Perspectives on Identity, Image, Reputation, Corporate Branding, and Corporate-level Marketing: an Anthology*. Routledge.

Barrow, S. and Mosley, R. (2005). *The Employer Brand: Bringing the Best of Brand Management to People at Work*. London: Wiley.

Baruch, Y. (2003). Career systems in transition: a normative model for organizational career practices. *Personnel Review*, 32(2), 231–51.

Beijer, S., Farndale, E., and van Veldhoven, M. (2009). The meaning of employee engagement: towards an integrative typology for HR research. Paper presented to the Dutch Association of Work and Organizational Psychologists (WAOP), Amsterdam, the Netherlands, 5 November.

Bergh, D. D., Ketchen, Jr, D. J., Boyd, B. K., and Bergh, J. (2010). New frontiers of the reputation performance relationship: insights from multiple theories. *Journal of Management*, 36, 620–32.

Boyd, B. K., Bergh, D., and Ketchen Jr, D. J. (2010). Reconsidering the reputation performance relationship. *Journal of Management*, 36, 588–609.

Briscoe, J. P., Hall, D., and Mayrhofer, W. (eds.) (2011). *Careers Around the World: A Global Perspective*. London: Routledge.

Burrell, G. and Morgan, G. (1979). *Sociological Paradigms and Organizational Analysis*. UK: Heinemann Educational Books Ltd.

Celani, A. and Singh, P. (2011). Signaling theory and applicant attraction outcomes. *Personnel Review*, 40 (2), 222–38.

Cerdin, J.-L. (2007). *S'expatrier en toute connaissance de cause*. Paris: Eyrolles.

Cerdin, J.-L. and Bird, A. (2008). Careers in a global context. In M. Harris (ed.), *Handbook of Research in International Human Resource Management*. Lawrence Erlbaum Associates, Inc., Publishers, pp. 207–27.

Chartered Insurance Institute (2012). What we talk about when we talk about trust: the future of trust in insurance and financial services. www.cii.co.uk/downloaddata/Trust_CII_2010.pdf [Accessed January 2014].

CIPD (2007). *Talent Management.* London: Chartered Institute of Personnel and Development.

—— (2009). *Employer branding: maintaining the momentum.* Hot Topics Report, June. Chartered Institute of Personnel and Development.

—— (2010). *Sustainable Organizational Performance: What Really Makes the Difference?* London: Chartered Institute of Personnel and Development.

Conway, N. and Briner, R. B. (2005). *Understanding Psychological Contracts at Work: A Critical Evaluation of Theory and Research.* Oxford: Oxford University Press.

Crawford, E. R., LePine, J. A., and Rich, B. L. (2010). Linking job demands and resources to employee engagement and burnout: a theoretical extension and meta-analytic test. *Journal of Applied Psychology*, 95 (5), 834–48.

Cronk, L. (2005). The application of animal signaling theory to human phenomena: some thoughts and clarifications. *Social Science Information/Information sur les Sciences Sociales*, 44, 603–20

Davies, G. and Chun, R. (2008). Employer branding and its influence on managers. *European Journal of Marketing*, 42 (5/6), 667–81.

Deephouse, D. L. and Carter, S. M. (2005). An examination of differences between organizational legitimacy and reputation. *Journal of Management Studies*, 42, 329–60.

Douglas Pugh, S. and Dietz, J. (2008). Employee engagement at the organization level of analysis. *Industrial and Organizational Psychology*, 1, 44–7.

Dowling, G. R. (2001). *Creating Corporate Reputations: Identity, Image and Performance.* New York: Oxford University Press.

Edwards, M. R. (2009). HR, perceived organizational support and organizational identification: an analysis after organizational formation. *Human Resource Management Journal*, 19, 91–115

Edwards, M. R. and Peccei, R. (2007). Organizational identification: development and testing of a conceptually grounded measure. *European Journal of Work and Organizational Psychology*, 16, 25–57.

Gittell, J., Seidner, R., and Wimbush, J. (2010). Relational model of how high-performance work systems work. *Organization Science*, 21 (2), 490–506.

Gouldner, A. W. (1957). Cosmopolitans and locals: towards an analysis of latent social roles. *Administrative Science Quarterly*, 2, 281–306.

Groysberg, B., Nanda, A., and Nohria, N. (2004). The risky business of hiring stars. *Harvard Business Review*, 82 (5), 92–100.

Groysberg, B., Sant, L., and Abrahams. R. (2008). When 'stars' migrate, do they still perform like stars? *MIT Sloan Management Review*, 50, 41–6.

Hatch, M. J. and Schultz, M. (eds.) (2004). *Organizational Identity: A Reader*. Oxford: Oxford University Press.

Hatch, M. J. and Schultz, M. (2008). *Taking Brand Initiative: How Companies can Align Strategy, Culture and Identity through Corporate Branding*. San Francisco: Josey Bass.

Highhouse, S., Brooks, M. E., and Gregarus, G. (2009). An organizational impression management perspective on the formation of corporate reputations. *Journal of Management*, 35, 1481–93.

Hofstede, G. (2001). *Culture's Consequences: Comparing Values, Behaviors, Institutions and Organizations across Nations*. Thousand Oaks, CA: Sage.

Holt, D. B. (2007). *How Brands Become Icons: the Principles of Cultural Branding*. Boston, MA: Harvard Business School Press.

House, R. J. and Javidan, M. (2004). Overview of GLOBE. In R. J. House, P. J. Hanges, M. Javidan, P. W. Dorfman, and V. Gupta (eds.), *Culture, Leadership, and Organizations: the GLOBE Study of 60 Societies*. London: Sage Publications, pp. 9–28.

Jiang, K., Lepak, D. P., Hu, J., and Baer, J. (2012). How does human resource management influence organizational outcomes? A meta-analytic investigation of the mediating mechanism. *Academy of Management Journal*, 55, 1264–94.

Joo, B. K. and McLean, G. N. (2006). Best employer studies: a conceptual model from a literature review and a case study. *Human Resource Development Review*, 5, 228–57.

Judge, T. A. and Bretz, R. D. (1992). Effects of work values on job choice decisions. *Journal of Applied Psychology*, 77 (3), 261–71.

Judge, T. A. and Cable, D. M. (1997). Applicant personality, organizational culture, and organization attraction. *Personnel Psychology*, 50 (2), 359–94.

Knox, S. and Freeman, C. (2006). Measuring and managing employer brand image in the service industry. *Journal of Marketing Management*, 22, 695–716.

Krasikova, D., Green, S., and LeBreton, J. M. (2013). Refining and extending our understanding of destructive leadership. *Journal of Management*, 39, 1308–38.

Kristof, A. L. (1996). Person-organization fit: an integrative review of its conceptualizations, measurement, and implications. *Personnel Psychology*, 49 (1), 1–49.

Langley, A., Smallman, C., Tsoukas, H., and Van de Ven, A. H. (2013). Process studies of change in organization and management: unveiling temporality, activity, and flow. *Academy of Management Journal*, 56, 1–13.

Lazarova, M., Cerdin, J.-L., and Liao, H. A. (forthcoming). The internationalism career anchor: a validation study. *International Studies of Management and Organization.*

Levin, D. L. and Cross, R. (2004). The strength of weak ties you can trust: the mediating role of trust in knowledge transfer. *Management Science,* 50 (11), 1477–90.

Lievens, F. (2007) Employer branding in the Belgian Army: the importance of instrumental and symbolic beliefs for potential applicants, actual applicants and military employees. *Human Resource Management,* 46, 51–69.

Lievens, F. and Highhouse, S. (2003). The relation of instrumental and symbolic attributes to a company's attractiveness as an employer. *Personnel Psychology,* 56, 75–102.

Lievens, F., Van Hoye, G., and Schreurs, B. (2005). Examining the relationship between employer knowledge dimensions and organizational attractiveness: an application in a military context. *Journal of Occupational and Organizational Psychology,* 78, 553–72.

Lievens, F., Van Hoye, G., and Anseel, F. (2007). Organizational identity and employer image: towards a unifying framework. *British Journal of Management,* 18, S45–S59.

Macey, W. H. and Schneider, B. (2008). The meaning of employee engagement. *Industrial and Organizational Psychology: Perspectives on Science and Practice,* 1, 3–30.

Martin, G. (2009a). Employer branding and corporate reputation management: a model and some evidence. In C. L. Cooper & R. Burke (eds.), *The Peak Performing Organization.* London & New York: Routledge.

(2009b). Driving corporate reputations from the inside: a strategic role and strategic dilemmas for HR. *Asia Pacific Journal of Human Resource Management,* 47, 219–35.

Martin, G. and Beaumont, P. B. (2003). *Branding and HR: What's in a Name?* London: Chartered Institute of Personnel and Development.

Martin, G. and Groen-in't Woud, S. (2011). Employer branding and corporate reputation management in global companies. In H. Scullion and D. G. Collings (eds.), *Global Talent Management.* London: Routledge. pp. 87–110.

Martin, G. and Hetrick, S. (2006). *Corporate Reputations, Branding and Managing People: a Strategic Approach to HR.* Oxford: Butterworth-Heinemann.

(2009). Employer branding and corporate reputation management in an international context. In P. R. Sparrow (ed.), *Handbook of International Human Resource Management,* Chichester: John Wiley and Sons, pp. 293–320.

Martin, G., Pate, J. M., and Bell, S. (2009). Images of organization: reputation management, employer branding and HR in NHS (Scotland). Paper presented to a joint HRM and Healthcare Division symposium, British Academy of Management Annual Conference, Brighton, 16th September.

Martin, G., Gollan, P., and Grigg, K. (2011). Is there a bigger and better future for employer branding? Facing up to innovation, corporate reputations and wicked problems in SHRM. *International Journal of Human Resource Management*, 22 (17), 3618–37.

Miles, S. J. and Mangold, W. G. (2004). A conceptualization of the employee branding process. *Journal of Relationship Marketing*, 3, 65–87.

(2005). Positioning Southwest Airlines through employee branding. *Business Horizons*, 48, 535–45.

Mintzberg, H. (1994). *The Rise and Fall of Strategic Planning: Reconceiving Roles for Planning, Plans, Planners.* Toronto: Free Press.

Oliver, D. and Roos, J. (2007). Constructing organizational identity multimodally. *British Journal of Management*, 18, 342–58.

Rich, B. L., LePine, J. A., and Crawford, E. R. (2010). Job engagement: antecedents and effects on job performance. *Academy of Management Journal*, 53, 617–35.

Rindova, V. P., Williamson, I. O., Petkova, A. P., and Sever, J. M. (2005). Being good or being known: an empirical examination of the dimensions, antecedents, and consequences of organizational reputation. *Academy of Management Journal*, 49, 1033–49.

Roberts, P. W. and Dowling, G. R. (2002). Corporate reputation and sustained superior financial performance. *Strategic Management Journal*, 23, 1077–93.

Rousseau, D. M. (1995). *Psychological Contracts in Organizations. Understanding Written and Unwritten Agreements.* Thousand Oaks, CA: Sage.

Salanova, M. and Schaufeli, W. B. (2008). A cross-national study of work engagement as a mediator between job resources and proactive behavior: a cross-national study. *International Journal of Human Resources Management*, 19, 226–31.

Schaufeli, W. B. and Bakker, A. B. (2004). Job demands, job resources, and their relationship with burnout and engagement: a multi-sample study. *Journal of Organizational Behavior*, 25, 293–315.

Schein, E. G. (1990). *Career Anchors: Discovering Your Real Values.* San Diego, CA: Pfeiffer & Company.

(2004). *Organizational Culture and Leadership.* San Francisco: Jossey-Bass.

Schultz, M., Hatch, M. J., and Larsen, M. H. (2002). *The Expressive Organization: Linking Identity, Reputation and Corporate Brand.* Oxford: Oxford University Press.

Schwartz, S. H. (1992). Universals in the content and structure of values: theoretical advances and empirical tests in 20 countries. *Advances in Experimental Social Psychology*, 25 (1), 1–65.

Simha, A. and Cullen, J. B. (2012). Ethical climates and their effects on organizational outcomes: implications from the past and prophecies for the future. *Academy of Management Perspectives*, 26, (4), 20–34.

Slaughter, J. E., Zickar, M. J., Highhouse, S., and Mohr, D. C. (2004). Personality trait inferences about organizations: development of a measure and assessment of construct validity. *Journal of Applied Psychology*, 89 (1), 85–103.

Sparrow, P. (ed.) (2009). *Handbook of International Human Resource Management: Integrating People, Process and Context*. Chichester, UK: John Wiley.

Sparrow, P. and Balain, S. (2009). Talent-proofing the organization. In C. Cooper and R. Burke (eds.), *The Peak Performing Organization*. London and New York: Routledge.

Sparrow, P., Hesketh, A., Hird, M., Marsh, C., and Balain, S. (2010). Reversing the arrow: using business model change to tie HR into strategy. In P. Sparrow, M. Hird, A. Hesketh, and C. L. Cooper (eds.), *Leading HR*. London: Palgrave.

Spence, M. (1973). Job market signaling. *Quarterly Journal of Economics*, 87, 355–74.

(1974). *Market Signaling: Informational Transfer in Hiring and Related Screening Processes*. Cambridge, MA: Harvard University Press.

Suazo, M. M., Martínez, P. G., and Sandoval, R. (2009). Creating psychological and legal contracts through human resource practices: a signaling theory perspective. *Human Resource Management Review*, 19 (2), 154–66.

Suutari, V. and Taka, M. (2004). Career anchors of managers with global careers. *Journal of Management Development*, 23 (9), 833–47.

Truffier, A. (2010). *What is the Legitimacy of Employer Branding within Multinational Companies Today?* Professional Masters Thesis.

Van Riel, C. B. (2003). The management of corporate communications. In J. M. T. Balmer and S. A. Geyser (eds.), *Revealing the Corporation: Perspectives on Identity, Image, Reputation, Corporate Branding and Corporate-level Marketing*. London: Routledge, pp. 161–70.

Wanous, J. P. (1980). *Organizational Entry: Recruitment, Selection, and Socialization of Newcomers*, 1st edn. Reading, MA: Addison-Wesley.

Weick, K. E. (2001). *Making Sense of the Organization*. Oxford: Blackwell.

Weiss, A. (1995). Human capital vs. signaling explanations of wages. *Journal of Economic Perspectives*, 9, 133–54.

Whetten, D. A. (2002). Modelling-as-theorizing: a systematic methodology for theory development. In D. Partington (ed.), *Essential Skills for Management Research*. London: Sage, pp. 45–71.

Whetten, D. A. and Mackey, A. (2002). A social actor conception of organizational identity and its implications for the study of organizational reputation. *Business & Society*, 41, 393–414.

Zinko, R., Ferris, G. R., Blass, F. R., and Laird, M. D. (2007). Toward a theory of reputation in organizations. In J. J. Martocchio (ed.), *Research in Personnel and Human Resources Management, Volume 26*. Emerald Group Publishing Limited, pp.163–204.

7 | A typology of talent-management strategies

IBRAIZ TARIQUE AND RANDALL SCHULER

7.1 Introduction

The previous chapters have looked at talent management through the lenses of strategy, expert knowledge, employer branding, and the supply chain. They have raised a number of challenges for the field of talent management. We now draw upon discussion from the field of human resource management (HRM), and also in particular international HRM (IHRM), which has also devoted much attention to the topic.

As the workforces around the world have become increasingly diverse, and multinational enterprises (MNEs) become much more global, the topic of *global talent management* (GTM) has received a remarkable degree of academic and practitioner interest. Several survey-based studies have been conducted by *consulting firms and professional associations* such as the Boston Consulting Group, McKinsey and Company, and the Hay Group. On the academic side, several books have been published such as *Global Talent Management* by Scullion and Collings (2011), and *Talent Management of Knowledge Employees* (Vaiman, 2010). As noted in Chapter 1, special journal issues on talent management such as the *International Journal of Human Resource Management* (Vaiman and Collings, 2013), *Journal of World Business* (Scullion, Collings, and Caligiuri, 2010), and the *Asia Pacific Journal of Human Resource Management* (McDonnell, Collings, and Burgess, 2012) have been published.

Despite the plethora of research and industry reports on issues related to GTM, there is currently a dearth of theory in this area and this chapter attempts to makes a contribution in this respect by examining issues surrounding the formation and alignment of talent-management strategies. We begin by discussing the conceptualization of GTM to show that an important part of GTM is a talent-management system (e.g., specific IHRM policies and practices), which plays an important role in attracting, retaining, developing, and mobilizing talent. We refer to the specific configurations of IHRM policies and practices within the talent-management system as a *talent-management strategy*. Next we explain the important differences between an organization's HR strategy and talent-management strategy and argue why it is important to have alignment between the two. Then we develop a topology that allows us to differentiate talent-management strategies into four types: nexus, extensive, bounded, and concentrated. This is followed by a discussion on the importance of a talent-management function to effectively manage the various talent-management strategies. Finally, we discuss areas for future research and implications for talent-management professionals.

7.2 Conceptualization of global talent management

Global talent management is emerging as an important area in the field of IHRM (Tarique and Schuler, 2010). There are five interpretations of GTM (Lewis and Heckman, 2006; Collings and Mellahi, 2009; Tarique and Schuler, 2010; Vaiman, Scullion, and Collings, 2012):

1. GTM is *identical to* the standard HR department practices and functions.
2. GTM is HR planning and projecting employee/staffing needs.
3. GTM focuses on high-performing individuals also known as high potentials.
4. GTM focuses on strategic or critical jobs.
5. GTM is a subset of strategic HRM.

Although there are different interpretations, the focus of GTM is on two important dimensions: individuals with high and/or critical levels of talent; and complementary IHRM policies and practices that are used to manage employees with high and/or critical levels of talent. A number of different definitions of GTM were presented in Chapter 1. For us, GTM can be defined as:

a subset of IHRM activities (systematically linked IHRM policies and policies) to attract, develop, retain, and mobilize individuals with high levels of current and potential human capital consistent for the strategic directions of the multinational enterprise to serve the objectives of multiple stakeholders. (Tarique and Schuler, 2010)

Imbedded in our definition is the importance of the subset of IHRM policies and practices that make up the talent-management system.

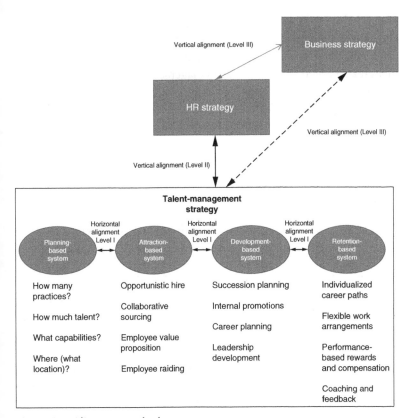

Figure 7.1 Alignment and talent-management strategy

Research is needed to understand how talent-management systems are configured and how they relate to the organization's HR and business strategies. This chapter attempts to address these questions by proposing the model in Figure 7.1.

7.3 Talent-management system and talent-management strategy

It is important to note that there are important differences between an organization's HR strategy and its talent-management strategy. First, HR strategy focuses on a broader range of employees whereas talent-management strategy focuses on employees with high levels of human capital. Second, HR strategy focuses on broader HR policies and practices that apply to all employees whereas talent-management strategy concentrates on policies and practices related to planning, attraction, development, and retention of employees with high levels of human capital. Third, talent-management strategy includes fewer practices than HR strategy.

As shown in Figure 7.1, talent-management systems can be defined in terms of four components or subsystems:

1. planning-based systems
2. attraction-based systems
3. development-based systems
4. retention-based systems.

The *planning-based system* includes policies and practices that estimate the type of competences (knowledge, skills, abilities, and personality) and individual-level capabilities that will be needed in various locations. The ultimate objective of a planning-based system is to maximize *talent positioning*, which refers to having the right talent at the right place at the right time with the needed competences and motivation at all levels and all locations of the firms (Guthridge, McPherson, and Wolf, 2009).

The *attraction-based system* includes policies and practices that relate to recruiting, selecting, and socializing top talent. Examples include opportunistic hiring practices, collaborative sourcing, employee value proposition practices, and employee-raiding practices. Effective attraction-based systems are able to attract applicants with the competences needed to perform a wide variety of strategic or critical jobs regardless of worldwide location (see Huselid, Beatty, and Becker, 2009). One way this can be achieved is by sending applicants signals such as being "employer of choice" and the "most admired company to work for." The objective here is to build a talent-management reputation that can attract the best people and then select them for positions rather than trying to select specific people for specific positions (Tarique and Schuler, 2010).

Practice and policies in the *development-based system* focus on providing top talent with the competences needed in their current and future positions. Examples of practices include succession planning, internal promotions, career planning, and leadership development. Some argue that a large part of talent management is talent development, because in an era of talent shortages, most of the time, the available competences in the labor markets fall short of the competences that firms need. The corporate-learning function is generally required to improve the quality of talent available and at the same time increase a firm's appeal as an employer.

The *retention-based system* focuses on policies and practices that address the challenges associated with talented employees changing jobs frequently, such as every two to three years. Examples of practices include developing individualized career paths, flexible work arrangements, performance-based rewards and compensation, and coaching and feedback. This is an important part of a talent-management system as retaining talent becomes a critical issue for all types of organizations, especially as organizations move toward developing a culture that signifies a strong commitment to talent management rewarding managers for improving talent retention (Schuler, Jackson, and Tarique, 2011).

It is obvious that the formation of a talent-management system can become a complex process as there are various configurations of policies and practices available within the four subsystems. There can be a range of possible configurations or bundles of policies and practices. Consistent with the thinking in the strategic HRM literature, a *talent-management strategy* refers to a specific configuration or a range of configurations of policies and practices within the talent-management system.

A critical part of a talent-management strategy is the issue of alignment, which refers to the fit between talent-management strategies and the other strategies of the organization. As shown in Figure 7.1, there are three levels of alignment.

Level I refers to horizontal alignment, which describes the fit among the four component of a talent-management strategy. A talent-management strategy is horizontally aligned when the four components (planning, attraction, development, and retention) support each other.

Level II refers to vertical alignment, which describes the fit between the talent-management strategy as a whole with the organization's HR strategy – that is the extent to which a talent-management strategy supports the HR strategy.

Level III refers to the fit between the talent-management strategy and the organization's business strategy – that is the extent to which a talent-management strategy supports the business strategy. There are two perspectives on how this relationship works. First, in organizations where HR is considered an important business partner or where HR contributes significantly to the overall business strategy, a talent-management strategy is required to support the HR strategy. In other words, HR strategy mediates the relationship between talent-management strategy and business strategy. Second, in organizations where HR is not a strong partner, talent-management strategy is more likely to contribute directly to the business strategy. This may happen in organizations where HR plays an administrative role, rather than that of a strategic partner, and the talent-management function is the strategic enabler that connects individual employee behavior to the organization's business goals.

7.4 Approaches to formulating talent-management strategies

The strategic HRM and the talent-management literatures provide several approaches that can be used to examine how talent-management strategies can be formulated. Here we examine four perspectives.

7.4.1 High-performance work systems

High-performance work systems (HPWS) are generally described as bundles or configurations of distinct but related HR practices that focus on improving skills, motivation, commitment, and effort in employees (Huselid, 1995; Boxall and Macky, 2007; Messersmith, Patel, and Lepak, 2011). Examples include formal information-sharing programs, formal job analysis, quality of work–life programs, profit-sharing plans, extensive training and development, performance-based compensation, and formal grievance procedures. Prior research has shown a strong relationship between HPWS and various measures of performance and effectiveness at the individual and organizational levels (Huselid, 1995; Boxall, 2012). High-performance work systems can be viewed as a particular type of talent-management system since they include HR practices that are or can be used to attract, develop, and retain employees with high levels of human capital (Vaiman, personal communication, February 10, 2013).

7.4.2 *Workforce differentiation/segmentation*

Strategic HRM scholars have developed a framework or approach labelled workforce differentiation or segmentation (Becker, Huselid, and Ulrich, 2001; Huselid, Becker, and Beatty, 2005; Becker, Huselid, and Beatty, 2009) that is consistent with the current focus of talent management. According to workforce differentiation, employees can be categorized into A, B, and C players with A players adding more value to the organization and hence treated differently. Furthermore, critical positions can also categorized into A positions and B positions, and A players placed in A positions and B players placed in B positions (Becker, Huselid, and Beatty, 2009). HR practices to manage A players can be viewed as a particular type of talent-management system.

7.4.3 *Human-capital theory*

As noted in Chapter 2, human-capital theory has been a dominant influence in the field of talent management. Human-capital theory (Becker, 1975) can be used to examine individuals with high levels of human capital to further our understanding and development of talent-management systems. This theory has been widely used in the field of HRM. According to this theory, human capital is a resource that organizations can invest in and is of value to the organization to the extent that it makes the organization productive (Strober, 1990; Lepak and Snell, 1999; Nafukho, Hairston, and Brooks, 2004; Kessler and Lülfesmann, 2006). At the heart of this theory is the notion of specific human capital and general human capital. Employees with specific human capital are valuable to their current employer and less valuable in the external talent markets. In contrast, employees with general human capital are less valuable to the current employer but can transfer the human capital to other employers. This theory can be used to examine how organizations and individuals use talent-management systems to make investments in specific and general human capital (Tarique and Schuler, 2010).

7.4.4 *9-Box assessment grid*

The 9-box grid or matrix assesses talent in terms of an employee's performance and his or her future potential in the organization

(Day, 2007; see also Figure 2.2(c) in Chapter 2). In this grid the y-axis rates employee current "potential" and the x-axis displays employee "future or growth potential." The matrix results in nine boxes that indicate if an employee is below, meeting, or exceeding current perform-ance and his/her future potential to the organization. Individuals in the upper-right quadrant (high potential/exceeding current performance) will then be identified as the organization's "talent pool." Each box (in the upper-right quadrant) identifies a particular group of employees that need specific talent-management practices. For instance, the upper-right box (in the upper-right quadrant) will include employees that are con-sidered extremely high potential with high performance. These employ-ees may need talent-management practices, such as stretch assignments, to prepare them for more leadership roles. In another example, the bottom-left box (in the upper-right quadrant) will include employees that need talent-management practices, such as coaching, to move to the next level (e.g., upper-right box). Overall the upper-right quadrant in the 9-box model plays an important role in identifying who is in the talent pool and the type of development needed to transit to the next level.

7.5 Typology of talent-management strategy alignment

It is possible to integrate the above perspectives, by showing how they influence talent-management strategy. This strategy is primarily guided by choices made across two axis:

1. the *extent of talent coverage* – defined as the scope or the number of employees that are part of the talent pool in an organization. For example, this can include "A" players (based on the workforce-differentiation framework), high-performance/high-potential employ-ees (based on the 9-box), or employees with specific human capital (based on human-capital theory)

2. the *extent of talent-management practices* – defined as the number and/or variety of talent-management practices needed to fully sup-port the organization's HR strategy. Number refers to the total number of practices in the talent-management system. Variety refers to the number of *different* talent-management practices in the talent-management system.

Both the extent of talent coverage and extent of talent-management practices create a varying degree of required alignment of the talent

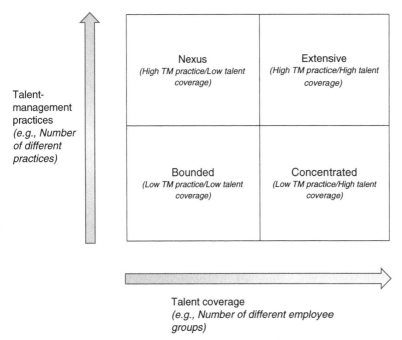

Figure 7.2 Typology of talent-management strategy alignment

management subsystems with each other, and with the overall HR strategy and business strategy.

The framework in Figure 7.2 can be used to describe an organization's talent-management strategy. The x-axis shows the extent of talent coverage (from low to high). The y-axis shows the extent of talent-management practices (from low to high). This framework can be used to categorize the talent-management strategy of an organization into four types:

1. extensive
2. nexus
3. concentrated
4. bounded.

The following provides a brief overview of these types of talent-management strategies.

Extensive talent-management strategy: this form of talent-management strategy has a greater extent of talent-management practices and a greater extent of talent coverage. This strategy requires greater alignment between talent-management practices and the talent pool. We would expect that an organization with this type of talent-management strategy is more likely to have a large talent-management function with considerably more control over talent-management decision making than nexus, concentrated, and bounded talent-management strategies.

Nexus talent-management strategy: this form of talent-management strategy has a greater extent of talent-management practices but a lower degree of talent coverage. A small group of tightly connected talented employees receive considerable exposure to talent-management practices. An organization with this type of talent-management strategy is more likely to have a talent-management function that exercises considerable control over a small group of talented employees.

Concentrated talent-management strategy: this form of talent-management strategy has a lower extent of talent-management practices and a greater extent of talent coverage. In this situation, a large group of talented employees are covered by few talent-management practices. An organization with this type of talent-management strategy most likely has a smaller talent-management function with a smaller group of talent-management professionals.

Bounded talent-management strategy: this form of talent-management strategy has a lower extent of talent-management practices and a lower degree of talent coverage. A small group of talented employees receives fewer talent-management practices. An organization with this type of talent-management strategy is more likely to have an extremely small talent-management function responsible for a very small group of talented employees.

The above typology allows academics and practitioners to categorize the talent-management strategies that organizations can pursue to manage talent. In addition the typology allows managers and researchers to design talent-management systems that are unique to each strategy and identify best practices among them. The notion of "best practices" is an emerging concept in GTM as it is directly tied to the convergence and divergence in talent-management systems when managing the talent-management function on a global basis.

7.6 Convergence and divergence in talent-management systems

Consistent with research done by Stahl and colleagues (2007, 2012) there are certain talent-management policies and practices that can be considered best practices. The notion behind this approach is that certain talent-management practices must be shared across all employees in the talent pool and across all four strategies in Figure 7.2. Examples may include leadership-development programs, recognition of star employees, and providing constant feedback (Blakely, 2012). However, the major concern with the best practices approach is that they can be copied and duplicated and thus can provide challenges to organizations in terms of retaining talent.

7.6.1 Country culture differences

National culture or country culture plays an important role in shaping the design of HR systems. We know from the IHRM literature that country culture shapes how HR policies and practices are designed, and how they influence employee behavior and performance (Gerhart and Fang, 2005; Briscoe, Schuler, and Tarique, 2012; Hassi, 2012). The convergence–divergence framework has been a frequent topic of study in the IHRM literature (Rowley and Benson, 2002; Brewster, 2007; Brewster, Wood, and Brookes, 2008; Mayrhofer, Brewster, Morley, and Ledolter, 2011). The notion of convergence refers to the extent to which HR policies and practices are similar across regions, countries, and cultures. Divergence, in contrast, suggests that HR practices are different across regions, countries, and cultures.

Several studies have begun to investigate talent-management practices in specific regions and countries, such as Poland (Skuza, Scullion, and McDonnell, 2013), South Africa (Koketso and Rust, 2012), Thailand (Piansoongnern and Anurit, 2010), India (Anand, 2011), Italy (Guerci and Solari, 2012), and New Zealand (Jayne, 2004). Although the research in this area is moving rapidly, it is not clear whether talent-management practices converge or diverge. The regional studies above generally argue that there are different conceptions of talent-management practice across these regions. These issues are picked up in the next two chapters. The divergence perspective then has support. Political and economic ideologies in certain regions and countries provide strong challenges to multinationals from adapting a best practice approach to talent management. Understanding of governmental pressures and local labor markets is necessary and talent-management practices need to be adjusted to the local conditions.

However, research by Stahl *et al.* (2012) supports the convergence perspective. It suggests that organizations are simultaneously focusing on integration and localization. They note that most organizations that operate on a global basis use similar approaches to managing talent and identify several reasons for using the convergence perspective.

- The talent pool is truly global and most companies now consider attracting talent from a global workforce. Location does not matter.
- Managing talent effectively is one of the biggest challenges that organizations face in most regions and countries. It is a universal concern that requires a standardized approach.
- There is considerable emphasis on best practices. A substantial body of data, information, and knowledge on best practices has emerged in the last few years allowing organizations to easily develop talent-management best practices.

The challenges that corporate HRM functions face in attempting to create more globalized integration, or appropriate levels of local responsiveness, in talent management, will be picked up in Chapter 9.

7.7 Directions for future research and implications for GTM professionals

In this chapter we have provided a framework of generic talent-management practices and how they must be aligned (Figure 7.1) and a typology that draws upon different underlying perspectives that have influenced thinking about talent management to identify four separate strategies that might be pursued (Figure 7.2). A key purpose of this chapter is to encourage and motivate future researchers to investigate more deeply the issues surrounding the formation and alignment of talent-management strategies. In this regard, our proposed framework and typology may serve as a fundamental first step toward future theory building in talent management. Several areas for future research remain.

Future research is needed to examine how talent-management sub-systems of planning, attraction, development, and retention operate together to support the organization's HR strategy and business strategy. Given the potential relationships among talent-management sub-systems, research is needed to examine which talent-management subsystems are most important for which HR strategies and business strategies.

Another area for future research is to explore how talent-management systems are designed and configured in each talent-management strategy. This chapter proposed a general conceptual framework (Figure 7.2) that can guide future research in this area. From a theoretical perspective, the conceptual framework provides insights into critical components of a talent-management strategy and how this strategy relates to two dimensions (i.e., the *extent of talent coverage* and the *extent of talent-management practices)*. Quantitative and qualitative studies are needed to determine whether the various strategies hold as described.

Strategic HRM research also suggests that the design of a talent-management system may be influenced by the characteristics of the exogenous environment. Although we note the importance of national culture, there are other factors that future researchers can examine such as globalization strategy. For example, to what extent do multinational organizations need to be sensitive to regional conditions and whether to design talent-management systems for the entire organization or adapt their talent-management practices to multiple regions and industries, each with their own special and unique needs.

Finally, future research is needed to measure the overall impact of talent-management systems on various measures of organizational effectiveness. Research on talent metrics (e.g., Boudreau and Ramstad, 2007) has identified talent metrics such as talent brand mapping, employee–recruit gap analysis, strategic readiness of individual talent, employee satisfaction, work motivation, employee commitment, and extra-role behaviors (Lawler, Levenson, and Boudreau, 2004; Becker, Huselid, and Beatty, 2009; Collings and Mellahi, 2009). In addition to these metrics, research is needed to measure the impact of talent-management systems on MNE's multiple stakeholders (Tarique and Schuler, 2010).

It is important to note that this chapter also has implications for managers facing talent-management issues. First, Figure 7.1 highlights the need for more integrated talent-management approaches and systems. Managers need to view a talent-management system in terms of four subsystems of planning, attraction, development, and retention – and how these subsystems work together to support each other and work together to form a "talent-management strategy" that supports HR and business strategies. Second, Figure 7.1 provides managers with a menu of talent-management practices that managers can use to "configure" various types of talent-management strategies. Third, the typology shown in Figure 7.2 allows managers to use talent-management strategies depending on the required talent coverage and the number of talent-management practices.

In conclusion, our chapter and our typology add value to the existing models and frameworks in talent management. Given the weakness of theory in this area, our proposed typology provides a good platform for future researchers in the area, and encourages new directions in practice and research that begin to examine talent-management strategies.

References

Anand, P. (2011). Talent development and strategy at telecom major Bharti Airtel. *Strategic HR Review*, 10 (6), 25–30.

Becker, B. E., Huselid, M. A., and Ulrich, D. (2001). *The HR Scorecard : Linking People, Strategy, and Performance*. Boston, MA: Harvard Business School Press.

Becker, B. E., Huselid, M. A., and Beatty, R. W. (2009). *The Differentiated Workforce : Transforming Talent into Strategic Impact*. Boston, MA: Harvard Business Press.

Becker, G. S. (1975). *Human Capital: a Theoretical and Empirical Analysis, with Special Reference to Education, 2nd edn.* New York, NY: National Bureau of Economic Research, Columbia University Press.

Blakely, A. (2012). Top 10 talent management strategies for 2012. *On Balance.* www.wicpa.org/Content/Files/PDF/On%20Balance/JanFeb12/Top10.pdf [Accessed 9 Janaury, 2014]

Boudreau, J. W. and Ramstad, P. M. (2007). *Beyond HR: the New Science of Human Capital*. Boston, MA: Harvard Business School Press.

Boxall, P. (2012). High-performance work systems: what, why, how and for whom? *Asia Pacific Journal of Human Resources*, 50 (2), 169.

Boxall, P. and Macky, K. (2007). High-performance work systems and organisational performance: bridging theory and practice. *Asia Pacific Journal of Human Resources*, 45 (3), 261.

Brewster, C. (2007). Comparative HRM: European views and perspectives. *International Journal of Human Resource Management*, 18 (5), 769–87. doi: 10.1080/09585190701248182.

Brewster, C., Wood, G., and Brookes, M. (2008). Similarity, isomorphism or duality? Recent survey evidence on the human resource management policies of multinational corporations. *British Journal of Management*, 19 (4), 320–342. doi: 10.1111/j.1467–8551.2007.00546.x.

Briscoe, D. R., Schuler, R. S., and Tarique, I. (2012). *International Human Resource Management : Policies and Practices for Multinational Enterprises, 4th edn.* New York, NY: Routledge.

Collings, D. G. and Mellahi, K. (2009). Strategic talent management: a review and research agenda. *Human Resource Management Review*, 19 (4), 304.

Day, D. V. (2007). Developing leadership talent. A guide to succession planning and leadership development. SHRM Foundation's Effective Practice Guidelines Series. www.shrm.org/about/foundation/research/documents/developing%20lead%20talent-%20final.pdf [Accessed 9 January, 2014]

Gerhart, B. and Fang, M. (2005). National culture and human resource management: Assumptions and evidence. *The International Journal of Human Resource Management*, 16 (6), 971–86. doi: 10.1080/09585190500120772.

Guerci, M. and Solari, L. (2012). Talent management practices in Italy: implications for human resource development. *Human Resource Development International*, 15 (1), 25.

Guthridge, M., McPherson, J. R., and Wolf, W. J. (2009). Upgrading talent. *McKinsey Quarterly*, 1, 61.

Hassi, A. (2012). The impact of culture on corporate training design: a review of the current state of knowledge. *International Journal of Human Resources Development & Management*, 12 (1/2), 119–39.

Huselid, M. A. (1995). The impact of human resource management practices on turnover, productivity, and corporate financial performance. *Academy of Management Journal*, 38 (3), 635–72.

Huselid, M. A., Becker, B. E., and Beatty, R. W. (2005). *The Workforce Scorecard : Managing Human Capital to execute Strategy*. Boston, MA: Harvard Business School Press.

Huselid, M., Beatty, D., and Becker, B. (2009). *The Differentiated Workforce: Transforming Talent into Strategic Impact*. Boston, MA: Harvard Business Press.

Jayne, V. (2004). Smart wars: the global battle for brains and management talent; Talent has become a global commodity. So can New Zealand keep it's share of sharp thinkers? What will keep top players at home or attract others to replace departing brains? In other words, how do we maintain our talent trade balance? *New Zealand Management*, 26–33.

Kessler, A. S. and Lülfesmann, C. (2006). The theory of human capital revisited: on the interaction of general and specific investments. *Economic Journal*, 116 (514), 903–23.

Koketso, L. P. and Rust, A. B. (2012). Perceived challenges to talent management in the South African public service: an exploratory study of the City of Cape Town municipality. *African Journal of Business Management*, 6 (6), 2221.

Lawler, E. E., Levenson, A., and Boudreau, J. W. (2004). HR metrics and analytics: use and impact. *Human Resource Planning*, 27 (4): 27–35

Lepak, D. P. and Snell, S. A. (1999). The human resource architecture: toward a theory of human capital allocation and development. *Academy of Management Review*, 24 (1), 31–48.

Lewis, R. E. and Heckman, R. J. (2006). Talent management: a critical review. *Human Resource Management Review*, 16 (2), 139.

Mayrhofer, W., Brewster, C., Morley, M. J., and Ledolter, J. (2011). Hearing a different drummer? Convergence of human resource management in Europe – a longitudinal analysis. *Human Resource Management Review*, 21 (1), 50–67.

McDonnell, A., Collings, D. G., and Burgess, J. (2012). Guest editors' note: talent management in the Asia Pacific. *Asia Pacific Journal of Human Resources*, 50 (4), 391–8.

Messersmith, J. G., Patel, P. C., and Lepak, D. P. (2011). Unlocking the black box: exploring the link between high-performance work systems and performance. *Journal of Applied Psychology*, 96 (6), 1105.

Nafukho, F. M., Hairston, N., and Brooks, K. (2004). Human capital theory: implications for human resource development. *Human Resource Development International*, 7 (4), 545–51.

Piansoongnern, O. and Anurit, P. (2010). Talent management: quantitative and qualitative studies of HR Practitioners in Thailand. *International Journal of Organizational Innovation (Online)*, 3 (1), 280–302.

Rowley, C. and Benson, J. (2002). Convergence and divergence in Asian human resource management. *California Management Review*, 44 (2), 90–109.

Schuler, R. S., Jackson, S. E., and Tarique, I. (2011). Global talent management and global talent challenges: strategic opportunities for IHRM. *Journal of World Business*, 46 (4), 506–16.

Scullion, H. and Collings, D. (eds.) (2011). *Global Talent Management*. London: Routledge.

Scullion, H., Collings, D. G., and Caligiuri, P. (2010). Global talent management. *Journal of World Business*, 45 (2), 105–8.

Skuza, A., Scullion, H., and McDonnell, A. (2013). An analysis of the talent management challenges in a post-communist country: the case of Poland. *International Journal of Human Resource Management*, 24 (3), 453–70.

Stahl, G. K., Bjorkman, I., Farndale, E., *et al.* (2007). Global talent management: how leading multinationals build and sustain their talent pipeline. Faculty & Research Working Paper. Fontainebleau, France: INSEAD.

Stahl, G., Björkman, I., Farndale, E., Morris, S., Paauwe, J., and Stiles, P. (2012). Six principles of effective global talent management. *MIT Sloan Management Review*, 53 (2), 25–32

Strober, M. H. (1990). Human capital theory: implications for HR managers. *Industrial Relations*, 29 (2), 214.

Tarique, I. and Schuler, R. S. (2010). Global talent management: literature review, integrative framework, and suggestions for further research. *Journal of World Business*, 45 (2), 122–33.

Vaiman, V. (ed.) (2010). *Talent Management of Knowledge Employees: Embracing Non-traditional Workforce*. UK: Palgrave Macmillan.

Vaiman, V. and Collings, D. G. (2013). Talent management: advancing the field. *International Journal of Human Resource Management*, 24 (9), 1737–43.

Vaiman, V., Scullion, H., and Collings, D. (2012). Talent management decision making. *Management Decision*, 50 (5), 925–41.

PART III

Globalizing the strategic talent-management agenda

8 The strategic role of HR in the United States and China: relationships with HR outcomes and effects of management approaches

JOHN W. BOUDREAU AND EDWARD E.
LAWLER III

8.1 Introduction

The previous chapter laid out some of the developments in talent management when seen in a global context. In this chapter we look at the strategic context in the largest emerging market – that of China – through comparison of practices with those in the United States. Corporations in China and the United States differ greatly in many ways. United States' firms typically are older and more global, thus it is not surprising that some research suggests that Chinese HRM policies and practices differ from Western HRM practices. In particular, there is evidence that HR functions allocate less time to strategic activities and play a less strategic role (Wei, 2010). However, there is some evidence of a two-speed system in China, whereby a small number of firms have highly sophisticated systems, while a much larger proportion has only very basic HR systems. This has been attributed to the difference between the relatively advanced management systems of large state-owned enterprises and the more basic systems characterizing smaller private firms.

The development of Chinese HRM has occurred in several phases (see Wei, 2010). During a Soviet-style traditional phase (from 1949 to 1979), there was little HR presence in organizations because much of HR management was dictated by state rules that required similar treatment across organizations, and with little worker movement across them (Naughton, 1996; Warner, 1996). This phase was followed by a reform phase (from 1979 to 1995), following the Third Plenary Session of the 11th Central Committee in late 1978. It allowed private ownership and foreign investment. It included greater profit incentive for enterprises, allowed for more experimentation with employment arrangements, and allowed the importation of HR practices by the Western firms that were investing in China (Wei, 2010). In the 1990s, there were changes in Chinese corporate and labor laws. These included abolishing the jobs-for-life requirement in favor of specific labor contracts, compensation linked to performance and skill, and employment-based pension and insurance arrangements (Warner, 1996; Wei, 2010). Thus China, as compared to the United States and other Western nations, has had less experience with a legal and social environment that motivates significant investments and advancements in HR, and a shorter time during which the strategic value of the HR profession has been recognized. Thus we might expect that in China HR functions and leaders currently play a less strategic role in their organizations.

It is possible that Chinese organizations and HR leaders have had the chance to learn from the best practices of the West, and thus might be equally or even more advanced than their Western counterparts. Convergence theory has proposed that cross-national systems converge as industrialization and technologies carry knowledge of new approaches and their effects (Kerr, 1983), particularly the transfer of international best practices. However, the evidence of convergence remains mixed (Björkman, 2002; Rowley and Benson, 2002; Brewster, Mayrhofer, and Morley, 2004; Wood *et al.*, 2012).

Recent studies of Chinese organizations' HRM practices have suggested that there is some convergence, but there are also some important differences (Collins, Zhu, and Warner, 2012). For many years now studies have suggested that the Chinese system emphasizes criteria such as work attitudes, diligence, and team spirit more than Western systems (Nyaw, 1995), and that Chinese companies rely on less specific criteria in performance assessment, leaving more to individual interpretation (Verburg *et al.*, 1999). Thus, there is reason to believe that we may see differences between Chinese and US organizations in the array and combination of HR practices that they use and in the activities of the HR function.

A significant reason for the evolution of HR practices in China has been that the dominant organizational ownership and management approach in organizations has changed. There has been a good deal of writing about the impact of ownership arrangements on the professional practice of HR in China (e.g., Ding and Akhtar, 2001). It describes four types of ownership: state-owned enterprises (SOEs),

Chinese private companies (CPCs), foreign-directed investment entities (FIEs), and joint ventures (JVs).

State-owned enterprises were the dominant ownership approach from the 1940s to the 1970s, offering little discretion in employment and social welfare arrangements; they were controlled by state economic planners. Beginning in the late 1970s, SOEs were encouraged to increase productivity, leading to reforms designed to be more sensitive to labor and economic market forces. As Wei (2010: p. 44) noted: "a distinct feature of HRM of SOEs at this period is the mixture of old and new: managers have greater discretion over personnel issues... but senior positions are still assigned by the state; performance-linked pay practices have been incorporated... but a major proportion of salary still depends on tenure and seniority; training for technical and managerial development is more frequent though political education is still an integral part of corporate training" (Cooke, 2005; Zhu, 2005).

Joint ventures were quite popular during the 1970s as capital investment increased rapidly. Joint ventures were often formed through part-ownership of former SOEs by foreign investment entities. Thus the organization and HRM practices were often a compromise between the older traditional approach of the SOEs, and the more Western approaches of the investing organization (Beamish, 1993), with some suggesting integration of HRM practices as a reason for the underperformance of JVs (Glover and Sin, 2000). Foreign-directed investment entities are fully owned by a foreign investor and thus have more freedom in choosing their organization and management approaches. It has been suggested that the greater recognition of performance and performance-based incentives is one reason for talent moving from SOEs to JVs and FIEs (Ding and Warner, 2001).

Chinese private companies are companies managed by Chinese citizens rather than foreign investors. They tend to be younger businesses but important to China's economic growth, with some reports projecting a proportion of over 70% of gross domestic product (GDP) (ACFIC, 2006). These firms are smaller and managed more through personal relationships than formal management policies. They are concentrated in low-technology, labor-intensive sectors such as manufacturing and exporting, and face greater hurdles of obtaining financing and other privileges offered to SOEs and FIEs. Thus CPCs may offer less comprehensive HR strategies (Cooke, 2005).

There are few parallels between the Chinese ownership categories and those in the United States. A prior survey showed that a very large proportion of larger Chinese companies are SOEs, so they comprised 75% of the sample (Wei, 2010: p. 60). Thus while ownership category has been proposed as a potential factor in the variation of HR practices by past research, the current Chinese organization distribution suggests that ownership category does not differ very much among large companies. Thus, in comparing US and Chinese firms, this chapter reports on a study that compares large firms regardless of their ownership category.

The study included a variable that reflects the perceived management operating approach of the organization. The management approaches included operating as a bureaucracy, low-cost operator, global competitor, innovator, or through sustainability. We elaborate on this later in the chapter. For now, we propose that examining the management approach of organizations may provide a direct perspective on the organizations' support for advanced HR. Because we measured size and organization approach in both samples, these variables allow us to examine the emergence of HR practices in China and the United States, and their patterns with regards to organization size and management approach.

8.2 Sample, methodology, measures, and outcomes

The data reported in this chapter come from a survey conducted in 2010, of HR leaders in the United States and China (Lawler and Boudreau, 2012). These data form part of a larger research initiative in which similar survey data were collected from US HR executives in the years 1995, 1998, 2001, 2004, 2007, and 2010. For China, the questionnaire was translated by Chun Hui Huo, a Chinese HR researcher. All the 2010 survey data were collected using the internet. We restricted our analysis to companies with more than 1,000 employees. HR executives were given a link and asked to respond. We received completed surveys from 172 US companies and from 215 companies in China.

The survey contained items concerning the characteristics of the HR function in corporations and how the corporation is managed (for a copy of the complete survey, see Lawler and Boudreau, 2012). Items to measure the effectiveness of the HR function and its role in corporations were also included.

HR strategic role. The survey contained an item requesting respondents to answer the question, "Which of the following best describes the relationship between the Human Resource function and the business strategy of your corporation?" Four options were offered: 1 = "Human Resource plays no role in business strategy," 2 = "Human Resource is involved in implementing the business strategy," 3 = "Human Resource provides input to the business strategy and helps implement it once it has been developed," and 4 = "Human Resource is a full partner in developing and implementing the business strategy." There was a notable tendency for Chinese HR managers to more frequently report playing "no role" or an "implementation role," and less frequently a "full partner" role, than their US counterparts. The US sample responses showed 4.3% chose "no role," 17.4% chose "an implementing role," 47.3% chose "input and implementing," and 31% chose "full partner role." The Chinese sample showed 15.5% chose "no role," 41.3% chose "implementing role," 37.6% chose "input and implementing," and 5.6% chose "full partner."

The picture in China appears not to have changed in recent times, despite the continued and rapid development there. In a 2007 study, Wei (2010) used the same items and surveyed 171 HR leaders in China. His 2007 sample showed 9.6% chose "no role," 46.6% chose "implementing role," 28.1% chose "input and implementing," and 15.7% chose "full partner." The relative frequencies in our 2010 sample and the Wei 2007 sample are similar. Taken together, the results from the two surveys reaffirm that Chinese HR leaders are less involved in strategy than US HR leaders. Indeed, if the comparison to the Wei sample in 2007 is valid, then the strategic role of Chinese HR leaders may have, in fact, decreased during the period of the global economic downturn. This is interesting because data from the Cranet survey for 2011 (Cranet, 2011) show that in Taiwan (which although sharing many cultural traits with mainland China, of course differs in institutional, managerial, and economic context) 51% of HR managers claim to be involved in the development of business strategy from the outset.

HR functional effectiveness. The overall effectiveness of the HR function was measured using the average of the ratings of effectiveness (1 = not meeting needs... 10 = all needs met), on 11 items describing various HR activities: (1) providing HR services, (2) being an employee advocate, (3) analyzing HR and business metrics, (4) managing outsourcing, (5) operating HR centers of excellence, (6) operating HR shared service units, (7) working with the corporate board, (8) providing change consulting services, (9) being a business partner, (10) helping to develop business strategies, and (11) improving decisions about human capital. The mean was 6.4 for the US sample and 5.2 for the China sample, a statistically significant difference ($p < .05$) that shows that the US HR functions were rated as more effective.

Organizational effectiveness. The effectiveness of the organization was measured with one item, asking "How would you gauge your organization's performance relative to its competitors?" Respondents chose from the following options: 1 = Much below average, 2 = Somewhat below average, 3 = About average, 4 = Somewhat above average, 5 = Much above average. The mean response for the US sample was 3.87, while the mean response for the China sample was 3.58. The difference between the responses for the two countries was significant ($p \leq .05$).

Overall then, the pattern is consistent. The Chinese HR leaders consistently rate their organizations lower on effectiveness and the strategic role of HR. Why might this pattern arise? Our survey data revealed a particularly interesting reason having to do with the management approach taken by organizations.

8.3 Organization's management approach

We asked respondents to describe their organization's management approach. Table 8.1 shows the approaches, and the proportion of HR executives choosing each response (for more details on the definition of the approaches see Lawler and Worley, 2011; Lawler and Boudreau, 2012). Chinese HR executives are similar to their US counterparts regarding their ratings of the bureaucratic management approach. This is interesting in light of the propositions of prior researchers that Chinese SOEs are characterized by a bureaucratic approach. It seems plausible that our sample contains a large proportion of SOEs considering Wei's (2010) finding that a similarly solicited sample of 171 Chinese HR leaders produced about 76% who said they worked in SOEs. In our results, the Chinese HR leaders rate their organizations significantly higher only on the "low-cost operator" approach. They rate them significantly lower on the "high involvement," "global competitor," and "sustainable" approaches.

Table 8.1 *Organizational management approach: the United States versus China*

To what extent do these describe how your organization operates?	Country	Little or no extent = 1	Some extent = 2	Moderate extent = 3	Great extent = 4	Very great extent = 5	Mean of 5-point scale
Bureaucratic (hierarchical and top–down)	USA	12.8%	29.9%	24.6%	27.8%	4.8%	2.8
	China	9.8%	30.7%	31.2%	23.7%	4.7%	2.8
Low-cost operator (minimum compensation, low-cost focus)	USA	40.0%	29.2%	21.6%	7.6%	1.6%	2.0
	China	9.3%	36.0%	31.3%	16.8%	6.5%	2.8*
High involvement (participative, flat, high career commitment)	USA	9.1%	25.7%	26.2%	29.4%	9.6%	3.0
	China	13.0%	33.5%	31.6%	19.1%	2.8%	2.7*
Global competitor (complex work, hire the best, low career commitment)	USA	20.4%	28.5%	23.1%	21.0%	7.0%	2.7
	China	28.4%	32.6%	24.2%	11.6%	3.3%	2.3*
Sustainable (agile, both financial and sustainability goals)	USA	4.8%	18.2%	27.8%	38.0%	11.2%	3.3
	China	5.6%	28.4%	29.8%	28.4%	7.9%	3.0*

* Significant differences between countries ($p \leq .05$).

Early Chinese economic successes were often built upon being a low-cost global supplier of manufactured goods. The research noted above proposed that the evolution of Chinese organizations has proceeded from purely state-controlled SOEs to more market-driven SOEs as well as growing JVs, FIEs, and CPCs. It may be that the larger Chinese organizations are evolving from a purely bureaucratic approach patterned after state control to a more market-driven approach, but one still characterized by a low-cost emphasis.

A further test of this possibility is whether organizational size is differently associated with management approach in China and the United States. We examined the relationship between management approach and organization size in both countries. For the US sample, there were no significant correlations between organization size (number of employees) and ratings of the different management approaches. The Chinese sample reflects a similar pattern – with one exception: there is a significant, positive correlation between organization size and the extent to which HR leaders characterized the organization as "low-cost competitor." This suggests that in China, organizational size is more associated with taking a low-cost approach than it is in the United States As we shall see, this has significant implications for the likelihood that Chinese organizations develop advanced strategic HR practices.

Our results show a similar pattern to prior research. Compared to US HR leaders, Chinese HR leaders report less of a full partner role in strategy, lower HR functional effectiveness, and lower organizational effectiveness. Moreover, Chinese HR leaders work in organizations that operate more as low-cost competitors, and less as global competitors, high-involvement, and sustainable organizations. For research on talent management in a Chinese context, this may mean that until Chinese HR functions and leaders play a more prominent role, the mechanisms through which talent management investments affect organizational outcomes may be different. For example, Bowen and Ostroff (2004) suggest that HRM practices work through both content and process, and note the importance of employee perceptions. In organizations with strongly strategic HR leaders and functions, it seems likely that such perceptions will be shaped more by the intentions of the HR function, than in organizations where this role is weaker. Measuring HRM programs through perceptions of HR leaders may be less valid in a Chinese context.

The traditional management systems in China may be ones that hinder the implementation of strategic HR because they are characterized by practices and structures that are less HR friendly. In research focusing on the US sample (Boudreau and Lawler, forthcoming), we found that the management approach has a strong effect on virtually all measures of HR advancement and effectiveness. We need to examine the effect of an organization's management approaches on how HR spends its time and how HR engages in strategic activities, to see if this pattern also exists in China.

8.4 Time spent: China and the United States both perceive HR's progress incorrectly

We asked respondents to indicate the percentage of time their HR function currently spends on five categories of HR activities, ranging from maintaining records and auditing, to acting as a strategic partner. We also asked them to recall the percentage allocation that existed five to seven years ago. Table 8.2 shows the results.

Looking at the current time allocation, Chinese HR leaders report HR spending more time than their US counterparts on the administration and auditing of records and compliance. They report spending less time as strategic partners. HR leaders in the US report HR spending 26.1% of its time maintaining records and auditing/controlling compliance, 47.1% of its time providing and developing human resources services, and 26.8% of its time acting as a strategic business partner. In China, the estimates are about six percentage points higher for maintaining records and auditing/controlling. They are about twelve percentage points lower for acting as a strategic business partner.

The last column of Table 8.2 contains the results from a survey by Wei (2010) using the same questions. It reports the responses of 171 Chinese HR managers. The responses to this independently conducted survey with a different sample are quite similar to our 2010 survey, suggesting that these measures are relatively stable and reliable between 2007 and 2010.

The two left columns of the table show that when recalling their time allocation from five to seven years ago, US HR leaders recall significantly less time being spent maintaining records now than in the past (23.2% in the past vs. 13.6% currently). They recall spending about the same percentage of time on auditing/controlling, and providing and

Table 8.2 *How HR spends its time now and five to seven years ago: comparing the United States and China*

Please estimate the percentage of time your HR function spends performing these roles

Country	Five to seven years ago		Current		Wei (2010)
	USA	China	USA	China	China
Maintaining records Collect, track, and maintain data on employees	23.2%	31.5%	13.6%	19.4%	22.8%
Auditing/controlling Ensure compliance to internal operations, regulations, and legal and union requirements	15.7%	21.2%	12.5%	20.1%	20.4%
Human resources service provider Assist with implementation and administration of HR practices	32.8%	27.1%	30.4%	29.5%	34.5%
Development of HR systems and practices Develop new HR systems and practices	14.4%	11.0%	16.7%	16.0%	16.9%
Strategic business partner Member of the management team. Involved with strategic HR planning, organizational design, and strategic change	13.9%	9.2%	26.8%	15.0%	14.0%

developing HR services, and significantly less time on strategic partnership in the past than is the case now (13.9% in the past vs. 26.8% currently). For the Chinese HR executives, the general pattern of recollection is similar. They recall much greater time spent on maintaining records in the past than currently (31.5% vs. 19.4%) and less time spent on strategic partnership in the past (9.2% vs. 15.0%). Based on these perceptions, HR leaders in both China and the United States might quite understandably feel that they might have reduced their time on administrative records maintenance, and reallocated the time to strategic partnership activities.

In the United States, our research suggests that the sense of progress is actually due to the misperception of how time was spent in the past (see Lawler and Boudreau, 2012). In prior studies of US HR leaders (based on our survey run every three years since 1995), each survey found virtually identical current time allocations, as well as virtually identical recollections of time spent five to seven years ago. So although US HR leaders perceive spending more time on administrative activities and less time on strategic partnership activities in the past, the data suggest that the actual allocation has not changed. The past is consistently and incorrectly perceived to have had less strategy and more records administration than it actually had.

We did not collect prior data for the Chinese sample of HR leaders. However, some longitudinal perspective can be gained by comparing the results from the Wei (2010) sample. This suggests a similar pattern to the United States. Specifically, our sample of Chinese HR leaders in 2010 recalled a far different pattern of time allocation than their ratings of how they currently spent their time. Yet the Wei (2010) data show that a similar sample of Chinese HR leaders in 2007 rated their actual time allocation as more similar to the 2010 allocation, than to the 2010 recollections of Chinese HR leaders. Like the US HR leaders, the Chinese HR leaders may perceive progress based on a misperception of the past.

We have coined the term "stubborn traditionalism" (Boudreau and Ramstad, 2007, Lawler and Boudreau, 2012; Boudreau and Lawler, 2013) to describe the evolution of the HR profession, reflecting the widespread impression and frequent finding that HR's progress is slower than often perceived, and possibly slower than needed to retain its relevance. These results suggest that in both the United States and China, perceptions of HR leaders about the progress of the profession may be subject to the same misperceptions. One explanation may be that the admonishment that HR must evolve to a strategic-partner role, and shift its time from "administrative" to "strategic" activities is now so globally widespread that HR leaders in most regions tend to believe that such a shift has taken place. Research on HR's role may be more accurately based on actual estimates of time spent, activities undertaken, skills achieved, etc., than on opinions about HR progress.

8.5 Time spent and performance outcomes

Table 8.3 shows the correlations among the responses to the time-spent question and measures of HR and organizational effectiveness. The pattern is broadly the same for all three outcomes within each country, but the strength of the relationships differs between countries. For both the US and Chinese samples, the greater the reported time allocated to "maintaining records," and "auditing and controlling," the lower the reported level of HR's role in strategy, HR's effectiveness, and organizational performance. The negative correlation with organizational performance is even stronger for the Chinese sample.

However, the other three categories of time allocation show interesting differences between the countries. "Providing HR services" is negatively related to all three outcomes in the US sample, but not significantly related to any outcomes in the Chinese sample. "Developing HR systems and practices" is not significantly related to the outcomes in the US sample, but is strongly and positively related to all three outcomes in the Chinese sample. Finally, while "strategic business partner" is significantly and positively related to all three outcomes in the US sample, it is unrelated to the outcomes in the Chinese sample. There is of course good reason to assume that an HR business partner role is very much an artifact of Western HR practice, and that the traditional three-box model that differentiates transactional, centers of excellence, and strategic HR business partner roles has low adoption in Chinese organizations.

Correlations cannot reveal causal direction, so it is possible that these relationships occur partly because when the outcomes occur (HR plays a greater role in strategy, achieves effectiveness, or is a part of a well-performing organization), it causes HR to spend time differently. However, it seems likely that the relationship exists in part because when HR spends more time on certain activities, it contributes

Table 8.3 *Time spent and key performance outcomes for the United States and China*

Please estimate the percentage of time your HR function spends performing these roles	USA			China		
	Correlation with HR role in strategy	Correlation with HR effectiveness	Correlation with organizational performance	Correlation with HR role in strategy	Correlation with HR effectiveness	Correlation with organizational performance
Maintaining records Collect, track, and maintain data on employees	-.18*	-.42***	-.12	-.36***	-.31***	-.24***
Auditing/controlling Ensure compliance to internal operations, regulations, and legal and union requirements	-.17*	-.30***	-.13	-.04	-.21*	-.18**
Human resources service provider Assist with implementation and administration of HR practices	-.18*	-.24**	-.23*	.02	.07	.10
Development of HR systems and practices Develop new HR systems and practices	.05	.12	.16^t	.24***	.32***	.24***
Strategic business partner Member of the management team. Involved with strategic HR planning, organizational design, and strategic change	.31***	.54***	.27**	.22**	.15^t	.10

Significance level:
^{t} $p \leq .10$
* $p \leq .05$
** $p \leq .01$
*** $p \leq .001$

to a stronger HR role in strategy, stronger HR functional effectiveness, and better organizational performance.

It appears that the path toward achieving better HR outcomes and effectiveness is somewhat different in China than in the United States. In the United States, time spent on service provision is negatively related to HR effectiveness and organization performance. However, in China it is not. Time spent developing HR systems and practices in China, is positively related to HR effectiveness and organizational performance, while in the United States it is not. Perhaps this reflects a relative lack of HR program development and availability in Chinese organizations, making time spent by HR on these dimensions more important and impactful.

Regarding time spent on a strategic partnership, the results for China show that it is unrelated to HR effectiveness and organizational performance, yet it is positively and significantly related to these outcomes for the US sample. Perhaps HR strategic partnership activity is recognized or valued more by the line leaders and other members in the United States, relative to China. Perhaps HR leaders in the United States have had more time to develop satisfactory HR systems, so that they have a platform and permission to be a strategic partner. On the other hand, the development and delivery of HR services in China may be at an earlier stage and has not yet progressed to the point where an HR strategic partnership is widely understood and valued by key executives and HR professionals.

The results suggest that it is quite feasible for HR activities to impact HR and organizational effectiveness in both the United States and China, but in different ways. Greater time on building the infrastructure of HR services and practices seems more potent in China, while strategic partnership is relatively more potent in the United States. Both the "services" and "strategy" paradigms can add value depending on organizational needs. It may be quite sufficient in some contexts for HR to focus much more on insuring that business units receive the HR programs they want or need, and that they are delivered well. Excellence in such service delivery need not necessarily go hand in hand with HR being deeply involved in shaping or even understanding strategy. For example, sometimes a business unit merely needs a working system to recruit talent, not an HR partner equipped to debate which talent characteristics best fit the strategy. Delivering great recruitment services may be far more impactful than delivering great strategic insight.

In the predominant Western view, it is often implied that if HR "merely" delivers services, without a strong connection to strategy, that there is little value. It appears possible that differences in where HR makes its most "pivotal" contribution (Boudreau and Ramstad, 2007) may vary across regions and with the evolutionary stage of organizations and HR.

8.6 Management approach and how HR spends its time

Table 8.4 shows the correlations between time spent and the use of each management approach. For the first four HR activities, both the US and Chinese samples show similar patterns. When respondents rate "bureaucratic" or "low-cost operator" higher, they also tend to report spending more time on maintaining employee records and less time on HR systems development. Also, in both China and the United States, when respondents rate "high involvement," "global competitor," and "sustainable" higher, they report less time spent on maintaining records and auditing, and more time spent on developing HR systems. This suggests a common pattern between China and the United States in the value that organizations with different approaches derive from HR activities, and in the way that different organizational approaches allocate resources for HR activities.

When it comes to time spent on strategic partnership (the bottom row of Table 8.4), the US and Chinese samples differ. In the United States, the more an organization is characterized by a "bureaucratic" or "low-cost operator" approach, the less time is spent on strategic business partnership, while the "sustainable," "global competitor," and "involvement" approaches are positively and significantly associated with time spent on strategic partnership. In the Chinese sample, time spent on strategic partnership is unrelated to the organization's management approach.

As noted earlier, the Chinese sample spends less time on strategic partnership activities, and time spent in this role has a lower association with all HR outcomes in China than it does in the United States. Perhaps for this reason, Chinese organizations do not attend to the strategic partnership role to the same extent as their US counterparts. This reinforces the earlier observation that HR's presence as a strategic partner may play a very different structural role in China versus the United States, not only in the time spent, but also in the way it

Table 8.4 HR time allocation and organization's management approach

Please estimate the percentage of time your HR function spends performing these roles	Bureaucratic (hierarchical and top–down)		Low-cost operator (minimum compensation, low-cost focus)		High involvement (participative, flat, high career commitment)		Global competitor (complex work, hire the best, low career commitment)		Sustainable (agile, both financial and sustainability goals)	
Country	USA	China	USA	China	USA	China	USA	China	USA	China
Maintaining records Collect, track, and maintain data on employees	.19*	.18**	.30***	.17*	-.23**	-.21**	-.12	-.16*	-.11	-.25***
Auditing/controlling Ensure compliance to internal operations, regulations, and legal and union requirements	.12	-.01	.09	.11	-.18*	-.07	-.06	-.23***	-.17*	-.23***
Human resources service provider Assist with implementation and administration of HR practices	.14^t	-.07	.10	-.10	-.04	.02	-.06	-.07	-.02	.01
Development of HR systems and practices Develop new HR systems and practices	-.11	-.16*	-.20**	-.14*	.16*	.21**	.23**	.19**	.09	.26***
Strategic business partner Member of the management team. Involved with strategic HR planning, organizational design, and strategic change	-.24**	.03	-.20**	-.04	.16*	.10	.03	.30***	.11	.25***

Significance level:
^{t} $p \leq .10$
* $p \leq .05$
** $p \leq .01$
*** $\wedge \leq .001$

contributes to the underlying organizational approach. This may have implications for how the HR delivery system and structure has, and will, evolve differently in the two regions.

Thus while US HR leaders apparently face greater challenges in acting as a strategic partner in "bureaucratic" and "low-cost operator" organizations, this is not the case with HR leaders in China. It is possible that as the strategic-partnership role evolves in China, we may see a greater association with an organization's management approach, because Chinese organizations will see the value of such activities, and different types of Chinese organizations will support or demand them. It may also be that Chinese HR management may evolve with a lighter emphasis on HR's strategic role, perhaps adopting a model in which leaders outside of HR are more accountable for understanding the connection between their talent and strategy, and formulating talent strategies to fit their current and future challenges.

8.7 HR's strategy activities

We have seen that the United States and China vary in the time spent on strategic-partnership activities and in how those activities relate to organizational success and management approaches. This raises the issue of whether the two countries also differ in the types of strategy activities they engage in. We asked respondents to rate the extent to which their HR function engages in eight strategy activities. Table 8.5 shows to what extent the average organizations engage in eight HR strategy activities in the United States and China. Chinese HR leaders rate seven of the eight activities significantly lower than their US counterparts, reinforcing the pattern of a generally less extensive strategic role for the Chinese HR leaders. The one activity on which the HR leaders' ratings are not significantly different is "help identify new business opportunities." This item is also the lowest rated by both the US and Chinese HR leaders, so there may be a "floor" effect that caused the two ratings to converge at a very low level.

The relative extent to which HR engages in these activities is similar in both countries. Specifically, in both countries the more traditional HR activities (strategy implementation and organization design) are rated highest, while activities related to strategy formulation and business decisions are rated lowest. Thus in both the United States and China, HR is more extensively involved in strategic activities focused

Table 8.5 *HR strategy activities: comparing the United States and China*

With respect to strategy, to what extent does the HR function. . .?	USA	China
Help identify or design strategy options	2.8	2.2*
Help decide among the best strategy options	2.9	2.3*
Help plan the implementation of strategy	3.6	2.5*
Help identify new business opportunities	2.0	2.1
Assess the organization's readiness to implement strategies	3.2	2.6*
Help design the organizational structure to implement strategy	3.6	3.0*
Assess possible merger, acquisition, or divestiture strategies	2.7	1.9*
Work with the corporate board on business strategy	2.6	2.1*

Response scale: 1 = little or no extent; 2 = some extent; 3 = moderate extent;
4 = great extent; 5 = very great extent
* $p \leq .05$ test of mean differences

on implementing strategy after it is formed than in actually formulating the strategy itself.

Does the extent and kind of HR strategy activity matter to key organizational outcomes? Table 8.6 shows the relationship between the ratings of the extent that each HR strategy activity takes place, and the ratings of HR's role in strategy, HR effectiveness, and organizational performance.

In both countries, all of the strategy activities are significantly and positively correlated with both HR's role in strategy and HR's functional effectiveness. The correlations in the Chinese sample are somewhat lower, but still statistically significant.

When it comes to organizational performance, in both countries the correlations are positive but smaller than those with HR's role in strategy and HR effectiveness. This is not surprising given the many factors that influence organizational effectiveness. It is much less likely to be influenced by HR activities than is the effectiveness of the HR function and HR's role in strategy.

The strength of the correlations with organizational performance is different in the two countries and somewhat surprising. Considering the greater extent of strategy activity in the US sample, and the greater relationship in the US sample between time spent on strategy and organizational performance, one might expect that the extent of the strategy activities in Table 8.7 would be more strongly related to

Table 8.6 *HR strategy activities and HR outcomes*

With respect to strategy, to what extent does the HR function...?	USA			China		
	Correlation with HR role in strategy	Correlation with HR effectiveness	Correlation with organizational performance	Correlation with HR role in strategy	Correlation with HR effectiveness	Correlation with organizational performance
Help identify or design strategy options	.65***	.45***	.15	.35***	.47***	.15*
Help decide among the best strategy options	.70***	.53***	.14	.41***	.48***	.16*
Help plan the implementation of strategy	.58***	.55***	.11	.42***	.46***	.13^t
Help identify new business opportunities	.52***	.47***	.12	.24***	.43***	.20**
Assess the organization's readiness to implement strategies	.54***	.59***	.13	.50***	.48***	.20**
Help design the organizational structure to implement strategy	.58***	.62***	.12	.39***	.44***	.18*
Assess possible merger, acquisition, or divestiture strategies	.38***	.55***	.18^t	.26***	.45***	.20**
Work with the corporate board on business strategy	.58***	.51***	.09	.41***	.47***	.18*

Response scale: 1 = little or no extent; 2 = some extent; 3 = moderate extent; 4 = great extent; 5 = very great extent

Significance level:

^{t} $p \leq .10$

* $p \leq .05$

** $p \leq .01$

*** $p \leq .001$

215

Table 8.7 HR strategy activities and organization's management approach

With respect to strategy, to what extent does the HR function...?	Bureaucratic (hierarchical and top–down)		Low-cost operator (minimum compensation, low-cost focus)		High involvement (participative, flat, high career commitment)		Global competitor (complex work, hire the best, low career commitment)		Sustainable (agile, both financial and sustainability goals)	
Country	USA	China	USA	China	USA	China	USA	China	USA	China
Help identify or design strategy options	-.21**	-.20**	-.11	-.06	.27***	.44***	.00	.37***	.26***	.41***
Help decide among the best strategy options	-.22**	-.21**	-.07	-.03	.30***	.42***	.06	.34***	.32***	.41***
Help plan the implementation of strategy	-.26***	-.19*	-.17*	.02	.39***	.39***	.11	.30***	.32***	.32***
Help identify new business opportunities	-.12	-.06	-.10	-.05	.27***	.28***	.13^t	.33***	.19*	.28***
Assess the organization's readiness to implement strategies	-.25***	-.14^t	-.16*	-.04	.42***	.40***	.14^t	.30***	.22**	.38***
Help design the organizational structure to implement strategy	-.27***	-.11	-.21**	-.05	.44***	.36***	.21**	.30***	.20**	.34***
Assess possible merger, acquisition, or divestiture strategies	-.28***	-.03	-.20**	.01	.27***	.27***	.17*	.32***	.19*	.22**
Work with the corporate board on business strategy	-.19*	-.18*	-.14^t	-.09	.38***	.32***	.07	.21**	.22**	.22**

Significance level:
^{t} $p \leq .10$
* $p \leq .05$
** $p \leq .01$
*** $p \leq .001$

organizational performance in the US sample. Yet in the US sample the correlations range from .11 to .18 with only one reaching significance at $p < .10$. For the Chinese sample, the range of correlations is somewhat higher (from .13 to .20), and all but one reached significance at $p < .05$. However, none of the differences between the Chinese and US correlations reached statistical significance. Thus it does not appear that the extensiveness of these strategy activities is more strongly associated with organizational performance in the United States than in China.

8.8 Organization's management approach

Does an organization's management approach associate with the extent of HR's strategic activity? Table 8.7 contains the correlations of the eight strategy activities with ratings of the organization's management approach in both the United States and China.

The overall pattern of correlations is similar across both countries. As with earlier findings regarding time spent, the more an organization is characterized as "bureaucratic "or a "low-cost operator" the less extensive are HR strategy activities. The more an organization is characterized as "high involvement," "global competitor," or "sustainable" the more extensive are HR strategy activities, in both the United States and China. Thus it appears that the management approach creates a similar pattern of encouragement or discouragement for HR strategy activities across both countries. It is simply less likely that HR will engage in these strategic activities in "bureaucratic" and "low-cost operator" organizations in both countries.

There are some intriguing differences between the countries. Consider the findings for the "low-cost operator" approach. The ratings of this approach are more likely to be significantly negatively associated with strategy activities in the United States than in China. As noted earlier, this management approach was significantly associated with organizational size only in the China sample. It seems possible that if the route to growth in China has more often been through the "low-cost operator" approach, then this approach may have little effect on HR's strategic activity. Large organizations may have the resources and capacity to value HR's strategic activity, and in China such organizations are more likely to be low-cost operators. In contrast, if "low-cost operator" is less often a growth strategy in the United States, then it may mean that US organizations adopting this approach devote fewer resources to HR and allow it less opportunity for strategy activities.

Consider the findings for the "global competitor" approach. The correlations of the strategy activities with this approach are stronger and more frequently statistically significant for China than for the United States. It seems possible that the US-based companies that are global competitors may have progressed through the stage at which deep HR strategy involvement occurs, and have moved toward a model of shared services and a more pragmatic approach to careers ("we employ you as long as you can add value"). On the other hand, China-based "global competitor" organizations may be at an earlier growth stage in which deep involvement by HR in strategy issues is more necessary and accepted. It may also be that there is simply a more HR-involved approach and perspective among the global competitors in the Chinese sample than the US sample.

Table 8.1 showed that, compared to US HR leaders, Chinese HR leaders more strongly described their organizations as "bureaucratic," and less strongly described them as "global competitors," "high involvement," and "sustainable." The results in Table 8.7 suggest that this pattern may partially explain the lower level of many strategy activities in Chinese HR functions. In both China and the United States, advanced strategy activities are more extensive under management approaches that occur less often in China. Thus US HR leaders more frequently find themselves in organizations that operate in ways that may be more "friendly" to HR strategy activities.

These results from the United States and China, as well as the larger pattern of results in our survey data (Boudreau and Lawler, forthcoming; Lawler and Boudreau, 2012) suggest that certain organizational approaches (e.g., "bureaucratic" and "low-cost") present a "headwind" against which HR must battle to achieve strategic partnership, advanced strategy activities, high professional skill levels, etc. Other organizational approaches (e.g., "sustainable" and "innovation") present a "tailwind" that seems to support such achievements. The fact that the former approaches appear more often in the Chinese sample may mean that Chinese HR leaders and organizations may find it more difficult to advance HR through the Western pattern of strategic partnership. It may also be that the place to look for more advanced HR in China may be not only a function of organizational size or longevity, but of management approach. Future research might attend to the role of the organization's management approach in HR evolution in China, versus other countries.

8.9 Conclusions

Chinese and US HR organizations show interesting similarities and differences. Our results clearly reinforce prior studies that suggest that Chinese HR is at a different stage than HR in the United States. Chinese HR functions spend a smaller proportion of their time on strategic partnership and engage in advanced strategy activities less often. This may be partially explained by the fact that time spent on strategic partnership is less strongly related to organizational performance in China. Yet time spent on auditing and maintaining records was negatively related to organizational performance in both countries, and the Chinese HR leaders reported spending more time there than US organizations. In both the United States and China there appears to be a case that increasing the proportion of time spent on strategy will enhance key HR outcomes, though the impact of increased time on strategic partnership seems to be less in China.

Chinese HR leaders more often characterized their organizations as "low-cost operators," and less often as "global competitor," "high involvement," and "sustainable" organizations. This is related to the greater proportion of time Chinese HR functions spend on HR administration, because in both the United States and China, being a "low-cost operator" was positively related to HR administration and the other three management approaches were negatively related to it. Interestingly, the proportion of time spent on strategic partnership was unrelated to the management approaches in China. So the lower proportion of time spent on strategic partnership by Chinese HR functions may not be a consequence of their management approach.

When it comes to advanced strategy activities, our results reinforce past research suggesting that Chinese HR functions engage in such activities less extensively. Interestingly, the relative extensiveness of the activities suggests that in both China and the United States, HR is more likely to implement the strategy than to form it.

Advanced strategy activities were related to HR and organizational outcomes in both the United States and China. The relationship with organizational performance was more statistically significant in the

Chinese sample. Thus the implication that more extensive engagement in advanced strategy activities may enhance HR and organizational outcomes is similar for both countries.

Management approaches do affect the extent of advanced strategy activities. Both the "low-cost operator" and "bureaucratic" approaches are being negatively associated with these activities in both countries. The greater prevalence of these management approaches in China may partially explain their less extensive use. An interesting finding was that the "low-cost operator" approach was more strongly associated with organizational size in China than in the United States, and had less of a negative association with advanced strategy activities in China than in the United States. Chinese HR leaders in "low-cost operator" companies may be seeing the advantages of size in ways that their US counterparts do not.

Overall, while China appears to show a pattern of HR activity that is at an earlier stage of development, both China and the United States show evidence that progress toward strategic partnership and active strategic roles is associated with stronger HR and organizational outcomes. Both samples also show evidence that an organization's management approach matters. Thus in both China and the United States, HR may advance more quickly in organizations that operate as "global competitors," "sustainable," and "high involvement" than as "bureaucratic" and "low-cost operators." A key to the advancement of HR in China may well be how the use of management approaches evolves.

8.10 Implications for practice

This chapter has analyzed the extent and nature of HR strategy activity in US and Chinese companies. The findings reinforce past research, in that HR executives in China remain less active in business strategy than are US HR executives. In both countries the extent and nature of HR strategic activity is associated with HR effectiveness and organizational performance, albeit with some differences. It appears that one reason for the differences in the strategic role of HR between the two countries is the extent to which organizations adopt management approaches that are positively associated with the opportunity for HR to engage in strategic activities. Moreover, organizations in China often have organizational design and HR practices that are less "friendly" to strategic HR.

Given this, organizations operating globally will likely wish to accommodate the differences between HR approaches and practices in the United States and China. Indeed, in data not reported here, we found that this same pattern of differences exists when Chinese companies are compared to their counterparts in a variety of Western countries, including those in Europe and in Canada. It appears that in many ways Chinese HR operates in a more operational and less strategic role than in the United States and other Western countries. This may mean non-HR Chinese leaders will be less accustomed to having HR play a leadership role in strategy and a strategic role in the enterprise. There is likely to be a greater need for education and acceptance building with HR constituencies in China in order to advance a greater strategic role for the HR profession. It may also be that Chinese leaders outside of HR will learn to take on a greater role in HR strategy, if lacking an HR function that is as prepared to take this role.

A significant finding is that the management approach taken by the organization associates strongly with the degree to which HR engages in strategic activities and spends time on strategy. This was true in both countries, though the pattern differed somewhat. It appears that organizations that accomplish their objectives by operating as "low-cost operators" or "bureaucracies" are less likely to see strategic and more advanced HR roles, while those operating as "global competitors," "sustainable" organizations and with high employee involvement are more likely to see such roles. This poses a conundrum for organizations and the HR profession. Should HR leaders who wish to play an advanced HR role try to join organizations whose operating approach is more "friendly" to strategic HR, or is it possible to change organizations whose approaches are inherently less HR friendly? Do organizations that operate as "bureaucratic" or "low-cost" have different needs for strategic HR? Our data are at the early stage, but it does appear that both HR and non-HR leaders as well as HR scholars, may wish to measure and account for the management approach of organizations as they consider the likelihood and effect of strategic HR activities.

Understanding and measuring the management approach of organizations may also provide ways to compare US and Chinese organizations that add to what has been done before. Specifically, a good deal of prior research on Chinese HR has emphasized ownership arrangements such as state-owned or joint ventures. Such categories are less meaningful in the United States and other Western countries, but our data suggest that measuring the organization's management approach may provide similar insights while being more comparable across regions. Though our data are at the company level, it seems plausible that such measures might also reveal differences between organizational units at the regional or national level. Thus leaders may find it useful to map their units according to the prevalent management approach, as they consider the viability of strategic HR in different regions of their organization.

References

All-China Federation of Industry and Commerce (2006). *Report on Non-state Sector Economic Development (2005/2006)*. Beijing: Social Science Academic Press (China).

Beamish, P. W. (1993). Characteristics of joint ventures in the People's Republic of China. *Journal of International Marketing*, 1 (1), 29–48.

Björkman, I. (2002). The diffusion of human resource management practices among Chinese firms: the role of western multinational corporations. *Asia Pacific Business Review*, 9 (2), 43–60.

Boudreau, J. W. and Lawler, E. E., III (2013). Stubborn traditionalism in HRM: causes and consequences. *Center for Effective Organizations Working Paper*. University of Southern California.

Boudreau, J. W. and Ramstad, P. M. (2007). *Beyond HR: the New Science of Human Capital*. Boston, MA: Harvard Business School Press.

Bowen, D. E. and Ostroff, C. (2004). Understanding HRM–firm performance linkages: the role of the "strength" of the HRM system. *Academy of Management Review*, 29 (2), 203–21.

Brewster, C. J., Mayrhofer, W., and Morley, M. (eds.) (2004). *Trends in Human Resource Management in Europe: Convergence or Divergence*. London: Butterworth-Heinemann.

Collins, N., Zhu, Y., and Warner, M. (2012). HRM and Asian socialist economies in transition: China, Vietnam and North Korea. In C. J. Brewster and W. Mayrhofer (eds) *A Handbook of Comparative HRM*. Cheltenham: Edward Elgar, pp. 598–619.

Cooke, F. L. (2005). *HRM, Work and Employment in China*. London, UK: Routledge.

Cranet (2011) Cranet survey on comparative human resource management: international executive report. Cranfield University: Cranet Network.

Ding, D. Z. and Akhtar, S. (2001). The organizational choice of human resource management practices: a study of Chinese enterprises in three cities in PRC. *International Journal of Human Resource Management*, 12 (6), 946–64.

Ding, D. Z. and Warner, M. (2001). China's labour-management system reforms: breaking the "three old irons" (1978–1999). *Asia Pacific Journal of Management*, 18 (3), 315–34.

Glover, L. and Sin, N. Y. M. (2000). The human resource barriers to managing quality in China. *International Journal of Human Resource Management*, 11 (5), 867–82.

Kerr, C. (1983). *The Future of Industrial Societies: Convergence or Continuing Diversity?* Cambridge, MA: Harvard University Press.

Lawler, E. E. and Boudreau, J. W. (2012). *Effective Human Resource Management: a Global Analysis*. Stanford, CA: Stanford University Press.

Lawler, E. E. and Worley, C. G. (2011). *Management Reset: Organizing for Sustainable Effectiveness*. San Francisco, CA: Jossey-Bass.

Naughton, B. (1996). *Growing out of the Plan: Chinese Economic Reform, 1978–1993*. Cambridge, UK: Cambridge University Press.

Nyaw, M. K. (1995). Human resource management in the People's Republic of China. In L. F. Moore and P. D. Jennings (eds.), *Human Resource Management on the Pacific Rim*. Berlin, Germany: Walter de Gruyter, pp. 187–216.

Rowley, C. and Benson, J. (2002). Convergence and divergence in Asian human resource management. *California Management Review*, 44 (2), 90–109.

Verburg, R. M., Drenth, P. J. D., Koopman, P. L., Van Muijen, J. J., and Wang, Z. M. (1999). Managing human resources across cultures: a comparative analysis of practices in industrial enterprises in China and the Netherlands. *International Journal of Human Resource Management*, 10 (3), 391–410.

Warner, M. (1996a). Economic reforms, industrial relations and human resources in the People's Republic of China: an overview. *Industrial Relations Journal*, 27 (3), 195–210.

  (1996b). Human resources in the People's Republic of China: the "three systems' reforms." *Human Resource Management Journal*, 6 (2), 32–43.

Wei, S. (2010). *HR Practices and Challenges in Chinese Firms: Comparison with Western Firms*. Thesis submitted for Masters of Business. Brisbane, Queensland, Australia: Queensland University of Technology.

Wood, G., Psychogios, A., Szamosi, L. T., and Collings, D. G (2012). Institutional perspectives on comparative HRM. In C. J. Brewster and W. Mayrhofer (eds.) *A Handbook of Comparative HRM*. Cheltenham: Edward Elgar, pp. 27–50.

Zhu, C. J. (2005). *Human Resource Management in China: Past, Current and Future HR Practices in the Industrial Sector*. London, UK: Routledge.

9 Emerging markets and regional patterns in talent management: the challenge of India and China

JONATHAN DOH, RICHARD SMITH, STEPHEN
STUMPF, AND WALTER G. TYMON, Jr.

9.1 Introduction

The business context of growth in emerging markets has considerable implications for talent-management strategies. There is a changing balance of economic power from developed to developing countries, accompanied by a new geographical demography that is giving rise to enormous talent pools in the emerging markets of Asia, Africa, and Latin America. In particular, China and India have emerged as the two most dynamic of the BRIC economies (Brazil, Russia, India, and China). These giant labor and consumer markets have attracted large shares of foreign investment, have developed strong indigenous industrial and service sectors, and have experienced rapid market growth, resource acquisition, and deployment. Both countries have served as springboards for the growth of emerging market multinationals, as large heretofore domestic companies globalize. This chapter has three objectives. First, it addresses the need for talent management in the Indian and Chinese context and the challenges associated with talent management in those regions. Second, it considers the state of talent-management practices in China and India and how they have evolved in recent years. Third, it explores the implications of that evolution for management practice and research and our understanding of talent practices generally in the next wave of emerging markets economies.

Economic development in both China and India has led to a focus on those factors that enable growth such as the availability of natural resources, investment funding, favorable regulatory policies, and a supportive infrastructure. China and India are the world's most populous countries. They have sustained the highest annual GDP growth rates over the past decade among all major economies – 9% for China and 6 to 7% for India. Both have exerted strong influence and leverage among the ten emerging-market countries in the G-20. China is the world's largest source of net capital outflows and India is the world's largest recipient of foreign outsourcing of computer-based services. China and India are each heavily dependent on imported oil. They are the second and fourth largest importers, respectively. These two countries are by far the most important emerging markets in terms of economic and demographics factors.

Increasingly, one of the critical global differentiators for organizations is the human capital of a nation (Florida, Mellander, and Stolarick, 2008). The type and availability of talent will be a key factor in determining the industries and business that can be supported and competitive. With the rapid economic expansion, the level of available skills and talent has increased in both quantity and quality as both economies work to advance the sophistication of production and services provided.

Porter, Ketels, and Delgado-Garcia (2007) suggest that the human-capital capabilities of an emerging nation will evolve through several stages. These stages progress with additional capabilities brought on by furthering education and talent development. These stages include:

- Factor driven – basic manual labor for the production of simple commodities or the extraction of natural resources. Competition on price in labor-intensive environments with limited focus on talent development as labor is seen as a commodity. Over time, new technologies will be introduced to improve productivity, which will begin to increase the importance of managing talent and retaining key talent.
- Investment driven – manufacturing of more sophisticated products and increasing skill development as the needs for productivity and use of technologies increase. As capabilities are increased so are the needs for technical and managerial skills. Talent management becomes important in ensuring quality and increasing efficiency.
- Innovation driven – the ability to provide innovative services and products with the use of technology and advanced methods. Knowledge-based focus creates high demand for talent with technology skills and more sophisticated managerial capability. The issues associated with retaining, attracting, and managing talent can be acute.

In the case of India and China, the pace of development through these stages has been rapid as the early basic manufacturing in the 1990s quickly led to increased foreign direct investments in many sectors. With the improved access to services through the Internet, the services sector has provided additional fuel to the need for more sophisticated skills and human capital in both countries. Now we find research centers and advanced technology designs being located in China and India due to the availability of talent.

Of course, for India and China, the sheer size of the population creates an interesting backdrop for economic growth. The focus on education is increasing with enrollments in tertiary education now at 25% for China and 13% for India (Economist, 2012). While these percentages pale in comparison to 83% enrollment level in tertiary education for the United States, the population differences create larger numbers of future graduates in both countries.

Human capital will be of increasing importance with significant implications for the management of talent (Heckman and Yi, 2012): attracting, retaining, developing, and managing people becomes a critical issue for business leaders. As Schuler, Jackson, and Tarique (2011) point out in their work on global talent management, many issues associated with managing talent in emerging markets pose difficult challenges. It is not uncommon for there to be limited talent when and where it is needed, which creates many challenges in adjusting to the dynamics in markets such as China and India. In this chapter there are five main themes or sections. First, we begin by reviewing the talent-management challenges in India and China. Second, we focus on how rapid economic growth is creating pressures for more formalized and institutionalized talent practices, while also being responsive to the unique social and cultural settings of these countries. Third, we review literature that has tracked the evolution of talent practices in these regions, focusing on how those practices have changed to reflect the increasing globalization of their economies. Fourth, we explore practices by foreign MNEs operating in China and India as well as indigenous companies, many of which are becoming global themselves. Finally, we conclude with a discussion of implications of this review, and an exploration of how this literature can help us understand talent practices in the "next wave" emerging economies of Asia, Latin America, and Africa.

9.2 Talent challenges in emerging markets: the case of India and China

The rapid economic development and business growth in China and India have created challenges in the attraction, development, and retention of talent (Beechler and Woodward, 2009). Even following the global financial crisis, the focus on talent has continued in both China and India where the rising bar for skilled talent continues. In some industries the widespread talent shortages are more acute as the number of qualified graduates in specialized areas (e.g., logistics) can be a challenge for many organizations (Shi and Handfield, 2012). Some of the noted underlying talent issues facing organizations in India and China include: demographic trends of ageing generations, change in skill specialization, rising expectations from multinational enterprises (MNEs), convergence of local and global HRM standards, and the supply/demand imbalance.

9.2.1 Demographics and diversity

The challenges of demographics and diversity continue to be significant in China and India. The increasing numbers of new graduates entering the workforce each year, the average age of working adults, and the projected pools of future talent all combine to create a fast-evolving environment. Based on the US Census Bureau Research, the population of India will continue to rise, creating more workforce entrants and an increasing supply of skills to the market. China, on the other hand, will begin to decline in population after 2020 due to the reduction in birth rates (Wolf *et al.*, 2011). The working population will continue to be younger in India than China and will eventually overtake China in both population and working-age adults as shown in Figure 9.1.

This eventual shift in working age can be an important long-term consideration for leaders while also balancing immediate business needs for the right skills. As China has placed increased emphasis on education for over a decade, the number of college graduates in China will continue to increase.

In addition, these workforce demographics will not only lead to many young, professional organizations, but will also exacerbate the generational differences within a workforce. The predominance in

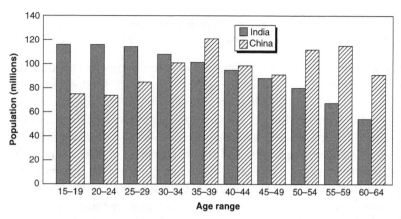

Figure 9.1 Age breakdown of working-age populations in China and India in 2025 (Source: US Census Bureau, 2010)

some firms will be people in generation X and generation Y due to the relatively recent economic and skill development. Without years of tradition or assumptions on the ways of working, architects of talent programs will need to consider the needs of a workforce with values and an orientation of the younger generation. Where generations are mixed, conflicts can arise due to different expectations of talent development and talent management (Smola and Sutton, 2002).

The increased emphasis on education and expansion of universities in China and India are paving the way for the development of future talent, but companies must be ready with talent programs to address the recruitment and retention needs that will continue to surface as organizations compete for top talent. The pyramid of talent has long been reported as an issue in China as the economic growth has outpaced the personal development growth of future managers. This acute need for managerial experience has forced companies to lower the bar for manager expectations or import leadership talent. As a result, a growing percentage of Chinese companies are forced to find foreign talent to supplement their needs (Lane and Pollner, 2008). In India, the same general issue with the lack of leadership experience occurred in the services sector as the demand for information technology (IT) services and business process outsourcing (BPO) services have grown rapidly over the last decade. The result was a rapid influx of talent and programs to accelerate leadership development across the services sector in India.

9.2.2 *Skill specialization*

Employers in China and India are increasingly seeking employees with higher and more specialized skills as both countries move from basic labor for manufacturing or services to a strong focus on knowledge work. This is fueled in part by foreign direct investments in R&D centers, advanced technical design centers, and centers of expertise. These give rise to new levels of specialized skills in the medical, engineering, and science fields that may not have been a focus in the past. The increase in demand for knowledge workers (Chen and Hoskin, 2007) has created shortages of specializations in the areas of research, accounting, medical, pharmaceutical, and management talent. While the number of college graduates is increasing, the availability of highly skilled graduates in the sciences, technology, and innovation is lacking as the skill levels are often not up to international standards (Simon and Cao, 2009). As a result, it will take time and extensive educational and apprenticing efforts for the supply of these specialized skills to catch up with the demand. Although the talent situation in China and India has been uneven, these two countries have led the greater Asian region, and many MNEs have been increasing their expectations of talent levels available in emerging economies based on positive experiences in China and India. These expectations often leave HR leaders struggling to keep up with demands for specialized skills that cannot be found at the scale needed to support ongoing operations. Targeted talent-management programs will need to find ways to address the more challenging skill segments in organizations in both India and China.

9.2.3 *Science and technological development and education*

Investment and education are being increasingly recognized by developed and developing countries as important stimuli to increase the supply of skilled science and technology talent. A report from the Rand Corporation (2010) underscores that despite some popular conceptions, China and India have a long way to go in terms of catching up to the United States, Europe, and Japan in this regard. Concerns are especially pronounced for India (Rand, 2010).

One important measure of the future potential of a country in science and technology is the level of R&D investments. While non-OECD countries account for a growing share of global R&D investment, and the United States' and EU's shares in global R&D have decreased by 3% and 2%, respectively, the share of global R&D attributable to non-OECD countries is still a relatively modest 18.4% (OECD, 2008). Investment in R&D (R&D intensity) is approximated by gross expenditures in R&D (GERD) as a percentage of GDP. Gross expenditures in R&D as a percentage of GDP have been increasing in real terms at 3.2% average rate worldwide for the past three decades. As a percentage of GDP, the United States invests 2.6%, Japan 3.1%, South Korea 2.5%, Taiwan 2.1%, the EU 1.8%, China 1.0%, and India 0.8%. In terms of total investment in R&D, China is the third largest R&D spender worldwide after the United States and Japan, with an annual GERD growth rate of 18% since 2000. Gross expenditures in R&D can be decomposed into four performing sectors: business (BERD), government (GOVERD), higher education (HERD), and private non-profit (PNPERD) (Rand Corporation, 2010).

Within the total GERD, China's BERD has increased from 0.25% of GDP in 1996 to around 1.01% in 2006 and total BERD has grown to half that of the EU – about 60% of the total – due to increase in business investments in the past three decades. This increase reflects, in part, the restructuring of formerly state-owned enterprises and is consistent with China's decrease in GOVERD. China's annual HERD growth rate (9–10%) is ranked second in the world since 2001 (OECD, 2008). India's GERD is around 0.8% of GNP, compared with more than 2% in developed countries. Of India's total GERD, 70.5% is GOVERD (62% central and 8.5% state government), 4.2% is HERD, and 25.3% is BERD (5.0% from public-sector industries and 20.3% from private-sector industries). India's 11th five-year plan, covering 2008 to 2013, calls for India to triple its investment in science and technology to 2.5% of GDP, although it is unclear as to whether this is a realistic goal. Business expenditures in R&D (BERD) have diminished since the beginning of 2000, with the high-tech recession in early 2000 and thereafter.

Another important measure of a nation's potential contribution to science and technology investment and growth is the percentage of employees in science and technology occupations. For example, for the period 1995 to 2006, growth in employees in science and technology occupations in the EU, United States, Japan, Taiwan, and South Korea has substantially outpaced those of China and India, and in India, employees in science and technology occupations actually fell during the period. Further, for the period 1985 to 2006, science and engineering doctoral degrees as a percentage of overall doctoral degrees awarded remained relatively flat, averaging about 65% through the period, roughly the same as the United States but less than Taiwan. In this calculus, India (and the EU and Japan) lagged significantly (Rand Corporation, 2010). While India graduates 350,000 engineers per year, the quality of these graduates varies widely. In 2004, India had 974 private engineering colleges – many of questionable quality – and only 291 public institutions.

China graduates 600,000 engineers per year, although higher enrollments, reduced teacher salaries, reductions in the number of tech schools, and increases in class sizes have resulted in a deterioration in quality. According to China's National Development and Reform Commission, 60% of university graduates in 2006 were not able to find work. China has set the following goals, to be accomplished by 2020: raise GERD to at least 2.5% of GDP; raise total factor productivity (TFP) to 60% of GDP growth.

9.2.4 Interaction levels

Interaction levels are changing as businesses in both India and China move from basic labor-intensive industries to those of more knowledge-based organizations. Employees are often expected to work across borders and communicate with other employees, customers, suppliers, and even alliance partners. As organizations in China and India move from basic level production of products and services to more complex areas of design, innovation, or high-level service, the need for global collaboration and communication becomes more critical. This requires cross-cultural competences that may not be available in the market (Price and Turnbull, 2007). In addition to skills in working across cultures, language barriers can create challenges for cross-border work among Asian countries.

Increased global mobility has been cited as a way for increasing competence and cultural awareness of working across borders. While global mobility has had an impact on the ability of people to move across borders and relocate outside their home countries (Tung and Lazarova, 2006), mobility in China and India tends to be intranational due to the size of the country and demographic factors and restrictions on international mobility.

9.2.5 *The convergence of HRM standards*

Increasing convergence of HRM standards continues in these regions as MNEs bring Western practices into developing countries. The increased cross-border interaction puts pressure on HRM practices as employees collaborate across borders leading to a level of convergence expectation and ways of working (Paik, Chow, and Vance, 2011). Multinational enterprises and regional leaders in China and India have an opportunity to gain a competitive advantage by using HR practices that can improve the standards and focus on talent management (Gupta and Govindarajan, 2002).

As eastern MNEs quickly develop and adopt Western HRM practices, they will push the convergence of the HRM standards to a global, common expectation among employees. This is often furthered by the adoption of HRM systems that address the needs of talent management, which can become a competitive differentiator (Becker and Huselid, 2006). As the experiences of employees across multiple types of organizations with various talent-management practices continue to grow and the competition based on talent management increases, we expect to see more convergence and perhaps innovation in HRM standards in China and India.

9.2.6 *Imbalances in supply and demand*

The rapid growth in global commerce has created a war for scarce talent in India and China. Notwithstanding the recent global economic recession, this continued imbalance for scarce skills persists and drives up the competition for needed skills, which creates challenges with retention, development, and attraction of key talent. The "war for talent" has been highlighted by many in light of the situation in China and India (Lane and Pollner, 2008; Beechler and Woodward, 2009; Gupta and Wang, 2009).

The attraction of talent in China and India continues to be a key challenge for both local companies and MNEs operating in these locations. As more MNEs move operations to India and China, even after the economic crisis of 2008 to 2010, the need for additional and specialized talent in these countries is acute. In addition, the ongoing growth of domestic companies and the focus on the domestic growth in China and India have channeled talent to other areas of the economy.

Of course, these create unique, yet ongoing challenges with the recruitment, retention, development, and career management for talent in China and India.

9.3 Talent practices in India and China

Research findings support the premise that talent-management practices have positive effects on employees and company performance, at least in Western countries (Arthur, 1994; Huselid, 1995; Delaney and Huselid, 1996; Delery and Doty, 1996; Ferris *et al.*, 1998; Ichniowski and Shaw, 1999; Guthrie, 2001;Collins and Clark, 2003). When firms apply talent-management practices that respond to their external environment and leverage their internal capabilities, they can achieve superior performance (Wright and McMahan, 1992; Lado and Wilson, 1994; Huselid, 1995).

Devanna *et al.* (1982) argue that HRM is a key element in strategy implementation. Schuler and Jackson (1995, 1999) highlight HR activities, such as performance appraisals and development programs, as essential to managing people so as to achieve organizational goals. What is not as clear is whether these practices yield similar employee and organizational outcomes in developing and emerging economies (Parker *et al.*, 2003).

One key element of talent management, particularly in rapidly growing emerging markets is employee retention. Factors affecting retention include:

1. growth in the economy and low unemployment
2. demographic trends affecting the supply of labor
3. poor performance or a low organizational growth rate
4. the organization's reputation and socially responsible behaviors
5. employer talent-management practices (e.g., performance management, professional development, quality of supervision)
6. attitudes and beliefs of the new professional (e.g., pride in the organization, satisfaction with the organization)
7. characteristics of the employee (e.g., length of service, age, gender, education).

Many of these factors are beyond the role or control of the HR function (e.g., state of the economy, labor market conditions, demographic trends), and others are likely to change slowly making it difficult to study the effects of HR changes (e.g., organizational performance and growth) (Maertz and Campion, 1998; Griffeth, Hom, and Gaertner, 2000; Ng and Butts, 2009; Vandenberghe and Bentein, 2009). Yet the findings relating retention to these factors over economic cycles are clear: organizations experience *higher turnover rates* in fast-growing economies, in tight labor markets, when demographic factors restrict the flow of talent, with weak organizational performance, and with slow growth.

In their in-depth analysis of national human resource development in India and China, Alagaraja and Wang (2012) note both countries share similar macro-level challenges and opportunities. Both have moved from centrally planned economies to transitional economies in the late 1990s, before becoming fully decentralized economies in the past decade. However, beyond this specific country contexts cannot be ignored. We examine research and findings within each of the specific country contexts of India and China.

9.3.1 The Indian context

Singh (2004) surveyed 82 Indian firms and found a significant relationship between two HR practices – professional development and reward systems – with perceived organizational and market performance. A Corporate Executive Board (2006) study on HR practices included 58,000 employees from 90 member organizations and 10 countries. The study reported the percentages of respondents rating various practices in their top five for enhancing their psychological commitment to their organization. Top practices for India were: people management (14%), recognition (20%), development opportunities (29%), and meritocracy (10%). For the United Kingdom they were: people management (17%), recognition (18%), development opportunities (31%), and meritocracy (16%). For the United States they were: people management (8%), recognition (7%), development opportunities (18%), and meritocracy (12%). People management, recognition, and development opportunities were more important to employees in India and the UK than in the United States, with meritocracy least important in India.

A recent survey of executives in India indicates a strong belief that robust HR practices in employee development are critical to building and sustaining a workforce needed to capitalize on business opportunities (Malkani, Pandey, and Bhagwati, 2007). HR practices that build workforce talent will determine whether or not companies are successful in harnessing India's demographic dividend (Knowledge@Wharton, 2008). For HR practices to yield tangible benefits to the firm in terms of employee career success, performance, and potential, they must be designed, executed, and perceived to be effective (Delery and Doty, 1996; Sparrow and Budhwar, 1997).

Consistent with this previous literature, Budhwar and Debrah (2009) suggest that future research should focus on factors that contribute to the efficient management of knowledge workers. Globalization and competitive pressures are pushing organizations in India to move toward Western systems. Budhwar and Debrah (2009) note a discernible trend toward talent-management practices targeted toward individual performance and rewards in India. With this shift, we hypothesize that more individualized talent-management practices will influence employee and employer assessments of individual employees – particularly for knowledge workers.

Stumpf, Doh, and Tymon (2010) and Tymon, Stumpf, and Doh (2010) conducted a large-scale talent-management study of the attitudes of 2,732 new professionals from 28 companies in India. They identified how the perceptions of talent-management practices contribute to more proud and satisfied professionals, and the factors that prompt these professionals to intend to leave, and their retention one year later (Steel, 2002). They focused on talent-management practices that organizations implement as part of their human resource strategy independent of uncontrollable exogenous factors. First, they explored how specific talent-management practices affect new professionals' pride in the organization and satisfaction with it. The practices, derived from both a review of the literature and discussions with company executives, were the organization's performance-management practices, professional-development practices, manager relationships with employees, and the organization's socially responsible behaviors (Turban and Greening, 1996). They then explored the likely effects of these practices on new professionals' intentions to leave and turnover as mediated by their pride in and satisfaction with the organization (Maertz and Campion, 1998; Griffeth, Hom, and Gaertner, 2000). Separately, they examined the degree of globalization of the firm (national, international, and global) on talent-management practices used and their effectiveness.

The four talent-management practices studied – performance-management practices, professional-development practices, manager support, and socially responsible actions – had a positive relationship with pride in and satisfaction with the organization; yet the size of these relationships varied substantially. Pride in the organization was most strongly associated with socially responsible actions (56% of the variance in pride was shared with socially responsible actions), and then by performance-management practices (42% shared variance), professional-development practices (36%), and manager support (21%). Satisfaction with the organization was most strongly associated with professional development (49% shared variance), socially responsible actions (48%), performance management (42%), and manager support (33%). The effects of the talent-management practices on retention were significant, but substantially less strong than they were on pride and satisfaction (from 8% to 13% shared variance with intention to leave; from 7% to 11% with turnover). The new professionals' pride in and satisfaction with the organization were more strongly related to intention to leave (pride, 12% shared variance; satisfaction, 26%) and turnover (pride, 10%, satisfaction, 23%).

Of the new professionals that strongly agreed with the quality of the performance-management practices – 42.6% expressed strong pride in the organization, 48.0% expressed satisfaction, 21.8% felt they would leave within two years, and 11.1% ultimately left within one year. Of those new professionals that did not agree or only slightly agreed with the effectiveness of the organization's performance-management practices – only 11.4% felt strong pride in the organization; 6.8% felt strong satisfaction with the organization, 42.7% expressed a strong intention to leave within two years, and 32.2% actually left within a year. A 21.1% difference in attrition rate translates into about a million dollars greater human resource expense to replace these professionals for every 50 positions in the firm. A similar pattern existed with respect to the professional-development practices, manager support, and social responsibility.

The new professionals' perception of these practices and their pride in and satisfaction with the organization have a strong relationship with their intention to leave and subsequent turnover. Of those expressing strong pride in the organization, 19.5% still expressed a strong intention to leave; only 10.3% left as of a year later. Of those expressing strong satisfaction with the organization, 14.4% express a strong intention to leave; only 6.5% left as of a year later. Professionals expressing satisfaction with the organization and pride in it are the least likely to leave – resulting in some of the lowest attrition rates reported in developing countries. It is perceived effectiveness of the firm's HR practices that lead to such satisfaction and pride.

The firms studied by Stumpf, Doh, and Tymon (2010) and Tymon, Stumpf, and Doh (2010) varied significantly in the extent to which these practices were enacted – with those new professionals in firms perceived to be effective in executing one or more of these practices being less likely to intend to leave, or actually leave (see Table 9.1). Having high levels of professional-development practices and manager

Table 9.1 *India talent-management survey: company differences on workplace study variables*

Company information	Organizational practice ratings	Employee affect	Intention to leave[1]
Cluster 1 (5 firms)	Average performance management High professional development High manager support Average social responsibility	High pride High satisfaction	Lowest (5%–10% turnover)
Cluster 2 (7 firms)	High performance management Average professional development Average manager support High social responsibility	High pride High satisfaction	Low (9%–15% turnover)
Cluster 3 (3 firms)	Average performance management High professional development Average manager support Average social responsibility	Average pride Average satisfaction	Average (16%–22% turnover)
Cluster 4 (13 firms)	Low performance management Low professional development Average manager support Low social responsibility	Low pride Low satisfaction	High (21%–36% turnover)

[1] These figures report an employee's active search for alternate employment and intention to leave within one year. We conducted a follow-up communication to determine actual employee departure and intention to leave was highly correlated with actual departure ($r = .69$).

support yielded the greatest retention. The importance of manager support provides evidence for Becker and Huselid's (2006) contention of the critical role of line managers in managing talent and implementing a workforce strategy – with high levels of performance-management practices and social responsibility yielding the next best levels of retention. However, this was contingent on these new professionals also feeling high levels of pride in and satisfaction with the organization. The incremental benefit to a firm that was perceived to do all four practices "exceptionally" well by its new professionals was modest compared to firms doing at least two of these practices well.

Their results support the idea that the influence of social responsibility is through its positive effect on new professionals' pride in and satisfaction with the organization (Burke and Logsdon, 1996). Within the literature, a consensus has emerged that "virtuous" firms are often rewarded in the marketplace for being socially responsible (Margolis and Walsh, 2003; Orlitzky, Schmidt, and Rynes, 2003). One common thread is the role of social responsibility in building and enhancing firm reputation – the opinions about an entity that results in a collective image of it (Bromley, 2001). In addition, research suggests that a good corporate reputation can increase current employees' motivation, morale, and satisfaction (Branco and Rodrigues, 2006; Riordan, Gatewood, and Bill, 1997). This research provides further support for the important role of a firm's reputation for social responsibility in the talent-management domain. This research specifically provides evidence of its importance among employees in emerging markets, and specifically its importance for professionals working in India. In emerging markets, with India as an example, many employees have experienced poverty first hand. The social responsibility of their employer matters greatly to these professionals (Ready, Hill, and Conger, 2008). They are committed to a stakeholder perspective of the corporation, whereby the success of the firm must provide benefits to the larger community. Only when they see this virtuous cycle occurring, do they feel pride and satisfaction as employees of the firm, and become committed to it. This suggests social responsibility needs to be a critical component of employer branding in India for effective talent management. Martin and Groen-in't-Woud (2011) argue that today effective employer branding is essential in global HR talent management.

In addition, social responsibility and managerial support may work together in improving retention in Indian firms. Consider, for example, Tata Steel, a global firm that is part of the Tata Group. Tata Steel created a leadership competence framework to help identify high-potential managers. Knowing the importance employees placed on the organization's commitment to social responsibility, Tata included such competences as "shows sensitivity and genuine concern for the eco system." They assessed the potential of managers around these dimensions to be groomed for more responsible assignments. One outcome is that Tata ranked highest among companies considered to have a larger purpose.

Because the relationship of satisfaction with the organization with intention to leave is strong, taking actions to increase employees' satisfaction tends to improve retention. One's pride in the organization is highly related with one's satisfaction with it. Elements of pride include being proud of the work you do and of the organization's reputation, being willing to speak highly of the organization's products and services, and being confident in this organization's ability to "do the right thing."

Organizations that may not have strong performance-management practices or strong professional-development practices, can still affect their employees' pride, satisfaction, intentions to leave, and retention through the support their managers provide to the employees and the social responsibility their organization exhibits. Socially responsible actions, in particular, are associated with a strong sense of pride in the organization (62.5%) and satisfaction with the organization (62.4%). Taken together, we believe managerial support and socially responsible actions represent talent-management practices that can positively impact attraction, development, and retention – the three key IHRM activities for global talent management identified by Tarique and Schuler (2010).

9.3.2 The Chinese context

Akhtar, Ding, and Ge (2008) examined HRM practices and their effects on company performance in 465 Chinese enterprises. Data were collected through two surveys among general managers and HRM directors on product/service performance of their companies and a range of HRM practices. Findings indicate that a set of strategic HRM practices (training, participation, results-oriented appraisals, and internal career opportunities) affect both product/service performance and financial performance. Employment security and job descriptions contributed uniquely to product/service performance, whereas profit sharing contributed uniquely to financial performance.

Gong and Chang (2008) investigated HRM in the Chinese context, comparing the presence of HR practices and their impact on performance by different ownership and governance structures. They found that the provision of career opportunities in domestic private firms and Sino-foreign joint ventures was similar to that in wholly foreign-owned firms, but greater than that in state-owned firms, and such provision was positively related to employee organizational commitment, citizenship behaviors, and firm performance. Additionally, they found that the provision of employment security was greater in state-owned than in non-state-owned firms. Employment security was positively related to employee organizational commitment, but not to citizenship behaviors or firm performance.

Ngo, Lau, and Foley (2008) examined HR practices in China to assess their impact on firm performance and the employee relations climate. Data were collected through a survey of 600 Chinese enterprises located in four different regions (Beijing, Shanghai, Guangdong, and Sichuan), which represented different industries and ownership arrangements. The levels of adoption of HR practices were lower in state-owned enterprises than in foreign-invested enterprises and privately owned enterprises. HR practices were found to have positive effects on financial performance, operational performance, and the employee relations climate. The moderating effect of ownership type was significant for financial performance only.

Cooke (2011) indicates Chinese firms have become more strategic in linking their HRM practices to organizational performance and that there is growing evidence of the adoption of Western HRM techniques. Cooke notes that HRM practices in China are becoming more mature, systematic, and relevant to organizational needs, and reflect labor-market trends. These practices include more sophisticated recruitment methods such as assessment centers and psychometric tests, the introduction of mentoring and coaching, and the use of performance-management systems and employee financial participation. In addition, evidence suggests that well-performing domestic private Chinese firms are adopting commitment-oriented HRM practices. The ability of private firms to align their HR strategy with employee expectations appears to be an important factor in managing talent effectively. Furthermore, Cooke notes an increasing number of studies have found a positive relationship between HRM practices and outcomes, such as increased motivation, job satisfaction, commitment, organizational citizenship, and reduced turnover intent in Chinese firms. However, Cooke also observes that the HR function itself in China remains far from being strategic and effective.

9.3.3 Multinational context

In their study of multinationals operating in the UK/Netherlands and India or China, Farndale *et al.* (2011) found that effective performance-management processes (from training to pay raises, from job rotation to bonuses) had an impact on employee engagement. The range of organizational actions that stimulate employee engagement and retention have been shown to also support firm financial performance. In a study of 50 multinational companies, Towers Perrin–ISR documented the impact of employee engagement on financial performance (Towers Perrin, 2008). Senior management's ability to demonstrate genuine interest in employees was the top engagement driver globally. Among the youngest employees (aged 18–24), the ability of the organization to develop leaders at all levels was the top engagement driver while the availability of excellent career advancement opportunities was the top driver among those aged 24 to 34. Over 12 months, companies with higher levels of engagement outperformed those with less engaged employees in three key financial measures: operating income, net income growth, and earnings per share. These companies also experienced higher levels of retention. These findings provide added support to the relationship among employer practices, employee engagement, and retention.

Some companies in India and China are investing in these HR practices, often integrating several of the levers we have discussed here into a broader performance-management initiative. For example, the Ingersoll Rand Engineering Centre worked with early-career technical employees to identify individuals with the potential to become business and technical leaders. As part of the process, the company worked with an HR consulting firm to create a 360-degree online tool, manage the assessment and feedback process, and provide consultative advice on mentoring and coaching. By doing so, they were able to find the best candidates as early as possible to jumpstart the development process.

In addition, employees were assigned mentors, drawn from the ranks of global leadership, to provide support in implementing individual development plans. This combination of leadership assessment and mentoring was recognized as one of the top five global best practices by the company, according to the firm (Doh *et al.*, 2011).

Infosys Technologies Limited developed a "Performance Engagement Skills" coaching program for 108 selected leaders from across the Infosys Development Centres. The 12 workshops included role-playing exercises, a development matrix based on the Infosys competence model, and an interactive electronic refresher course with key concepts for use after the program was over. These 108 managers were tasked with cascading the skills to over 1,000 managers throughout the organization for integration into their respective development centers. As Nandita Gurjar, Group HR Head for Infosys, explained, "Performance coaching is a key capability required in our senior managers to strengthen the high-performance work ethic. Tools such as 'appreciate inquiry' and 'coaching' help sustain employee engagement throughout the year rather than a one-time intervention. This helps us to focus more on the 'how' of getting results rather than just the results themselves" (N. Gurjar, personal communication, 2009).

Although it is too early to tell if these actions are paying off, studies suggest that investments such as these can help to create an environment characterized by managerial support and employee development, and reduce the incidents of unplanned turnover. These traditionally Western talent-management approaches seem to be working in a non-Western culture.

At the same time, the most successful companies in India and China are implementing talent-management practices with the cultural context in mind. Ramaswami and Dreher (2010) note that to be effective, management practices and their implementation depend on the cultural fit between the values and assumptions of the practice and those of the individuals practicing them. They note that knowledge of culturally similar aspects of HR practices can help in the design of career management or developmental initiatives by considering employees' cultural backgrounds. In this regard, they cite Bjorkman and Budhwar's (2007) finding that MNEs in India that adapt HR practices to fit local cultural norms had a positive relationship with organizational performance.

In India, for example, managerial support can involve what has been described as a nurturant-task leadership style (Sparrow and

Budhwar, 1997). The strong element of nurturing is consistent with a culture high in "power distance" – with Indians and Chinese more comfortable with, and accepting of, power differences within a hierarchy than in the West (Hofstede, 2001). In addition, in high "context cultures" such as India and China, managers need a higher level of emotional competence in order to be sensitive to others' emotions, to show empathy, and to value relationships (Sharma, 2012). Likewise, a company's visible commitment to social responsibility in the local community in which new professionals work can be particularly salient. These professionals are reminded on a daily basis of the reality of economic inequality. For them, the pride that results (or does not result) from the social responsibility of their firms is rarely far from their minds.

In conclusion, there is likely to be an increased emphasis on, and diffusion of, the talent-management practices discussed across firms in India and China. Successful firms are leveraging their social responsibility reputations, implementing equitable performance-management practices, attending to the professional development of employees, and training managers to provide the support necessary to lead professionals successfully. Successful companies operating in India and China have adopted fairly sophisticated systems that reflect these global best practices to meet the human-capital challenges they face. With continued intense global competition, we foresee these talent-management initiatives becoming more widespread.

While the Indian and Chinese business environments are distinctive in many ways, the similarities in Asian and South Asian cultures, cultures sometimes characterized as "high context" (i.e., communications and interactions depend heavily on context), may suggest our findings have broader applicability (Hall, 1976). As MNEs from the United States and Europe continue their penetration of emerging markets, and as emerging markets' MNEs broaden their scope to other emerging and developing countries, understanding the critical role of talent-management practices in employee satisfaction and retention will continue to be an important element of firm strategy and success.

9.4 Implications for practice and research

This chapter has identified some of the talent-management challenges in China and India and reviewed some of their talent-management practices. In this section, we draw some implications for practice from our review for the future of talent management in China, India, and in the "next wave" emerging economies, especially for managers from developed economies engaged in talent-management activities in India and China.

First, societal and cultural forces continue to influence talent-management practices in China and India such that approaches from Western, developed economies might not always be successful. Further, as noted by Alagaraja and Wang (2012), India and China share some macro-level challenges and opportunities, including transitions from centrally planned economies. For example, a Corporate Executive Board (2006) study on HR practices in ten countries found that people management, recognition, and development opportunities were more important to employees in India and the UK than in the United States, with meritocracy least important in India. Moreover, there are important differences between India and China, for example in India, managerial support may take the form of a nurturant-task leadership style (Sparrow and Budhwar, 1997), a practice consistent with the more paternalistic Indian culture.

Second, notwithstanding these differences, the overall trend is toward convergence such that practices in India and China are becoming more similar to those in the West. This finding is supported by a wide range of studies and insights, although the degree of convergence may vary widely based on industry sector, size and age of the firm, historical presence in the market, and many other factors. This means managers must tread carefully when seeking to implement talent-management practices from the "home" developed country market to the "host" emerging market.

Finally, managers should serve as conduits through which best practices from one market might inform approaches in another, leveraging the potential for fruitful transfer of practices while cognizant of the need to adapt and adjust them to local context.

9.5 Implications for research

As employers in China and India continue to compete for limited talent, employers will look for new ways to attract and retain people. Baum and Kabst (2013) completed a cross-national analysis on attracting applicants to show that some differences seem to exist across countries. More work is needed to review how a global employer would vary the employee-value proposition by country or how a local employer would best evaluate the value proposition for prospective employees. Studies exploring the employee-value proposition in China and India are limited and could be of great benefit to firms in these regions. A recent study in Zhejiang, China found that the focus on organizational attractiveness and employer-brand equity might have a key role in intention to accept a job as a part of the recruitment process (Jiang and Iles, 2011). Likewise, studies on India have highlighted the impact of HR and management practices that can impact performance and retention (Stumpf, Doh, and Tymon, 2010). Additional studies that explore talent attraction and retention of key talent would be of value to practitioners and further our understanding of potential regional differences in talent management.

As IHRM practices continue to converge in emerging markets such as China and India, we can expect talent-management practices to continue to be refined for each local market. Research that highlights various components of the employee-value proposition would help us better understand the nuances surrounding talent issues in these locations.

Diversity in the workforce poses a number of areas for future exploration related to gender diversity, national diversity, and even employee mindset. While the number of women in the workforce continues to be fewer than that of men around the world, the number of women in the workforce in China (67%) is much higher than that of the United States (58%) and the world average (52%) (World Bank, 2012). India on the other hand has many fewer women in the workforce (33%) relative to other countries. Hewlett and Rashid point out the value and challenges associated with female talent in emerging markets where women are typically less likely to be employed outside the home (Hewlett and Rashid, 2010). More research is needed to understand potential solutions that allow women to enter the workforce, and develop careers that address the needs for talent. Employers may not be aware of a bias within their organization or culture that may be limiting their full talent potential with women employees or potential employees. Additional focus on gender diversity in China and India could help address some inherent limitations for maximizing the potential for talent.

Cooke and Saini (2012) reviewed the importance of diversity across Chinese and Indian companies and found significant differences between the two regions. Chinese organizations generally do not see diversity management as an issue or may see it as a way of avoiding conflict. Indian organizations are more likely to be familiar with the idea and value of diversity. As the general idea of diversity becomes more prominent in India and China through the convergence of IHRM practices, additional focus will be needed on how the context of diversity may differ and practices used to enhance the management of talent. Recent studies in China highlight the need for more focus on functional diversity (Qian, Cao, and Takeuchi, 2012).

Diversity in India has been reviewed in different ownership structures and industry sectors (Cooke and Saini, 2010), yet more work is needed to understand the differences and challenges with diversity in leadership and the workforce. While the definition and thinking about diversity may vary by culture, it could hold potential areas for business benefit that have been otherwise untapped.

9.6 Conclusions

In our conclusions we highlight some of the implications for the next set of emerging markets. Since Goldman Sachs coined the BRIC acronym in 2003, identifying Brazil, Russia, India, and China as the largest, most rapidly developing countries with the greatest economic potential (Goldman Sachs, 2003), attention has turned to other dynamic economies in the developing world. In 2005, Goldman Sachs (2005) designated the BRIC successors, otherwise known as the Next-11 (N11). This grouping comprises Bangladesh, Egypt, Indonesia, Iran, South Korea, Mexico, Nigeria, Pakistan, the Philippines, Turkey, and Vietnam. The N11 countries share the characteristics of rapidly growing populations combined with significant industrial capacity or potential, although in some ways there is more variability in terms of their size, performance, and potential than among the BRICs (Goldman Sachs, 2007). For example, at the end of 2011, the four major countries (Mexico, Indonesia, South Korea, and Turkey) contributed to 73% of all N-11 GDP – US$13.5 trillion. Many analysts view Southeast Asia as the next region poised for rapid growth and global economic opportunity, and there are several forces at play that support this view.

First, like India, Southeast Asian countries still have a favorable demographic situation in that they feature a relatively high proportion of working age and a relatively low proportion of non-working age population. This contrasts with most developed countries, and within the emerging markets, China, which has seen declining birth rates resulting in surprisingly slow population growth and an ageing population. The Philippines, Malaysia, Indonesia, and Vietnam still have about 25 to 35 years left before this population pyramid begins to bulge and invert (Bloom and Canning, 2004). In addition, Southeast Asian countries are investing more heavily in science and engineering education. In Thailand, where until recently most students pursued liberal arts degrees, the government has placed additional emphasis on training engineers and scientists (Benson and Rowley, 2004). In Indonesia, relatively basic educational attainment has resulted in high youth unemployment. And as in China, in Vietnam, about 80% of the new graduates in engineering don't have basic practical skills (Benson and Rowley, 2004). In addition, business education, which first took off in Hong Kong and Singapore, has now proliferated in other parts of China, India, and increasingly Southeast Asian countries. The three leading business schools in Singapore – National University of Singapore, Nanyang Technological University, and Singapore Management University – are increasingly reaching out to other parts of Southeast Asia, offering programs geared toward different geographies and populations.

The prominence of family-owned companies in Southeast Asia also poses a challenge, as very few managers have been trained to international standards. This extends to the HR function, where few companies in Southeast Asia have HR managers with specific training in HR practices. The integration of information communication and technology has resulted in increased outsourcing to many Southeast Asian economies, and has helped modernize some HRM practices (Lynn, 2009).

As in India and China, HR practices in Southeast Asia tend to mix and integrate the more formal "hard" systems that have been in place in the developed countries, with more ambiguous and less structured programs that are indicative of the Asian cultural experience (Boxall, 1992). As such, we can expect that HR practices in Southeast Asian countries, like China and India, will tend to balance the more individualistically driven approaches of the West, with the more collective ones of the East. This means firms may continue to face challenges of retaining and rewarding the best employees, and dealing with mediocre performers whose status may have been protected in earlier more paternalistic systems. As such, many countries will continue to shift from a talent-management approach that stresses egalitarian and community values to those that focus on individual accomplishment and reward skills (Benson and Rowley, 2004).

As Western MNEs partially shift the focus of their investments from China and India to other emerging markets such as Malaysia, Vietnam, and Indonesia, they will continue to stimulate this transition. Moreover, as Chinese and Indian multinationals that have adopted some of these traditionally Western approaches increase their presence in Southeast Asia, they will also accelerate the incorporation of Western notions of individual merit, reward, and promotion, albeit balanced by Asian respect toward community, stability, and harmony.

References

Akhtar, S., Ding, D. Z., and Ge, G. L. (2008). Strategic HRM practices and their impact on company performance in Chinese enterprises. *Human Resource Management*, 47 (1), 15–32.

Alagaraja, M. and Wang, J. (2012). Development of a national HRD strategy model: cases of India and China. *Human Resource Development Review*, doi: 10.1177/1534484312446190.

Arthur, J. B. (1994). Effects of human resource systems on manufacturing performance and turnover. *Academy of Management Journal*, 37, 670–87.

Baum, M. and Kabst, R. (2013). How to attract applicants in the Atlantic versus the Asia-Pacific region? A cross-national analysis on China, India, Germany, and Hungary. *Journal of World Business*, 48 (2), 175–85.

Becker, B. E. and Huselid, M. A. (2006). Strategic human resources management: where do we go from here? *Journal of Management*, 32, 898–925.

Beechler, S and Woodward, I. (2009). The global war for talent. *Journal of International Management*, 15, 273–85.

Benson, J. and Rowley, C. (2004). Conclusions: changes in Asian HRM – implications for theory and practice. In J. Benson and C. Rowley (eds.), *The Management of Human Resources in the Asia Pacific Region: Convergence Reconsidered*. London: Frank Cass, pp. 174–82.

Bjorkman, I. and Budhwar, P. (2007). When in Rome...? Human resource management and the performance of foreign firms operating in India. *Employee Relations*, 29 (6), 595–610.

Bloom, D. and Canning, D. (2004). Global demographic change: dimensions and economic significance. *Harvard Initiative for Global Health Working Paper Series* 1. Cambridge, MA.

Boxall, P. F. (1992). Strategic human resource management: beginning of a new theoretical sophistication? *Human Resource Management Journal*, 2, 60–79.

Branco, M. C. and Rodrigues, L. L. (2006). Corporate social responsibility and resource-based perspectives. *Journal of Business Ethics*, 69, 111–32.

Bromley, D. B. (2001). Relationships between personal and corporate reputations. *European Journal of Marketing*, 35, 316–34.

Budhwar, P. and Debrah, Y. A. (2009). Future research on human resource management. *Asia Pacific Journal of Management*, 26, 197–218.

Burke, L. and Logsdon, J. M. (1996). How corporate social responsibility pays off. *Long Range Planning*, 29 (4), 495–502.

Chen, W. and Hoskin, J. (2007). Multinational corporations in China: finding and keeping talent. *Society for Human Resource Management*, October 2007, 1–4.

Collins, C. J. and Clark, K. D. (2003). Strategic human resource practices, top management team social networks, and firm performance: the role of human resource practices in creating organizational competitive advantage. *Academy of Management Journal*, 46, 740–51.

Cooke, F. L. (2011). *Human Resource Management in China: New Trends and Practices*. New York, NY: Routledge.

Cooke, F. L. and Saini, D. S. (2010). Diversity management in India: a study of organizations in different ownership forms and industrial sectors. *Human Resource Management*, 49 (3), 477–500.

(2012). Managing diversity in Chinese and Indian organizations: a qualitative study. *Journal of Chinese Human Resource Management*, 3 (1), 16–32.

Corporate Executive Board (2006). *Attracting and Retaining Critical Talent Segments: Identifying Drivers of Attraction and Commitment in the Global Labor Market*. Washington, DC.

Delaney, J. T. and Huselid, M. A. (1996). The impact of human resource management practices on perceptions of organizational performance. *Academy of Management Journal*, 39, 949–69.

Delery, J. E. and Doty, D. H. (1996). Modes of theorizing in strategic human resource management: tests of universalistic, contingency, and configurational performance predictions. *Academy of Management Journal*, 39, 802–35.

Devanna, M. A., Fombrum, C., Tichy, N., and Warren, L. (1982). Strategic planning and human resource management. *Human Resource Management*, 21, 11–17.

Doh, J., Smith, R., Stumpf, S., and Tymon, W. (2011). Pride and professionals: retaining talent in emerging economies. *Journal of Business Strategy*, 32 (5), 35–42.

Economist (2012). *World Figures 2012*. London: The Economist Newspaper Ltd.

Farndale, E., Hailey, V. H., Kelliher, C., and van Veldhoven, M. (2011). A study of the link between performance management and employee engagement in Western multinational corporations operating across India and China. Final report. Tilburg University.

Ferris, G. R., Arthur, M. M., Berkson, H. M., Kaplan, D. M., Harrell-Cook, G., and Frink, D. D. (1998).Toward a social context theory of human resource management–organizational effectiveness relationship. *Human Resource Management Review*, 8, 235–64.

Florida, R., Mellander C., and Stolarick, K. (2008). Inside the black box of regional development: human capital, the creative class and tolerance. *Journal of Economic Geography*, 8 (5), 615–49.

Goldman Sachs (2003). Dreaming with the BRICs: the path to 2020. Global Economics Paper 99.

(2005). How solid are the BRICs? Global Economics Paper 134.

(2007). The Next-11: more than an acronym. Global Economics Paper 153.

Gong, Y. and Chang, S. (2008). Institutional antecedents and performance consequences of employment security and career advancement practices: evidence from the People's Republic of China. *Human Resources Management*, 47, 33–48.

Griffeth, R.W., Hom, P.W., and Gaertner, S. (2000). A meta-analysis of antecedents and correlates of employee turnover: update, moderator tests, and research implications for the next millennium. *Journal of Management*, 26, 463–88.

Gupta, A. and Govindarajan, V. (2002). Cultivating a global mindset. *Academy of Management Executive*, 16, 116–26.

Gupta, A. and Wang, H. (2009). *Getting China and India Right: Strategies for Leveraging the World's Fastest Growing Economies for Global Advantage*. Josey-Bass, Hoboken NJ.

Guthrie, J. P. (2001). High-involvement work practices, turnover, and productivity: evidence from New Zealand. *Academy of Management Journal*, 44, 180–90.

Hall, E. T. (1976). *Beyond Culture*. New York: Doubleday.

Heckman, J. J. and Yi, J. (2012). Human capital, economic growth, and inequality in China. National Bureau of Economic Research, Working Paper No. 18100. May, 2012.

Hewlett, S. A. and Rashid, R. (2010). The battle for female talent in emerging markets. *Harvard Business Review*, 88 (5), 101–5.

Hofstede, G. H. (2001). *Culture's Consequences: Comparing Values, Behaviors, Institutions, and Organizations across Nations*, 2nd edn. Thousand Oaks, CA: Sage.

Huselid, M. A. (1995). The impact of human resource management practices on turnover, productivity, and corporate financial performance. *Academy of Management Journal*, 38, 635–72.

Ichniowski, C. and Shaw, K. (1999). The effects of human resource management practices on economic performance: an international comparison of US and Japanese plants. *Management Science*, 45, 704–21.

Jiang, T. and Iles, P. (2011). Employer-brand equity, organizational attractiveness and talent management in the Zhejiang private sector, China. *Journal of Technology Management in China*, 6 (1), 97–110.

Knowledge@Wharton (2008, September 18). India's corporations race to train workers and avoid being left in the dust. http://knowledge.wharton.upenn/india.

Lado, A. A. and Wilson, M. C. (1994). Human resource systems and sustained competitive advantage: a competency-based perspective. *Academy of Management Review*, 19, 699–727.

Lane, K. and Pollner, F. (2008). How to address China's growing talent shortage. *McKinsey Quarterly*, 3, 32–40.

Lynn, L. (2009). Technology development in Asia. In H. Hasegawa and C. Noronha (eds.) *Asian Business and Management*. Palgrave, pp. 55–76.

Maertz, C. P. and Campion, M. A. (1998). 25 years of voluntary turnover research: a review and critique. In C. L. Cooper and I. T. Robinson (eds.) *International Review of Industrial and Organizational Psychology*. London: John Wiley, pp. 49–86.

Malkani, D., Pandey, J., and Bhagwati, A. B. (2007). *The High-performance Workforce Study 2007: India*. Mumbia: Accenture.

Margolis, J. D. and Walsh, J. P. (2003). Misery loves companies: rethinking social initiatives by business. *Administrative Science Quarterly*, 48, 268–305.

Martin, G. and Groen-in't-Woud, S. (2011). Employer branding and corporate reputation management in global companies: a signalling model and case illustration. In H. Scullion, and D. G. Collings (eds.), *Global Talent Management*. London: Routledge, pp. 87–110.

Ng, T. W. H. and Butts, M. M. (2009). Effectiveness of organizational efforts to lower turnover intentions: the moderating role of employee locus of control. *Human Resource Management*, 48 (2), 289–310.

Ngo, H-Y., Lau, C-M., and Foley, S. (2008). Strategic human resource management, firm performance, and employee relations climate in China. *Human Resources Management*, 47 (1), 73–90.

Organization for Economic Cooperation and Development (2008). *OECD Science, Technology and Industry: Outlook 2008*. Paris: OECD.

Orlitzky, M., Schmidt, F., and Rynes, S. (2003). Corporate social and financial performance: a meta-analysis. *Organization Studies*, 24, 403–41.

Paik, Y., Chow, I. H-S., and Vance, C. M. (2011). Interaction effects of globalization and institutional forces on international HRM practice: illuminating the convergence–divergence debate. *Thunderbird International Business Review*, 53, 647–59.

Parker, C. P., Baltes, B. B., Young, S. A., *et al.* (2003). Relationships between psychological climate perceptions and work outcomes: a meta-analytic review. *Journal of Organizational Behavior*, 24, 389–416.

Porter, M. K. C., Ketels, C. H. M., and Delgado-Garcia, M. (2007). *The Microeconomic Foundations of Prosperity: Findings from the Business Competitiveness Index in the Global Competitiveness Report*. Palgrave Macmillan.

Price, C. and Turnbull D. (2007). The organizational challenge of global trends: a McKinsey global survey. *McKinsey Quarterly*, May.

Qian, C., Cao, Q., and Takeuchi, R. (2012). Top management team functional diversity and organizational innovation in China: the moderating effects of environment. *Strategic Management Journal*, 28 May, 2012. doi: 10.1002/smj.

Ramaswami, A. and Dreher, G. F. (2010). Dynamics of mentoring relationships in India: a qualitative, exploratory study. *Human Resource Management*, 49 (3), 501–30.

Rand Corporation (2010). *China and India 2025: A Comparative Assessment*. The Rand Corporation.

Ready, D. A., Hill, L. A., and Conger, J. A. (2008). Winning the race for talent in emerging markets. *Harvard Business Review*, 86 (11), 62–70.

Riordan, C. M., Gatewood, R. D., and Bill, J. B. (1997). Corporate image: employee reactions and implications for managing corporate social performance. *Journal of Business Ethics*, 16, 401–12.

Schuler, R. S. and Jackson, S. E. (1995). Understanding human resource management in the context of organizations and their environment. *Annual Review of Psychology*, 46, 237–64.

(1999). *Strategic Human Resource Management: A Reader*. London: Blackwell.

Schuler, R. S., Jackson, S. E., and Tarique, I. R. (2011). Framework for global talent management: HR actions for dealing with global talent challenges. In H. Scullion and D. G. Collings (eds.) *Global Talent Management*. Routlege.

Sharma, R. (2012). Measuring social and emotional intelligence competencies in the Indian context. *Cross Cultural Management*, 19 (1), 30–47.

Shi, Y. and Handfield, R. (2012). Talent management issues for multinational logistics companies in China: observations from the field. *International Journal of Logistics Research and Applications*, 15 (3), 163–79.

Simon, D. F. and Cao, C. (2009). Creating an innovative talent pool. *The China Business Review, Magazine of the US-China Business Council* November–December, pp. 34–42.

Singh, K. (2004). Impact of HR Practices on perceived performance in India. *Asia Pacific Journal of Human Resources*, 42, 301–17.

Smola, K. and Sutton, C. (2002). Generational differences: revisiting generational work values for the new millennium. *Journal of Organizational Behavior*, 23, 363–82.

Sparrow, P. R. and Budhwar, P. S. (1997). Competition and change: mapping the Indian HRM recipe against world-wide patterns. *Journal of World Business*, 32, 224–42.

Steel, R. P. (2002). Turnover theory at the empirical interface: problems of fit and function. *Academy of Management Review*, 27 (3), 346–60.

Stumpf, S. A., Doh, J. P., and Tymon, W. (2010). Capitalizing on human resource management in India: the link between HR practices and employee performance. *Human Resource Management*, 49 (3), 351–73.

Tarique, I. and Schuler, R. S. (2010). Global talent management: literature review, integrative framework, and suggestions for further research. *Journal of World Business*, 45, 122–33.

Towers Perrin (2008). Global workforce study 2007–2008. www.towersperrin. com/tp/showhtml.jsp?url=global/publications/gws/index.htmandcountry= global.

Tung, R. and Lazarova, M. (2006). Brain drain versus brain gain: an exploratory study of ex-host country nationals in Central and East Europe. *International Journal of Human Resource Management*, 17, 1853–72.

Tymon, W., Stumpf, S. A., and Doh, J. P. (2010). Exploring talent management in India: the neglected role of intrinsic rewards. *Journal of World Business*, 45, 109–21

Turban, D. B. and Greening, D. W. (1996). Corporate social performance and organizational attractiveness to prospective employees. *Academy of Management Journal*, 40 (3), 658–72.

Vandenberghe, C. and Bentein, K. (2009). A closer look at the relationship between affective commitment to supervisors and organizations and turnover. *Journal of Occupational and Organizational Psychology*, 82 (2), 331–48.

Wolf, C. Jr. *et al.* (2011). *China and India, 2025: A Comparative Assessment*. RAND Report. National Defense Research Institute.

World Bank (2012). World development indicators. July 9, 2012. The World Bank.

Wright, P. M. and McMahan, G. C. (1992).Theoretical perspectives for strategic human resource management. *Journal of Management*, 18, 295–320.

10 Globalizing the HR architecture: the challenges facing corporate HQ and international-mobility functions

PAUL SPARROW, ELAINE FARNDALE, AND HUGH SCULLION

10.1 Introduction

The preceding chapters have raised a number of important issues. In Chapter 7, Ibraiz Tarique and Randall Schuler showed that there are different philosophies about global best practice and divergence, and that the different practices under planning, attraction, development, and retention need to be aligned vertically to both the overarching HR strategy and the business strategy. They noted there is a core pressure on global talent management (GTM) to deliver a degree of vertical (global) integration *within* businesses across the internal labor (talent) markets (i.e., between the strategy, business model, and structure through to the talent-management practices). There is also a need for horizontal integration (i.e., across operating divisions) in order to shape requisite levels of transfer of knowledge and individuals across businesses. Then in Chapter 8 John W. Boudreau and Edward E. Lawler III argued that the study of GTM also needs to move beyond simplistic ideas about global convergence or divergence of practice. This theme was further developed in Chapter 9 by Jonathan Doh and colleagues, who reminded us of the power of local contexts (they looked at emerging markets) in shaping the nature and conduct of talent management, and the need for local responsiveness within those multinationals operating in such markets.

From these chapters, it becomes clear that there is a new economic topography within multinational corporations (MNCs), based much on the growth of emerging markets. A new demography of international mobility then begins to flow from this. This creates two fundamental challenges, discussion of which forms the focus of this chapter.

First, how do organizations manage the globalization of the talent management function itself? When studying the globalization of talent management, we are in effect looking at how organizations develop linkages between geographically dispersed units and use a series of integration modes to regulate functional activities across borders (Malbright, 1995). Kim, Park, and Prescott (2003: p. 327) define such functional global integration as the "coordination and control of individual business functions across borders." They found that the dynamics of this functional integration were "highly critical" in R&D, manufacturing, and marketing functions, seeing these functions as central to the global transfer and integration needed to achieve scale, scope, and learning economies.

Second, in globalizing the talent-management function, how does the organization accommodate the individual side of the equation? As the demography of international mobility continues to diversify, we are also seeing increasing variety in the forms of international work, which as a consequence leads to a growing importance of the role of the individual as a stakeholder in decisions about, and management of, global mobility (Dickmann and Mills, 2009; Howe-Walsh and Schyns, 2010). The management of international mobility also has to foster the appropriate network ties between the expatriate and their host and home support networks (Farh *et al.*, 2010). Rapid economic growth among developing nations, covered earlier in the book, also increases the need to accommodate idiosyncratic assignee objectives and motivations (Stroh *et al.*, 2005). Meyskens *et al.* (2009: p. 1448) argue that "while international talent grows in value, it is increasingly difficult to obtain, deploy and retain... Even though global talent management trends have evolved in practice, IHRM theorizing has not kept pace."

We look at these two processes to aid and assist the development of new insights into the theory of GTM.

10.2 Global talent management in comparative context

As the previous chapters make clear, talent-management practices, as with any other HR practices, are subject to the usual comparative management influences. Their desirability, execution, and chances of becoming embedded in day-to-day management are subject to cultural and institutional influences. This is particularly so, because as also made clear in the opening chapters, talent management often comes with ideological associations. Depending on the "version" of talent management pursued, it brings with it values of elitism and linkage to the business objectives of certain stakeholders. The "workability" of some of its core practices – such as the conduct of assessment centers or other techniques associated with the identification of potential, the skill, inclination and capability of line managers to take on responsibility for employment relationship, and coaching and development of talent – is very dependent on local managerial capability and attitude. Finally, the attractiveness of local markets in terms of their ability to deliver sufficient quantity and quality of talent (at whatever skill level) in terms of the sorts of capability, leadership, and competence models that the globalizing organization choses to seek, varies massively. Organizations have to make tradeoffs in terms of the time it takes to find the appropriate level of talent in a local market (the cost of search – in terms of resources assigned to search – and the opportunity costs of the time taken), the power of their brand to attract such limited labor versus the cost of attraction if the brand is not strong, and sometimes the political necessity of sourcing from the local labor market. They must factor in implicit calculations around the cost of labor, the trainability and speed to competence or acculturation, the risk of lost investment through active employee turnover, and so forth.

All of this we know, and such statements would not be new to any comparative management researcher, nor to any practitioner who has had significant international experience. Yet, at the same time, it will have been evident throughout this book that the HR strategies of many MNCs, of Western or emerging market origin, major domestic organizations that are in the process of globalizing, and even national public-sector organizations seeking talent from broadened labor markets, all use talent-management practices as one of the first targets for globalization.

Managing this movement from national and locally responsive practices to some form of more globally integrated practice, is a major challenge for such organizations. It involves a competition between employers as they begin to manage talent on a global basis to remain competitive.

Sparrow and Hiltrop (1997), interested in how HR professionals "transition" their HR systems from one mentality to another, argued that in reality, such professionals (and academic study) needed to accept and manage three realities:

1. They need to understand the ways in which HR in any geography is country specific, and the range of factors (broadly to do with

national culture, local institutional context, the variety of capitalism and national business models, and the typical strategic capability and role of HR in that geography) that will shape national practice.

2. They need to understand the forces at play that are, however, creating a dynamic for greater globalization. These factors might be generic integration such as e-enablement and creation of core processes, or the pursuit of so-called best practices, or the movement toward global production or service models within the firm, and so forth. The task at hand is to understand whether such forces are, at the most, actually changing the HR practice in reliable and sustainable ways or, at the least, making the local environment for previously unattractive HR ideas more receptive to change.

3. Finally, because HR is such a "political" process, but also one where an HR strategy for change is often "piggy-backed" and aligned pragmatically to other strategic initiatives, senior HR professionals can make choices about the broader initiatives that are taking place within the organization to which they might "tie" or "link" their efforts to globalize any particular HR practice. So, for example, there might be a global merger taking place, which creates the opportunity and space for the HR function to pursue integrative efforts that otherwise would not have been politically acceptable, or there might be a strategic drive to develop capability in a particular emerging market, which affords the opportunity to undertake some workforce planning for that geography, or there might be (as of late) a global financial crisis, which creates a questioning within a workforce or global management about what should be meant by talent.

At a broad level, the first type of knowledge reflects the many comparative HRM studies of talent management that have emerged (the locally responsive issue). The second type of knowledge reflects the competing forces that are requiring greater global integration (a more international HRM perspective on GTM). And the third type of knowledge is facilitated by seeing GTM as a bridge field that links what might be being done in the HR function to some of the broader strategic initiatives and imperatives that arise in the organization.

Following this logic, a critical area of research then should be to investigate the mechanisms through which multinationals attempt to manage these three dynamics. Given the national sensitivity of talent-management practices, there are a number of important questions that need addressing.

- If there are competing interpretations of talent management around the globe, yet strong pressures to converge around best practice, can we use notions of global integration and local responsiveness to signal the challenges faced by corporate functions in balancing their GTM practices?
- How does, or perhaps more pointedly how should, the corporate headquarters manage GTM?
- How do organizations accommodate the competing dynamics of global integration and local responsiveness into the structures of the talent function?

Several studies of talent management have focused on corporate strategies and practices implemented to attract and retain key talent and the need to build leadership to secure organizational capability (Sparrow, Brewster, and Harris, 2004; Gunnigle, Lavelle, and McDonnell, 2007; Collings, Scullion, and Dowling, 2009; Hartman, Feisel, and Schober, 2010; Scullion and Collings, 2011; Stahl, Björkman, and Morris, 2012). These practices typically include the use of talent pools, leadership competences, cultural-fit selection, 360-degree assessment, talent inventories, and leadership pipelines.

In the literature GTM is most commonly defined as adopting a differential, exclusive approach. For Collings and Scullion (2008: p. 102) it is "the strategic integration of resourcing and development at the international level, which involves the proactive identification and development and strategic deployment of high-performing and high-potential strategic employees on a global scale." Similarly, Mellahi and Collings (2010) consider it to involve three elements: identifying the key positions that contribute to a sustainable competitive advantage on a global scale; developing globally deployable talent pools to fill these roles; and differentiating the management of this talent pool that eventually fills these roles, while keeping them committed.

Sparrow, Brewster, and Harris (2004) found that GTM seemed to be associated with eight common strands of practice: (1) creating global HR network initiatives around talent management and capability development; (2) researching into "consumer insights" with current and potential employees, sister companies, external agencies, and benchmarking with external companies; (3) managing "talent pipelines" across countries in order to recruit "ahead of the curve;" (4) communicating brand and skills awareness across countries in graduate schools and businesses to get the people they needed; (5) developing internal talent pools around the world; (6) creating skilled and competent teams of assessors in different regional geographies; (7) managing recruitment suppliers on a global basis, introducing speed, cost, and quality controls, establishing master contracts to coordinate the messages conveyed and the use of preferred partners, ensuring audit trails to protect against legal issues associated with global diversity; and finally (8) e-enabling global information systems such as jobs notice boards, and redesigning websites to convey important messages about the employer brand.

For Stahl and colleagues (2007, 2012) GTM policies should be guided by six principles. (1) It requires the alignment of the talent strategy with the business strategy, values, and organizational culture. (2) The GTM systems have to be designed so that the various practices in the system support each other. The combination of practices should lead to a whole that is more than the sum of its parts. (3) The organization has to make talent management a critical part of the organizational culture. (4) It has to involve and encourage senior leaders and managers at all levels to be involved in the talent-management process. (5) The organization has to find the optimal balance between global integration (e.g., similar talent-management practices across regions) and localization (adapt talent-management practices to the local conditions). (6) The organization has to improve and differentiate itself in order to attract talent.

We need to understand the challenges that corporate HRM functions face in attempting to manage these tensions.

10.3 Globalizing the talent-management function itself

As organizations, and key functions such as those responsible for international mobility and talent management, move across the continuum between global integration and local responsiveness, the ability to manage the development of the function is affected by strategic capabilities, organizational infrastructures, and the strategic needs of local operations. A number of intra-organizational factors within the boundaries of the firm have to be managed as part of this globalization process (Björkman, 2006; Björkman and Lervik, 2007; Björkman *et al.*, 2009; Mäkelä, Björkman, and Ehrnrooth, 2009).

Sparrow (2012b) studied the process of functional globalization between international mobility and GTM functions. The study of global-mobility strategies found that even within a particular business sector "considerable insight to the business model is... needed before patterns of globalization, international mobility, costs, local factors and the associated role of the function are interpreted" (Sparrow, 2012b: pp. 2413). Moreover, "business model change... was often the real driver of the international mobility (IM) requirement in terms of the sorts of capabilities needed... Individual organizations were working to different business models and their IM strategies were influenced by these unique factors accordingly" (Sparrow, 2012b: p. 2423).

Coordinating this globalization is also complex because, in practice, a host of people and units interact with expatriates in order to manage the process of international mobility. These include home and host HR units or HR business partners, home and host line managers or business units, internal administrators, and outsourced specialist service providers (Danielsen and Molnar, 2007). Responsibilities across the life cycle of an international assignment are also distributed across several units. Business units typically select employees, handle performance management and training, provide career direction, enforce disciplinary action, and determine salary. Corporate HR functions develop, monitor, benchmark, and conduct internal satisfaction surveys, implement change, and address exceptions all with regard to policy. Expatriate administrators establish and approve policies and programs and obtain feedback as to whether they meet objectives. Vendors and specialist service providers have to adhere to contract terms and conditions. The expatriates themselves need to understand their new job duties and responsibilities, meet performance standards, and follow procedures before, during, and at the conclusion of the assignment. The trend toward the regionalization and localization of businesses and IHRM practices introduces yet more layers of complexity into the mix of relationships that the international-mobility function has to manage.

For Luo (2002) these pressures for integration that have to be managed include environmental and industrial forces, and these necessitate the deployment of business resources and global integration of dispersed businesses across national boundaries on a worldwide basis. However, while "pressures for local responsiveness are environmental and industrial forces that necessitate local context-sensitive strategic decision-making and quick responses to each local market or industrial setting," the balance at any one time is "constrained by administrative heritage, that is, organizational capability and internal infrastructure" (Luo, 2002: p. 190).

10.4 Global talent management as part of a global knowledge-management and capability-management process: the role of HR architectures

However, the examination of the role of, and delivery models used by, the corporate HR function in MNCs has been neglected in the IHRM literature, although it has received attention within the general HR strategy literature. The label of an "HR architecture" has been used by several US writers – including Dave Ulrich, Brian Becker, Barry Gerhart, Mark Huselid, Dave Lepak, Scott Snell, and Pat Wright – to explain how HR has to be delivered. This HR architecture is an organizational system that creates value. For Becker and Huselid (2006) the HR architecture refers to the combination of systems, practices, competences, and employee-performance behaviors that must be used in order to develop and manage the organization's strategic human capital. For them it is the whole system – the unique combination of the HR function's structure and delivery model, its HR practices and system, and the strategic employee behaviors that these create – that serves as the source of value creation. Multinational corporations use this HR architecture as a way of combining the necessary balance of coordination and control, integration of key service tiers and expert resources, and provision of access channels for delivery of service to end users, into an over arching "HR service-delivery model" (Evans, Pucik, and Björkman, 2010).

The choice of HR delivery model used to align HR operational functions with HR and business goals and objectives, ties international mobility into the broader HR strategy, but also reflects the potential constraint of administrative heritage. This choice of HR delivery model – and the internal infrastructure that it creates – is an organizational capability. This capability determines the organization's ability to respond effectively to changes in strategy – such as globalization and the global transfers of knowledge that globalization requires.

Sparrow (2012b) argues that the IHRM literature – and we also believe the GTM literature – needs to be seen as part of the broader global knowledge agenda and that we need to understand the ways in which the global HR architecture (including the GTM system) enables effective knowledge transfer, particularly with regard to the management of international mobility and GTM processes.

When analyzing the capabilities that are deemed necessary to support a knowledge-based enterprise, three integration mechanisms become important.

1. Knowledge acquisition and creation: generation of new knowledge fundamental to the long-term viability of the MNC.
2. Knowledge capture and storage: creation of an inventory of knowledge so the organization knows what knowledge it possesses, and where it resides. This requires the maintenance of current knowledge in usable form so that it remains valuable.
3. Knowledge flows/transfer and subsequent diffusion (vertically and horizontally within the organization and also across organizational boundaries): this enables the subsequent mobilization and flow of knowledge within the organization that creates knowledge-based value.

Global talent serves an important role in enabling this global knowledge management. The global integration of knowledge can only develop when organizations (or rather their talent) perceive, interpret, reconstruct, and communicate new information, and this requires that attention is given to the systems, structures, and cultures that are engineered through the actions of corporate human resource (CHR) functions. However, it has long been noted there has only been limited attention paid to the role of the CHR function in developing the strategies and practices, and roles, necessary to facilitate talent management on a global basis. This issue remains.

10.5 Four corporate HR roles in global talent management

Based on a review of the literature, Farndale, Scullion, and Sparrow (2010) found that the globalization of talent-management systems creates:

-   a need for new HR tools, methods, and processes
-   more attention to coordination systems to support global integration
-   an expansion of the territory that might legitimately be considered part of a GTM system
-   a series of unique but also interconnected corporate HR roles.

Building upon the arguments about capability from a global knowledge-management perspective outlined earlier in the chapter, organizations have to build a core competence – develop the ability – to transfer important capabilities globally. The building of this core competence requires a monitoring of the implementation of GTM policies and practices, an encouragement of an appropriate corporate culture, the establishment of supporting networks, and ensuring that all parts of the organization are sensitive to the needs of global mobility. The four roles, then, enabled the organization to create the necessary vertical integration between the strategy, business model, and organization structure, but also enabled horizontal integration between different strands of the global HR policy.

Farndale, Scullion, and Sparrow (2010) presented a conceptual model of GTM roles to explore how support for GTM strategies across the organization might be engendered and described four roles that may be adopted to facilitate GTM.

1. Champion of processes: developing and monitoring GTM practices and policies, strategy, and tools; ensuring these are implemented across the firm; monitoring GTM processes; and improving coordination of tools, techniques, and processes internally across functions.
2. Guardian of culture: ensuring a culture of mobility across the organization; incorporating values and systems in organizational strategies and activities to support global mobility of individuals; and breaking down silo mentalities that can exist between business divisions and geographic regions.
3. Manager of receptivity: encouraging the inflow and outflow of key talent across business entities; active management of key talent to ensure individuals are looked after; encouraging receiving units to manage diversity, careers, integration, and work–life balance; and encouraging sending units to share their talent for the good of the firm as a whole.
4. Network leadership and intelligence: developing appropriate networks inside and outside the organization to support the GTM process; being aware of developments in the internal and external labor market; mobilizing appropriate talent both internally and through external providers; and a sense of timing and context (sensitivity to what is going on at both local and global levels).

They argued, initially conceptually, that these four roles:

- are stable (regardless of the international context, changes in the external global context, or the organization's positioning on a centralization–decentralization continuum)
- are necessary for a firm to build a core competence of transferring capability – through talent – on a global basis.

Subsequent empirical investigation in two professional service firms examined these four roles (Sparrow, Farndale, and Scullion, 2013). They examined GTM processes in two case study firms from the financial and professional service sectors – sectors that provide highly specialized knowledge that facilitates the increasingly complex configuration and operation of global production networks. These firms, and the definition of talent within them, are driven by knowledge-based logics, creating value through their selection, development, and use of human capital on a global basis. However, in both sectors there are also important counter-globalization forces that result from three pressures: high levels of institutional embeddedness of corporate activities; the local nature of services provided; and sensitivity to the impact of the 2008 global financial services crisis. While the level of centralization was an important contingent variable for the four CHR roles, Sparrow, Farndale, and Scullion (2013) found that each of the four enabling CHR roles were used to achieve different goals. These goals were in turn a product of the level of GTM maturity the organization had in pursuing GTM strategies, and the needs of the business model.

They found that the *champion of processes* role, with its focus on monitoring GTM processes, was very important under a centralized system, but more limited under a decentralized system. The *guardian of culture* role focused on ensuring CHR support for creating a corporate culture of mobility across the firm by:

- incorporating values and systems to support global mobility of individuals throughout their career development into organizational strategies and activities (Brewster, Sparrow, and Harris, 2005)
- creating a "joined-up" approach to GTM across the whole organization (Gratton, 2005)
- breaking down silo mentalities between business divisions and geographic regions, the latter more challenging in the decentralized context (Scullion and Starkey, 2000).

The *manager of internal receptivity* role was most strongly evidenced under a decentralized system and was achieved by encouraging receiving units to manage diversity, careers, and integration, as well as encouraging sending units to share their talent for the good of the firm as a whole. Finally, the *network leadership and intelligence* role was important in a decentralized model but crucial under a centralized model. The political purpose to which network intelligence was directed included the building of local professional capability in GTM. The talent center of expertise (COE) had to weave connections with contiguous COEs, such as learning and development, creating "constellations" of connections between the talent specialists and others. In short, talent-management professionals had to use their social networks to forge a group of actors around any particular GTM issue, and through these networks create critical channels through which the policies could be "negotiated" to identify any new balance between the corporate HQ and local operations in the talent activities.

10.6 Global integration versus local responsiveness in the design of global talent management

One of the key issues in the practice of IHRM, then, is the need to manage the dual pressures of global integration and local responsiveness. This issue has been a central debate in the literature on human resource management within MNEs over the last two decades (Evans, Pucik, and Barsoux, 2002; Brewster, Sparrow, and Harris, 2005; Rosenzweig, 2006; Dickmann and Müller-Camen, 2006; Pudelko and Harzing, 2007; Björkman and Lervik, 2007; Farndale and Paauwe, 2007; Brewster, Wood, and Brookes, 2008; Farndale, Brewster, and Poutsma, 2008; Hartman, Feisel, and Schober, 2010; Chung, Bozkurt, and Sparrow, 2012; Festing *et al.*, 2012). This becomes especially critical to managing the complex problems of implementing talent-management systems in different countries (Farndale, Scullion, and Sparrow, 2010; Sparrow, Farndale, and Scullion, 2013).

Taylor, Beechler, and Napier (1996) identified three generic IHRM orientations at the corporate level of MNCs: exportive, whereby corporate HR actors attempt to transfer the parent company's HRM system to subsidiaries; adaptive, whereby they attempt to adapt subsidiary HRM system as much as possible to the local context; and integrative, in which "the best" approaches are sought from parent and subsidiary practices.

An organization's approach to GTM is largely defined by its corporate strategy and corporate structure, and whether operations are more centralized (globally integrated) or decentralized (locally responsive). Global talent-management strategies are also likely to vary as the organization passes through the various stages of the internationalization process. Scullion and Starkey (2000) argued that centralized firms have a greater need for coordination and integration of their international activities. They require greater central control over the mobility and careers of their international managers. They are therefore more likely to utilise a comprehensive set of GTM practices (e.g., management development, succession planning, career management, top-management rewards, and global mobility). However, where the business model is decentralized (often reflecting a multidomestic strategy) there is a weaker and more informal level of corporate control over GTM, and local operations decide their own approach.

The coordination of global transfers of managers and professionals tends to be more problematic in decentralized firms. There are tensions between the needs of the operating companies and the longer term strategic plans of the business. This is leading to increasing centralization of the management of this global mobility to improve control over developing the future leadership of the firm (Collings, Morley, and Gunnigle, 2008).

However, globalizing talent-management practices is very difficult. There are pragmatic problems of line of sight to all global talent and barriers against relocation – but for Minbaeva and Collings (2013) it is also based on a series of myths. Among these, they argue, while line managers are intimately involved in talent management, the global coordination of this activity necessitates a strong corporate HR role. Also, in a global context, a "position" approach to talent management rather than a "people" approach (see Chapter 2) becomes more important, but in order to understand the relative importance of these positions across countries, we need to know how they assist the implementation of a global strategy and what level of local and tacit knowledge is needed to be effective in the roles. Global talent management, through its focus on performance, assumes that there is a global consistency in performance evaluation – a very big assumption. It also assumes that there are relatively few barriers to international mobility, when we know there are many, and that high performance in one national context exports to other national contexts (which again from Chapter 2 is a questionable assumption). Finally, although Minbaeva and Collings (2013) do not say it, we can infer that organizations have to believe that investments in talent in one geography might create a different rate of return than in another because of the complex local labor market and institutional contexts that dampen or amplify the efforts of talented people. Rather than use the language of globally integrated and locally responsive, they also talk about the HR processes being core (relevant and necessary for all businesses) and differentiated (structured to meet the unique needs of specific businesses). To move on from these realities, they argue, we need to formulate theories "about (latent) mechanisms that can account for links among global strategy, GTM, core and differentiated architectures; the effectiveness of the implementation of GTM programmes; and global performance" (Minbaeva and Collings, 2013: p. 1772).

Recent studies, however, suggest that the way that corporate headquarters think about IHRM strategy and practices is very nuanced and complex.

1. Work by Edwards and colleagues has shown that complex patterns of transfer, negotiation, and combination of practice exist in the process of globalizing HRM (Edwards and Rees, 2008; Edwards and Tempel, 2010; Edwards, 2011; Edwards, Jalette, and Tregaskis, 2012).
2. Studies of Japanese multinational retail firms, both in their home country and in their subsidiaries in China, found that the way in which subsidiary HRM practices in MNCs were designed was too complex a phenomenon to be explained by the traditional standardization versus localization continuum (Gamble, 2010).
3. Chung, Sparrow, and Bozkurt (2014) found evidence of a hybridization approach in the globalization strategies of Korean MNCs, which involved careful choices of specific elements of HRM practices for global standardization, modification of global standards, or localization, in parent firms' approach to subsidiary HRM practices. Viable options were sought and selected from among the three orientations – global standardization, modification of standards, and pure localization – for each element of HRM practices.

4. Case studies examining HR globalization within Western MNCs make a distinction between standardization and optimization to capture the more nuanced and detailed approach MNCs adopt in their IHRM strategy. This has been seen in the globalization of HR at the functional level. At the element level Western MNCs reinforce this emerging view through the investigation of areas such as international recruitment (Sparrow, 2007), the evolution of international mobility functions (Sparrow, 2012a), and the development of global talent-management processes (Garavan, 2012; Sparrow, Farndale, and Scullion, 2013).

Standardization occurs when HRM processes designed at headquarters are applied to country operations either formally or tacitly based on the expectation of performance benefits, as seen by corporate headquarters (Martin and Beaumont, 2001). Optimization involves the discipline of adjusting a process based on multiple viewpoints so as to obtain a particular goal by setting or optimizing a specified set of parameters without violating some core constraints (Sparrow, Brewster, and Harris, 2004; Brewster, Sparrow, and Harris, 2005). Gamble (2010) similarly proposed the concept of "hybridization," which involved complex patterns of creating new management practices through simultaneous processes of highly selective adoption, transfer, and local adaptation.

In their study of a global bank and professional service firm, Sparrow, Farndale, and Scullion (2013) found that the global integration–regional responsiveness (GI–LR) balance varied for different components of GTM practice. For example, in the bank, although the leadership model that underpinned the definition of high potential was core, along with the measurement of potential, other components of GTM that surrounded this could vary across operations. So practices around the application of forced or shaped distribution to the core performance–potential matrix varied, along with the level of transparency around the attribution of talent status, the depth of vertical or horizontal segments to which talent processes were adapted, the design of career paths for talent, the use of coaching, and the ways in which talent processes were linked to resourcing or rewards.

For Sparrow, Farndale, and Scullion (2013) there were two key learning points from this.

1. The level of global integration could be seen to be based on successively deeper yardsticks: the need for explicit, mandated processes;

use of common language and calibration judgments; application of diagnostic explanatory and informational frameworks; achievement of educational outcomes, and actual behaviors.

2. At a micro-component level, for any GTM practice, different elements of that practice could be intentionally positioned at different levels on a GI–LR continuum.

The yardsticks used to create global integration or local responsiveness were applied differentially to different components that together constituted a particular GTM practice. Therefore organizations might arrive at a different GI–LR balance for each different aspect of their talent practice, such as the identification of potential, use of shaped distribution, leadership model that underpins attribution of talent, segments to which talent processes are applied, employment brand used for resourcing, or the values that underpin the brand. Even within a centralized and core talent process, there was huge latitude for variation in the components of practice that underpinned the core process.

Sparrow, Farndale, and Scullion's (2013) study suggests there are many interdependencies and complementarities between the four CHR roles in GTM. The roles are also contingent on strategic factors such as the business model and its level of centralization and decentralization, and subject to the impact of external context such as business crises. The GI–LR balance with regard to GTM is complex and varies on a component-by-component basis within each GTM practice. Therefore GTM strategy is highly embedded in the broader business structure, shifts in the direction of globalization within any particular business sector, and indeed also shifts in the epochs and episodes of internationalization. They argued that, in future, GTM research should be closely embedded in the strategic pathways of the firm.

10.7 Bringing the individual back into the equation

This linkage to the strategic context is clearly very important, but we end this chapter with a reminder that GTM research must also engage with the individuals who are deemed talent. It is not just the GTM function that is globalizing. It is also the people. Progress at both the functional and individual level has to be matched and aligned. Reflecting the observation in Chapter 2 that individuals have choices too in whether they will make the investments in their own career that might suit the organization's design, and that study of GTM needs to balance human-capital theory with approaches that capture individual motivations, Farndale *et al.* (2014) draw upon psychological contracting theory. They argue for a mutual-benefits perspective, as a more fruitful way of segmenting mobility populations. They note that the growing body of GTM literature that focuses on leveraging internal talent to address organizational goals pays little attention to the literature on expatriation assignments, which has emerged as an independent (though related) field of study on global mobility. This latter literature shows that there is variance emerging in the responses by MNCs to the GTM challenges they face. It focuses on the importance of expatriation assignments for MNCs and typically addresses their role in overcoming the lack of availability of management and technical skills in certain locations, meeting client demands, the need to control and coordinate operations locally (Collings and Scullion, 2012), the development of future managers and leaders (Javidan, Teagarden, and Bowen, 2010; Mendenhall *et al.*, 2012), the maintenance of trust in key foreign businesses, or their role in serving representational purposes (Li and Scullion, 2010).

However, the design of GTM systems solely around corporate needs and agendas has become more problematic. Organizations are given much more importance to alternative forms of international assignment such as short-term, commuter, and international frequent flyers (Collings, Scullion, and Morley, 2007; Collings *et al.*, 2010; Mayrhofer, Reichel, and Sparrow, 2012). There has also been a rise in the number of self-initiated expatriates (SIEs), defined as individuals who relocate voluntarily to a foreign country, without assistance, and are hired under a local, host-country contract (Biemann and Andresen, 2010; Vaiman, Scullion, and Collings, 2012; Al Ariss and Crowley-Henry, 2013). From an individual employee's perspective, there is now an equal, but different, variety of goals. These range from personal and career development (Baruch *et al.*, 2013), to a desire to follow family members to another country or a longing to experience the challenges of working overseas (Andresen, Biemann, and Pattie, 2013).

A significant challenge faced when managing this broadened set of internally mobile employees is that the competing needs, motivations, and goals of the organization's GTM function, and the individuals who may self-initiate their global mobility, needs to be understood. Organizations now have to balance both standardization and flexibility in their practices to achieve their GTM goals, both at the organization and individual levels. Global talent-management strategies now have to both accommodate *and* mutualize the greater individualization of arrangements being used to foster international mobility. HR policy makers now have to design and evolve more complex talent-management arrangements. They have to create a market around the management of talent and global mobility.

10.8 Conclusions and implications for practice

We have asked how do organizations manage the globalization of the talent management function itself? The answer lies in the way in which the activities of the GTM function are aligned with the broader strategic context of the organization – the different levels of internationalization that invariably exist across internal business divisions, the level of centralization and decentralization necessitated by the business model and structures, and the extent to which the GTM function is still operating transactionally – exporting people through assignments – or sees the movement of talent as just one element of a broader knowledge-management and capability-transfer strategy. In our discussion of centralization–decentralization within the structure – and the general trend toward centralization within GTM functions – we have built the argument that the business model typically brings with it the need for specialized knowledge, management through complex networks, a need for institutional embeddedness, and often the need to operate across relatively unique local markets. In some sectors these realities create a complex interplay between the level of centralization–decentralization that might be needed in a GTM system.

We see the properties of vertical and horizontal integration, mentioned earlier, as influencing whether global mobility is seen as either transactional or strategic, and they also create the opportunities for cross-work between talent functions, and the need to align talent-management practices with broader activity to do with organizational effectiveness or resourcing. Horizontal integration (the extent to which the business model requires significant integration across operating divisions) shapes the requisite levels of transfer of knowledge and individuals across businesses. Vertical (global) integration *within* businesses across the internal labor (talent) markets links GTM functions into the strategic pursuits of the firm.

We have also asked that when there are competing interpretations of talent management around the globe, yet strong pressures to converge around best practice, can we use notions of global integration and local responsiveness to signal the challenges faced by corporate functions in balancing their GTM practices? The answer is a qualified yes. Yes, to the extent that there must be some significant degrees of local responsiveness even in strategic talent practices. No, in that we argue that the assumption that the GI–LR dichotomy can be applied at the broad GTM system level – or HR architecture – seems to be inappropriate. We use the idea of micro-components to point out that surrounding any key GTM practices there is a range of associated conditions and applications to which the practice might be put that needs to be thought about holistically. If a GI–LR divide is to be used, it is best applied to each of the micro-components that together make the practice. We think the label optimization (or hybridization) might better describe what has to be done to GTM practices as they are used across different geographies.

We also asked how does or, perhaps more pointedly, how should, the corporate headquarters manage GTM? Here we have drawn attention to four corporate HR roles that become important. We argue that these roles together help create an organizational capability that assists in the globalization process. More recent empirical work has provided some guidance on how each of the four roles might be used, and their differential importance depending on whether the organization has a decentralized or centralized business model. The issue now is to expand such research into different business sectors and to better understand how each of the integration mechanisms that we have outlined operate, and with what performance benefits.

References

Al Ariss, A. and Crowley-Henry, M. (2013). Self-initiated expatriation and migration in the management literature. Present theorizations and future research directions. *Career Development International*, 18 (1), 78–96.

Andresen, M., Biemann, T., and Pattie, M. W. (2013). What makes them move abroad? Reviewing and exploring differences between self-initiated and assigned expatriation. *International Journal of Human Resource Management.* doi: 10.1080/09585192.2012. 669780.

Baruch, Y., Dickmann, M., Altman, Y., and Bournois, F. (2013). Exploring international work: types and dimensions of global careers. *International Journal of Human Resource Management*, 24 (12), 2369–93.

Becker, B. E. and Huselid, M. A. (2006). Strategic human resources management: where do we go from here? *Journal of Management*, 32, 898–925.

Biemann, T. and Andresen, M. (2010). Self-initiate foreign expatriates versus assigned expatriates: two distinct types of international careers? *Journal of Managerial Psychology*, 25 (4), 430–48.

Björkman, I. (2006). International human resource management research and institutional theory. In G. Stähl and I. Björkman (eds.) *Handbook of Research in International HRM*. Cheltenham, UK: Edward Elgar, pp. 463–74.

Björkman, I. and Lervik, J. E. (2007). Transferring HR practices within multinational corporations. *Human Resource Management Journal*, 17, 320–35.

Björkman, I., Barner-Rasmussen, W., Ehrnrooth, M., and Mäkelä, K. (2009). Performance management across borders. In P. Sparrow (ed.) *Handbook of International Human Resource Management*. Chichester: John Wiley and Sons, pp. 229–50.

Brewster, C., Sparrow, P. R., and Harris, H. (2005). Towards a new model of globalizing human resource management. *International Journal of Human Resource Management*, 16, 949–70.

Brewster, C., Wood, G., and Brookes, M. (2008). Similarity, isomorphism or duality? Recent survey evidence on the human resource management policies of multinational corporations. *British Journal of Management*, 19, 320–42.

Chung, C., Bozkurt, Ö., and Sparrow, P. R. (2012). Managing the duality of IHRM: unravelling the strategy and perceptions of key actors in South Korean MNCs. *International Journal of Human Resource Management*, 23, 2333–53.

Chung, C., Sparrow, P. R., and Bozkurt, O. (2014). South Korean MNEs' international HRM approach: hybridization of global standards and local practices. *Journal of World Business*. In press.

Collings, D. G. and Scullion, H. (2008). Resourcing international assignees. In M. Dickman, C. Brewster, and P. R. Sparrow (eds.) *International Human Resource Management: A European Perspective*. Abingdon: Routledge, pp. 87–106.

(2012). Global staffing: a critical review. In G. K. Stahl and I. Björkman (eds.) *Handbook of International Human Resource Management*. London, UK: Edward Elgar, pp. 141–57.

Collings, D. G., Scullion, H., and Morley, M. J. (2007). Changing patterns of global staffing in the multinational enterprise: challenges to the conventional expatriate assignment and emerging alternatives. *Journal of World Business*, 42 (2), 198–213.

Collings, D. G., Morley, M., and Gunnigle, P. (2008). Composing the top management team in the international subsidiary: qualitative evidence on international staffing in US multinationals in the Republic of Ireland. *Journal of World Business*, 43 (2), 197–212.

Collings, D. G., Scullion, H., and Dowling, P. J. (2009). Global staffing: a review and thematic research agenda. *International Journal of Human Resource Management*, 20 (6), 1253–72.

Collings, D. G., McDonnell, A., Gunnigle, A., and Lavelle, J. (2010). Swimming against the tide: outward staffing flows from multinational subsidiaries. *Human Resource Management*, 49 (4), 575–98.

Danielsen, T. and Molnar, L. (2007). The expatriate administrative structure: deciding what works best. *Benefits and Compensation International*, 36 (9), 1–4.

Dickmann, M. and Mills, T. (2009). The importance of intelligent career and location considerations: exploring the decision to go to London. *Personnel Review*, 39 (1), 116–34.

Dickmann, M. and Müller-Camen, M. (2006). A typology of international human resource management strategies and processes. *International Journal of Human Resource Management*, 17, 580–601.

Edwards, T. (2011). The nature of international integration and HR policies in multinational companies. *Cambridge Journal of Economics*, 35 (3), 483–98.

Edwards, T. and Rees, C. (2008). *International Human Resource Management: Globalisation, National Systems and Multinational Companies*. London: Financial Times/Prentice Hall.

Edwards, T. and Tempel, A. (2010). Explaining variation in the reverse diffusion of HR practices: evidence from the German and British subsidiaries of American multinationals. *Journal of World Business*, 45 (1), 19–28.

Edwards, T., Jalette, P., and Tregaskis, O. (2012). To what extent is there a regional logic in the management of labour in multinational companies? Evidence from Europe and North America. *International Journal of Human Resource Management*, 23, 2468–90.

Evans, P., Pucik, V., and Barsoux, J.-L. (2002). *The Global Challenge: Frameworks for International Human Resource Management*. New York, NY: McGraw-Hill/Irwin.

Evans, P., Pucik, V., and Björkman, I. (2010). *The Global Challenge: International Human Resource Management*. Boston, MA: McGraw-Hill.

Farh, L. C., Bartol, K. M., Shapiro, D. I., and Shin, J. (2010). Networking abroad: a process model of how expatriates form support ties to facilitate adjustment. *Academy of Management Review*, 35 (3), 434–54.

Farndale, E. and Paauwe, J. (2007). Uncovering competitive and institutional drivers of HRM practices in multi-national corporations. *Human Resource Management Journal*, 17 (4), 355–75.

Farndale, E., Brewster, C. J., and Poutsma, E. (2008). Co-ordinated vs. liberal market HRM: the impact of institutionalisation on multinational firms. *International Journal of Human Resource Management*, 19, 2004–23.

Farndale, E., Scullion, H., and Sparrow, P. R. (2010). The role of the corporate HR function in global talent management. *Journal of World Business*, 45 (2), 161–8.

Farndale, E., Pai, A., Sparrow, P. R., and Scullion, H. (2014). Balancing individual and organizational needs in global talent management: a mutual-benefits perspective. *Journal of World Business*. In press.

Festing, M., Knappert, L., Dowling, P. J., and Engle, A. D. (2012). Global performance management in MNEs: conceptualization and profiles of country-specific characteristics in China, Germany, and the United States. *Thunderbird International Review*, 54 (6), 825–43.

Gamble, J. (2010). Transferring organizational practices and the dynamics of hybridization: Japanese retail multinationals in China. *Journal of Management Studies*, 47, 705–32.

Garavan, T. (2012). Global talent management in science-based firms: an exploratory investigation of the pharmaceutical industry during the global downturn. *International Journal of Human Resource Management*, 23, 2428–49.

Gratton, L. (2005). Managing integration through cooperation. *Human Resource Management*, 44 (2), 151–8.

Gunnigle, P., Lavelle, J., and McDonnell, J. (2007). *Human Resource Practices in Multinational Companies in Ireland: a Large-Scale Survey*. Employment Relations Research Unit, University of Limerick.

Hartman, E., Feisel, E., and Schober, H. (2010). Talent management of western MNCs in China: balancing global integration and local responsiveness. *Journal of World Business*, 45 (2), 169–78.

Howe-Walsh, L. and Schyns, B. (2010). Self-initiated expatriation: implications for HRM. *International Journal of Human Resource Management*, 21 (2), 260–73.

Javidan, M., Teagarden, M., and Bowen, D. (2010). Managing yourself: making it overseas. *Harvard Business Review*, 88 (4), 109–13.

Kim, K., Park, J-H., and Prescott, J. E. (2003). The global integration of business functions: a study of multinational businesses in integrated global industries, *Journal of International Business Studies*, 34, 327–44.

Li, S. and Scullion, H. (2010). Developing the local competences of expatriate managers for emerging markets: a knowledge based approach. *Journal of World Business*, 45 (2), 190–6.

Luo, Y. (2002). Organizational dynamics and global integration. A perspective from subsidiary managers. *Journal of International Management*, 8, 189–215.

Mäkelä, K., Björkman, I., and Ehrnrooth, M. (2009). MNC subsidiary staffing architecture: building human and social capital within the organization. *International Journal of Human Resource Management*, 20 (6), 1273–90.

Malbright, T. (1995). Globalization of an ethnographic firm. *Strategic Management Journal*, 16, 119–41.

Martin, G. and Beaumont, P. (2001). Transforming multinational enterprises: towards a process model of strategic human resource management change. *International Journal of Human Resource Management*, 12, 1234–50.

Mayrhofer, W., Reichel, A., and Sparrow, P. R. (2012). Alternative forms of international working. In G. Stahl, I. Björkman, and S. Morris (eds.) *Handbook of Research into International Human Resource Management*, 2nd edn. London, UK: Edward Elgar, pp. 293–320.

Mellahi, K. and Collings, D. G. (2010). The barriers to effective global talent management: the example of corporate elites in MNCs. *Journal of World Business*, 45 (2), 143–9.

Mendenhall, M., Reiche, B. S., Bird, A., and Osland, J. S. (2012). Defining the "global" in global leadership. *Journal of World Business*. 47 (4): 493–503.

Meyskens, M., Von Glinow, M. A., Werther, W. B., and Clarke, L. (2009). The paradox of international talent: alternative forms of international assignments. *International Journal of Human Resource Management*, 20 (6), 1439–50.

Minbaeva, D. and Collings, D. G. (2013). Seven myths of global talent management. *International Journal of Human Resource Management*, 24 (9), 1762–76.

Pudelko, M. and Harzing, A.-W. (2007). Country-of-origin, localization, or dominance effect? An empirical investigation of HRM practices in foreign subsidiaries. *Human Resource Management*, 46, 535–59.

Rosenzweig, P. (2006). The dual logics behind international human resource management: pressures for global integration and local responsiveness. In G. Stahl and I. Björkman (eds.) *Handbook of Research in International Human Resource Management*. Cheltenham: Edward Elgar. pp. 36–48.

Scullion, H. and Collings, D. G. (2011). *Global Talent Management*. London: Routledge.

Scullion, H. and Starkey, K. (2000). In search of the changing role of the corporate human resource function in the international firm. *International Journal of Human Resource Management*, 11 (6), 1061–81.

Sparrow, P. R. (2007). Globalisation of HR at function level: four UK-based case studies of the international recruitment and selection process. *International Journal of Human Resource Management*, 18 (5): 144–66. (2012a). Globalizing the international mobility function: the role of emerging markets, flexibility and strategic delivery models. *International Journal of Human Resource Management*, 23 (12), 2404–27. (2012b). Global knowledge management and international HRM. In Stahl, G., Bjorkman, I., and Morris, S. (eds.) *Handbook of Research into International HRM*, 2nd edn. London: Edward Elgar, pp. 117–41.

Sparrow, P. R. and Hiltrop, J. M. (1997). Redefining the field of European human resource management: a battle between national mindsets and forces of business transition. *Human Resource Management*, 36 (2), 201–19.

Sparrow, P. R., Brewster, C., and Harris, H. (2004). *Globalizing Human Resource Management*. London: Routledge.

Sparrow, P. R., Farndale, E., and Scullion, H. (2013). An empirical study of the role of the corporate HR function in global talent management in professional and financial services firms in the global financial crisis. *International Journal of Human Resource Management*, 24 (9), 1777–98.

Stahl, G. K., Bjorkman, I., Farndale, E., *et al.* (2007). Global talent management: how leading multinationals build and sustain their talent pipeline. Faculty & Research Working Paper. Fontainebleau, France, INSEAD.

Stahl, G., Björkman, I., and Morris, S. (2012). *Handbook of Research in International Human Resource Management*, 2nd edn. Cheltenham: Edward Elgar.

Stroh, L. K., Black, J. S., Mendenhall, M. E., and Gregersen, H. B. (2005). *International Assignments: an Integration of Strategy, Research and Practice*. London: Lawrence Erlbaum.

Taylor, S., Beechler, S., and Napier, N. (1996). Toward an integrative model of strategic international human resource management. *Academy of Management Review*, 21, 959–85.

Vaiman, V., Scullion, H., and Collings, D. G. (2012). Talent management decision making. *Management Decision*, 50 (5), 925–41.

11 Strategic talent management: future directions

PAUL SPARROW, HUGH SCULLION,
AND IBRAIZ TARIQUE

11.1 Introduction: key learning points from the book

We complete this book by reviewing some of its key learning points, and summarizing the implications of these for the future development of practice and research. Chapter 1 provided a brief historical review of how the field emerged and developed and showed that while the field of strategic talent management is still very much in its infancy, it is becoming of growing significance to top managers as well as academics. We noted the range of recent special issues on the topic. It is also interesting to note that two out of the three most downloaded papers in 2013 from the *Journal of World Business* were about talent management. However, we also questioned what the contours of this new and emerging field will be, or should be.

In the opening chapters we asked a number of important questions about the emerging field of strategic talent management:

1. What do strategists think about the debates about talent management?
2. What should be the role of expert knowledge in the assessment of talent?
3. How should talent-management functions best think about strategic workforce planning and talent pipelines in an era of high levels of uncertainty?
4. How should the field of talent management best draw upon marketing concepts when articulating concepts such as employee-value propositions or employer brands?
5. How should organizations think about the strategic configuration of the talent-management practices that they need to put in place?

At the heart of these questions lies the reality that, by its very nature, strategic talent management must be a bridge field.

11.2 The creation of a bridge field

The field of strategic talent management is now taking shape with a very wide interdisciplinary basis. It is developing its own language. But as with any emerging field, it takes time for the best methodologies and models to emerge, and for researchers to learn what works, and what does not. Whether you are a practitioner wishing to integrate your talent activities across the range of management disciplines who wish to contribute to the debate, or an academic trying to shed some light on the underlying problems that practice will have to solve, it becomes clear from this book that you will need to widen your horizons and underlying knowledge base. A little knowledge is a dangerous thing, they say. HR professionals are being called upon to design strategic talent-management systems, and as such, are co-opting ideas from across a number of other management disciplines. They have borrowed ideas about resource portfolios and organizational capabilities from the field of strategy (which in turn invokes ideas about the management of strategic resources and organizational learning). They talk about talent pipelines and supply chain risks, which brings in ideas from the field of operations management. They talk about value propositions, brands that can be used to shape the employment experience, and market mapping – all ideas that originally come from the field of marketing.

If there is one contribution that we hope this book has made, it is to take us back to these cognate disciplines and understand how the ideas and concepts that we have borrowed really operate. If we are to manage through these ideas, let us be sure about their principles. Only then does it become clear whether we just need to borrow the *language* of strategy, operations, and marketing just to get an idea across, or whether we need to embed the *knowledge* of these fields into our practice as well. As we summarize later, the contributions in Chapters 2 to 7, all aimed at addressing this challenge of establishing a bridge field, should give HR practitioners and academics some pause for thought. When talent management is seen through the lenses of its cognate disciplines, some of its basic principles, practices, and theoretical underpinnings seem only half developed. The opening two chapters of the book showed that two theories have been dominant in this field – primarily human-capital theory with its arguments about talent as an investment on behalf of the firm – and to a much lesser extent expectancy theory with its portrayal of talent management as a two-way process requiring reciprocal investments from people in themselves on the return of investments. However, subsequent chapters have brought in the need for additional theoretical insights. From the field of strategy we have the resource-based view, from organizational learning we have the dynamic-capabilities perspective, from supply chain we have uncertainty and risk-management perspectives, from employer branding we have signalling theory and the demand–resources model of work engagement, from the fields of comparative management we have had reference to convergence theory, and the global integration–local responsiveness perspective.

At the beginning of the book we also laid out a second overarching development. This is the globalization of talent-management strategies. We argued that the talent-management agenda is increasingly driven by international dimensions, raising questions about the convergence–divergence of best practices across international operations, and the need for talent systems to accommodate the growth of emerging markets. We asked how can a talent-management function not only make itself more strategic, but how can it also globalize itself? How must it accommodate the competing dynamics of global integration and local responsiveness into the structures of the function?

We have argued that the contours of the field of strategic talent management are currently unclear. Chapter 2 showed how four different philosophies, or approaches, have come to dominate discussion of talent management. These can be called the people, practices, positions, and strategic-pools approaches. Each has helped to shape mainstream thinking in the area, but they are often presented as *competing* alternatives. We argued, however, that it was possible to reconcile when each philosophy should become more useful or dominant in the design of a talent system – they need not be seen as competing interpretations. Chapter 2 took each approach back to the debates on which it was based and showed that each was based on different sets of assumptions about how organizational effectiveness is created. Although a people perspective, with its fascination with "the war for talent" (Michaels, Handfield-Jones, and Axelrod, 2001), interest in elites and star talent, categorization of people across a matrix of high performance and high potential, has come to dominate much of the popular rhetoric, the chapter showed that few organizations in practice based the whole of their HR system on only one of the four perspectives we outlined. At the same time that they might be paying massive premiums for a handful of star managers, they are sending junior managers out to universities to attract graduate talent, and engaging in a wide spectrum of activity.

We also noted that notwithstanding the crucially important need for the use of some important and evidential HR analytics, talent management, at least as practiced by HR professionals, remains an artform, not a science. Indeed, Chapter 2 argued that it might need to remain an artform, at least until the world of practice takes up some of the more fundamental disciplines laid out in this book. Managers currently balance competing demands and priorities depending on the circumstances their firm faces. Although often based on imperfect information, they combine different ideas about talent management into their HR system, trading off priorities. Chapter 2 surfaced both the explicit and the hidden assumptions that were associated with each perspective on talent management. It raised some key critiques of the field, such as debates about whether it is individual stars or teams and systems that most impact organizational effectiveness, or whether elite versus egalitarian approaches are best. It identified the component practices that were most often associated with a talent-management strategy.

Chapter 2 also raised the importance of the question of "talent for what?" It argued that ultimately organizations have to make two bellwether judgments about the knowledge possessed by talent: is the individual capable of high-quality strategic thought; and does the "capital" that they possess enable them to make a potential contribution to value creation? This in turn raises questions about the sorts of competences that should be assessed by organizations, and the sorts of data about people that talent-management systems should be capturing. Chapter 2 also asked that we put the "strategy" back into talent management.

11.2.1 Lessons from the field of strategy

Part II of the book developed a number of important bridges to cognate academic fields. The first bridge that needs to be developed further is between talent management and the field of strategy. Chapters 2 and 3 made this evident. Importantly, by bringing in notions from the field of strategy, such as business models, Chapter 2 developed a contingency framework to show when the four different talent-management philosophies – people, practices, positions, and strategic pools – should each move more center stage within a talent strategy. Also, by drawing upon research on the problems of strategic leadership and the natural limitations of strategic decision makers, it called for a more collective perspective to be taken on talent management and strategic insight. It asked the question "what really makes a manager talented?" and in answering this, highlighted the importance of four different types of capital that became important. The bottom line of this analysis was that talent is forged uniquely within organizations, making export across organizations potentially risky. It argued that talent managers should focus less on just identifying talent, and more on getting effective brokerage out of the talent data they possess. They should focus less on the *talent* and more on the *management* side of the phrase *talent management*, i.e., by getting talent to talk to each other. HR functions need to proactively manage the talent data and treat talent systems as a "distributed capability system."

In similar vein, in Chapter 3, Cliff Bowman and Martin Hird picked up on the challenge we set to bring strategy back into assessment of what makes individuals talented. In outlining what strategists think about the debates about talent management, they presented a critique of many of the assumptions made by talent-management practitioners – especially those who adopt an elite model. They surfaced many of the key assumptions that we make about talent management, and then, by drawing upon research from the field of strategic management and the understanding it has developed around a resource-based view of the firm, they questioned whether it is really possible for organizations to actually "manage" talent. In examining how value is really created, they pointed out that the most valuable and firm-specific capabilities to which talent contribute are more easily built rather than bought. Moreover, organizational capabilities are also the result more of the collective interactions and interconnections between talent. Despite these words of caution, the chapter, however, argued that we can improve practice. It built on the strategic critique of practice by presenting six principles that should guide future changes to practice.

11.2.2 Lessons from the fields of organization learning and innovation

The second bridge that needs to be developed further is between talent management and the fields of organizational learning and innovation.

When Chapter 2 raised the "talent for what?" question and noted the importance of what we called "business model capital" – the intellectual understandings of the sort of organizational performance that is needed – this raised important questions about the role of expert knowledge in the assessment of talent. These were picked up in Chapter 4 by Greg Linden and David J. Teece. They presented another critique on practice. They argued that it gives far too much importance to the notion of general management potential and underplays the value of expert knowledge. This creates two challenges for practice.

1. Talent has to bring to bear a broader understanding of the firm's strategy, capabilities, and potential.
2. Expert talent needs to be managed and kept stimulated in quite different ways to general management talent.

The competitive advantage of organizations in high-talent industries is increasingly rooted both in the stock of experts they can access, but also in the organizational capabilities that such talent can harness. They made the case that in order to understand whether talent have appropriate strategic understanding and ability, we should look to research from the fields of organizational learning, strategy, and innovation management. Cutting across these fields is the idea of dynamic capabilities, they picked up on the ideas from the resource-based view of the firm articulated by Cliff Bowman and Martin Hird, and explained how it can be developed through an understanding of the dynamic-capabilities framework to identify two different categories of experts – the literati and numerate, and the entrepreneurial managers – who should be managed in talent systems. They also reaffirmed, as we have argued in Chapter 1, that there are risks in relying on a particular talented individual, especially if those talents do not translate into a set of replicable internal routines inside the organization.

11.2.3 Lessons from the field of operations management

The third bridge that needs to be developed further is between talent management and the field of operations management. In Chapter 5 Joseph R. Keller and Peter Cappelli built on another type of risk. Talent-management practitioners face a challenge. Their traditional workforce-planning models are based on assumptions of predictability, stability, and control when forecasting demand for talent and managing the pipelines to resource talent. These assumptions do not hold in an environment characterized by uncertainty in supply and demand. Consequently two fundamental questions need to be addressed.

1. How do organizations ensure a sufficient supply of human capital when both demand and supply are uncertain?
2. What are the different human-capital sourcing strategies available to firms, and when should each be used?

To design more appropriate talent-management systems, and in seeking a primary mechanism through which human resource management can affect the performance of the organization, they argued, practitioners must look to ideas from outside HRM. They need to understand the conceptual base of, and ideas from, the field of operations management, specifically about the efficiency, reliability, and responsiveness of supply chains. They made the case that a supply-chain perspective is a natural fit for advancing understanding about strategic talent management. Talent management is fundamentally concerned with anticipating the need for human capital and setting out plans to meet it. It is about finding the best ways to combine internal and external sourcing – development and hiring – in order to meet estimated demand in ways that minimize any costs associated with an oversupply or undersupply of human capital. They traced some of the historical experiences from which talent-management practices emerged, along with the early and ultimately redundant approaches taken to strategic workforce planning, and caution that history may be about to repeat itself. Talent-management practice in reality still tends to focus either on reactive hiring or internal development, but they argued there is a need to learn how to combine these approaches. They teased out the supply- and demand-side uncertainties that surround talent systems and demonstrate the mismatch costs that typically result. Chapter 5 then outlined what the *management* of talent must really be about. They argue that building an understanding of the alternative risk and uncertainty strategies that enable better management of reliability and responsiveness, through mitigation and contingency.

Making links back to the resource-based view of the firm outlined in Chapter 3, J. R. Keller and Peter Cappelli made the case that the ability to capture the full benefit of talent-sourcing strategies is greatest when supported by a complementary set of organization capabilities. These are capabilities – to do with knowledge sharing, HR analytics, and information management systems – that the talent-management function must master. They argued that in this endeavor, practice might be ahead of theory, believing that empirical research in strategic human resources and related fields has been much more cautious in embracing such an approach. However, the logic of supply-chain management must be used to improve talent management within organizations.

11.2.4 Lessons from the field of marketing

The fourth bridge that needs to be developed further is between talent management and the field of marketing. Chapter 6 by Graeme Martin and Jean-Luc Cerdin, as with Chapter 5, also took as its starting point the challenge of managing talent pipelines. It is clear that the field of talent management has expanded the role and contribution of HRM functions, but this also brings in a language from other related management disciplines – notably marketing. How should the field of talent management best draw upon these concepts when articulating concepts such as employee-value propositions or employer brands? This raises some important questions. First, have HRM professionals, in co-opting ideas like these, truly understood the underlying marketing research – have the ideas been transposed sensibly? Second, once you begin to import ideas about brand and draw upon marketing and communications expertise, where should these new multidiscipline talent-management professionals best sit in the organization – does it make sense to site a talent-management function still within HRM structures? Third, once you accept notions of employer brand, how do you work these ideas through into the longer term career management of talent?

Chapter 6 picks up on the notion of employer brands – which the authors defined as the ability of such brands to embody high-quality employment experiences and organizational identities that talent are happy to engage with and promote. The chapter made it clear that, broadly as a result of the global financial crisis, these ideas, originally applied to talent pipelines and the attraction of talent from outside the organization, have now been translated into ideas about the internal management of talent, the internal engagement of talent, and the need to address this engagement of talent through much better management of their career aspirations.

What is happening, they argued, is that as organizations begin to think much more seriously about how they sustain corporate reputations, they need to shift the focus between creating brand *differentiation*, which marks their organization as being different from others and creates a value proposition based on this differentness, toward creating organizational *legitimacy*.

Organizations must now tread carefully as they map early thinking about branding into the more difficult to navigate area of corporate reputation. As reputation, charisma, and authenticity – either of organizations as a whole or their leadership talent – become important, talent-management practitioners need to draw upon some new ideas to manage this new focus of talent-management practice.

Building on the arguments in Chapter 2 that much of the early practice of talent management – especially discussion of ideas about the need to present talent with an employee-value proposition but also of course the notion that a talent-management strategy can be aided by the development of an employer brand – had co-opted ideas from the field of marketing, Graeme Martin and Jean-Luc Cerdin introduced ideas from signalling theory – an idea that originated in the field of information economics – and employee-engagement theory – originating from the field of organizational psychology – to build a model that helps us think about the management of employment brands.

They identified the need to now link models of how employer brands are created and managed authentically, into the management of careers. They were critical of much of the rhetoric coming from HR practitioners linking talent management and employer branding, arguing it has very little chance of being regarded as authentic by employees on the ground. They also moved the book into important international dimensions, by demonstrating the challenges of managing employer brands in an increasingly global context.

11.2.5 *Configuring a talent-management system*

Having shown throughout Part II of the book that a more strategic talent-management agenda requires that practitioners think more deeply about the underlying and cross-disciplinary models and theories – such as the resource-based view of the firm and dynamic capabilities from the fields of strategic management, organizational learning and innovation management, and signalling and work engagement theory from the fields of branding, reputation management, and organizational psychology, Part II ended by asking how should organizations think about the configuration of talent-management practices that they need to put in place?

In Chapter 7 Ibraiz Tarique and Randall Schuler raised two fundamental challenges that must be dealt with when asking this question:

- how do organizations *configure* a talent-management system?
- how do they *align* this configuration of policies and practices to the broader HR and business strategy?

They answered these questions by concentrating on four generic processes of talent attraction, retention, development, and mobilization (the planning for and positioning of talent). In the context of the need to manage talent on a global basis, they pointed out that there are five different interpretations of global talent management (GTM). We discussed some of these different interpretations in Chapter 2. They argued that talent processes by default concentrate on those individuals who have high-value human capital, or the potential to develop it. There are multiple configurations of practice that can be engineered across these four generic processes. There are also different theoretical assumptions, derived from ideas such as high-performance work systems, employee differentiation, human-capital theory, and portfolio models of performance potential. There is a specific set of HRM policies and practices for such individuals that need to be aligned into a single talent strategy, managed by a dedicated function within HR. They discussed the differences between the HRM strategy and the talent strategy, and used this to identify four different types of talent strategy. Chapter 7 investigated the issues surrounding the formation and alignment of talent-management strategies. It proposed both a framework of generic talent practices and how they must be aligned, and a typology that draws upon different underlying perspectives that have influenced thinking about talent management to identify four separate strategies that might be pursued. The framework and typology represent a fundamental first step toward future theory building in the field of talent management. However, they also noted that there is a fundamental philosophical choice that has to be made by any talent function once they are operating on a global basis. Do we assume there is such a thing as best practices when we try and manage the talent strategy on a global basis, or do we believe that the problems of convergence and divergence in IHRM practices, also apply to the talent system? The regional studies that Ibraiz Tarique and Randall Schuler introduced in Chapter 7 generally argued that there are different conceptions of talent-management practice across these regions. Finally, Chapter 7 laid out some of the developments in talent management when seen in a global context. These global developments formed the focus of Part III of the book.

11.3 Globalizing the strategic talent-management field

11.3.1 Beyond simple ideas about convergence or divergence of talent-management practice

In Chapter 8 John W. Boudreau and Edward E. Lawler II made it clear that we need to move beyond simplistic ideas about global convergence or divergence of practice in the study of talent management. They looked at the strategic context in the largest emerging market – that of China – through comparison of practices with those in the United States. They pointed out that there is limited evidence to support the idea of convergence around best practices and highlighted that a two-speed system still operates in China, whereby a small number of firms have highly sophisticated systems, while a much larger proportion has only very basic HR systems. Chinese HR leaders are less involved in strategy than are US HR leaders. The chapter brought in important contingencies from strategy – such as whether the firm operates as a bureaucracy, low-cost operator, global competitor, innovator, or through sustainability. These different strategies are strongly associated with the degree to which HR engages in strategic activities and spends time on strategy. Chapter 8 made it clear that the predominant Western view implies that if HR "merely" delivers services, without a strong connection to strategy, there is little value. However, differences in where HR really makes its most "pivotal" contribution may vary across regions and also with the evolutionary stage of organizations and HR. The findings showed that when thinking about talent management in a Chinese context, the mechanisms through which talent-management investments might affect organizational outcomes will be different, at least until Chinese HR functions and leaders play a more prominent role. The chapter, however, also showed that Western HR functions still have a tendency to over-estimate their contribution – what they call the problem of "stubborn traditionalism" where the evolution of the HR profession is slower than often perceived, and possibly slower than needed for the function to retain its relevance. It raised the intriguing possibility that Chinese HR management might evolve with a lighter emphasis on HR's strategic role, possibly adopting a model in which leaders outside of HR are more accountable for understanding the connection between their talent and strategy, and formulating talent strategies to fit their current and future challenges.

11.3.2 Tracking the talent challenges in emerging markets

Then in Chapter 9 Jonathan Doh, Richard Smith, Stephen Stumpf, and Walter Tymon looked at the challenges of regional patterns in the emerging markets of India and China. They argued that growth in emerging markets has considerable implications for talent-management strategies. There is both a changing balance of economic power from developed to developing countries and a new geographical demography, giving rise to the potential for enormous talent pools. There is still an imbalance for scarce skills and this continues to drive competition for needed skills. The chapter reviewed the talent-management challenges in India and China and tracked the evolution of talent practices in the countries. It focused on how rapid economic growth is creating pressures for more formalized and institutionalized talent practices, side by side with the need to be responsive to the unique social and cultural settings of these countries. The chapter outlined demographic challenge and trends toward more skill specialization fueled by foreign direct investments in R&D centers, advanced technical design centers, and centers of expertise. It put to right popular misconceptions about educational development and points out that China and India have a long way to go in terms of catching up to the United States, Europe, and Japan. Despite the need to understand the different strategic evolution pathways of HR functions noted in Chapter 8, Chapter 9 argued there is evidence that increasing convergence of HRM standards continues in these regions as MNEs bring Western practices into developing countries. Key differences, however, persist – HR practices in Southeast Asia continue to mix and integrate the more formal "hard" systems in place in the developed countries, with more ambiguous and less structured programs indicative of the

Asian cultural experience. So, for example, the attention to employee-value propositions and approaches to diversity management inherent in Western conceptions of talent management are not yet evidenced in China and India.

11.3.3 *Understanding how to globalize the talent-management function*

In Chapter 7 Ibraiz Tarique and Randall Schuler showed that there are different philosophies about global best practice and divergence, and that the different practices under planning, attraction, development, and retention need to be aligned vertically to the both the overarching HR strategy and the business strategy. In the last of the issues-based chapters Paul Sparrow, Elaine Farndale, and Hugh Scullion built on this proposition in Chapter 10 by looking at the challenges faced by organizations – and specifically their corporate headquarters and international mobility functions – in their attempts to globalize their HR architecture. They asked, if there are competing interpretations of talent management around the globe, yet strong pressures to converge around best practice, can we use notions of global integration and local responsiveness to signal the challenges faced by corporate functions in balancing their global talent-management practices? They argued there were four stable roles needed to engender this vertical and horizontal integration, regardless of the international context. Organizations had to build a core competence – develop the ability to transfer important capabilities globally. This required a monitoring of the implementation of GTM policies and practices, encouraging an appropriate corporate culture, establishing supporting networks, and ensuring that all parts of the organization are sensitive to the needs of global mobility.

Chapter 10 raised debates about centralization or decentralization, noting a general trend toward centralization. It argued that a core pressure on global talent management is the need to deliver a degree of vertical (global) integration *within* businesses across the internal labor (talent) markets, between the strategy, business model, and structure through to the talent-management practices. But there is also a need for horizontal integration across operating divisions in order to shape requisite levels of transfer of knowledge and individuals across businesses. These properties of vertical and horizontal integration influenced whether global mobility was seen as either transactional or strategic, and also created the opportunities for cross-work between talent functions, and the need to align talent-management practices with broader activity to do with organizational effectiveness or resourcing.

Chapter 10 argued that a number of factors make the use of a centralization–decentralization axis overly simple in the field of global talent management. A range of factors created a complex interplay between the levels of centralization or decentralization, such as the pursuit of different business models, or different levels of evolution of the same business model, the need for specialized knowledge, the pursuit of international operations through complex networks, and the need for operations to be embedded in local institutional or unique local markets.

Chapter 10, in its observation that in the financial services sector firms were de-globalizing their talent management, and its note that some of the investments in emerging markets by Western firms may potentially be reversed, also made it clear that we must beware assuming that the globalization of talent-management systems is an inevitable development, or that it will run smoothly.

11.4 Conclusion: future research directions

Where does this leave us? We believe there is a clear direction now set for future research and practice. We end with three sets of conclusions, the first commenting on future research directions triggered by the challenges of emerging markets, the second signalling some future cross-disciplinary bridges to be built beyond the ones examined in this book, and the third commenting on some general developments that need now to be made.

11.4.1 The challenges of talent management in emerging markets

Notwithstanding the potential for disruptive events to lessen the pace at which organizations will globalize their talent-management systems, the importance of the emerging markets, shown in Chapters 8 and 9, can also be illustrated by the forecast that over the next two decades the combined gross national product of emerging markets will overtake that of the currently mature economies (Hoskisson *et al.*, 2000) resulting in a major shift in the center of gravity of the global economy away from the developed to the emerging economies (Horwitz and Mellahi, 2009), which has major implications for approaches to human capital and, more specifically, talent management. As well as the emerging markets attracting very large amounts of foreign direct investment (Tymon, Stumpf, and Doh, 2010), there has also been a significant growth of multinational companies (MNCs) headquartered in the emerging markets, particularly in India and China. Yet despite the increased national-level focus on skills development, talent shortages remain a real concern in these countries (Shi and Handfield, 2012) and firms increasingly look to overseas markets to attract talent (Lane and Pollner, 2008).

However, future research should engage not just with the Indian and Chinese contexts, but also other emerging markets such as the Central and Eastern Europe (CEE) region, which tends to be under-researched (some exceptions include Hartmann, Feisel, and Schober, 2010; Tymon, Stumpf, and Doh, 2010; Vaiman and Holde, 2011; Skuza, Scullion, and McDonnell, 2013). The increasing mobility of people across geographical and cultural boundaries has emerged as a key factor influencing the nature of the talent-management challenge in some emerging markets resulting in a serious brain drain that contributed to the shortages of skilled labor (Tung and Lazarova, 2006).

Recent research has pointed toward talent-management practices having positive effects on employee and company performance in Western economies; however, there is a need for more research on this relationship in emerging market economies (Parker *et al.*, 2003; Skuza, Scullion, and McDonnell, 2013). Future research should examine whether 'Western' talent-management practices will yield similar outcomes in the emerging markets while recognizing that emerging markets are not a homogeneous group and vary in terms of stages of economic development, regulatory environments, educational and skill levels, as well as national cultures (Tymon, Stumpf, and Doh, 2010). Recent research suggests that talent-management challenges are more acute and more complex in the emerging markets (Yeung, Warner, and Rowley, 2008) and that managerial practices are far from converging with Western models (Skuza, Scullion, and McDonnell, 2013). Talent management in many emerging economies is a relatively new concept and the limited research to date is largely focused on Western MNC subsidiaries that have taken the lead in talent-management initiatives (Vaiman and Holde, 2011).

Even following the global financial crises, the focus on talent management has continued and talent shortages in India and China are well documented (Tymon, Stumpf, and Doh, 2010), but talent shortages are also acute in other emerging markets such as the CEE countries with Bulgaria, Poland, and Romania experiencing difficulties in filling vacancies due to lack of available talent (ManpowerGroup, 2012; Skuza, Scullion, and McDonnell, 2013). Further research on talent management is needed on other emerging markets, other than the large BRIC economies of China and India, such as the so called Next-11 group (Goldman Sachs, 2007). This grouping comprises Bangladesh, Egypt, Indonesia, Iran, South Korea, Mexico, Nigeria, Pakistan, and the Phillipines, Turkey, and Vietnam. The N11 group of countries shows even more variability in terms of size, performance, and potential than among the BRICS (Vaiman and Collings, 2013). This highlights the need for further talent-management research in different national contexts.

Further research is required on the key barriers to the implementation of talent management in the emerging markets as in these countries talent management is a relatively new concept practiced mainly by MNCs and is still rarely implemented in domestic organizations (Horváthová and Durdová, 2011; Skuza, Scullion, and McDonnell, 2013). In particular, future research must examine the difficulties of adapting Western talent-management frameworks to the emerging markets (Skuza, Scullion, and McDonnell, 2013). Further research is required on how domestic talent strategy links in with the overall global strategy in the specific context of the emerging markets as this has received little attention in the literature. A key challenge facing many firms in emerging markets is their attempt to transform traditional personnel activities into strategic HRM approaches, and the lack of progress in this direction in some emerging markets is a major constraint on the emergence of talent management (Vaiman and Holde, 2011).

We also call for further research on strategic talent management in a wider range of organizations and industries. To date our understanding of talent management is largely based on MNEs (Mellahi and Collings, 2010; Sparrow, Farndale, and Scullion, 2013) and professional service organizations (Vaiman and Collings, 2013). There is little empirical research on talent management in SMEs despite their importance to many economies and recent research highlights the distinctive nature of the talent challenges in these type of organizations (Valverde, Scullion, and Ryan, 2013; Festing, Shäffer, and Scullion, 2013). Similarly there is a dearth of research on talent management in the voluntary and not-for-profit sectors and future research could examine the nature of talent-management issues and problems in this particular context (van den Brink, Fruytier, and Thunnissen, 2012). Finally the role of women in talent management has surprisingly been largely unexplored and we suggest the need for further research on female talent in both advanced and emerging markets (Hewlitt and Rashid, 2010).

11.4.2 Forging the next set of linkages: lessons from the field of economic geography?

The second set of conclusions relate to as-yet underexplored academic bridges. Building on from the previous discussions about strategic talent management acting as an important "bridge" field, we believe that in addition to the four bridges we highlighted, there would also be value in identifying some other links that have not been picked up in the book. An obvious bridge to explore is the link between talent management and economic geography, which represents a fifth important bridge to be built. The work of economic geographers, previously little mentioned in the IHRM literature, brings to bear a number of important strategic considerations that have a bearing on questions about centralization and decentralization in talent management. They have an understanding of how organizations deal with the mapping of geographical resources and have insights into the spatial distribution of such resources, and how global resources may be exploited and developed. They seem now to be bringing these insights to the analysis of talent management. A number of important studies have examined how labor markets operate across geographies. However, there is as yet little bridging between fields. Both international HRM researchers, and HR practitioners, are on the whole blind to the findings and insights that exist in these related fields, yet they offer the opportunity of important insights with important lessons for practice.

For example, Faulconbridge *et al.* (2009b) argue that in the new knowledge and weightless economies, claims made about the "war for talent" and global labor shortages tend to oversimplify how elite labor markets actually operate and are governed. Their study of 21 executive search firms and headhunter firms showed how they have become important intermediaries in elite labor markets – they have manufactured themselves a position of power. They both govern and regulate the management of global talent through their choice of global search locations, and can use their power to promulgate certain definitions of talent to determine who and what is classified as talent, and are admitted to the networks that provide access for executive positions, leading to a geographically prescribed "new boys network" within elite labor markets.

Important examples of work that could easily inform the study of global talent management would be: the work of Koser and Salt (1997) on the geography of highly skilled international labor; Beaverstock (2004) and Williams (2007) on knowledge management, tacit knowledge exchange across talent, and expatriation; Maskell, Bathelt, and Malmberg (2006) on building global knowledge pipelines; Beaverstock (2005) and Ewers (2007) on the creation of markets in global cities for high-skilled migrants; Jones (2007) and Faulconbridge (2007) on the globalization of law firms; Millar and Salt (2008) on the movement of global expertise; Faulconbridge *et al.*, (2009b) on the role of executive search firms in elite labor markets; Faulconbridge *et al.* (2009a) on international mobility through business travel; Salt and Wood (2012) on the impact of the global financial crisis on global talent mobility; and Currah and Wrigley (2004), Coe and Lee (2006), Christopherson (2007) on strategic locational decisions across a range of globalizing sectors.

Such work is important because it challenges some of the cosier assumptions that we might be tempted to make about the trajectory of globalization.

11.4.3 General research opportunities in talent management

Finally, having summarized the key learning across the various contributions to this book, we end with a third set of conclusions about the state of the field and its future evolution.

• It is surprising how narrow is the evidence base we have to work from. Most of the empirical studies on global talent management are based on descriptive statistics and reliance on trends – there is a need to move beyond descriptive statistics. Several studies have used qualitative methodologies such as interviews and case studies to collect information from individuals involved in talent management. These are informative, but we now need such case studies to be conducted against more controlled strategic contexts, and drawing upon a broader base of stakeholders beyond those responsible for the design of talent systems. Where claims have been made about potential returns on investment, the few studies that have been conducted in this area rely on correlation analysis. Little research, beyond the anecdotal, exists on the "effectiveness" of strategic talent management. Research is needed to determine the extent to which talent management systems relate to HR, financial, and market-based outcomes. In future, more theory-driven research is needed to examine the causal chain that explains how talent-management systems should relate to organizational effectiveness and proximal and distal performance outcomes.

- There are some important research agendas now emerging around the globalization agenda. Stahl *et al.* (2012: 30) note: "many organizations are moving toward greater integration and global standards while simultaneously continuing to experience pressure to adapt and make decisions at local levels." In recent years we have seen the emergence in some organizations of the chief global talent management officer (CTMO) to coordinate and facilitate organization-wide global talent management practices. More research is needed to examine this new role. Similarly, at the heart of global talent management has been the assumption that organizations should treat highly valuable and most talented employees differently. Thus it is important for organizations to identify who the talented individuals are, done for example by dividing employees into "A," "B," and "C" player categories and providing different global talent-management practices for each. Is this approach to managing talent universal, and applicable beyond Western multinationals?

- Even in using such language and asking such questions, some would argue that they do not fit the reality of the organizations they wish to study or need to influence. They would argue that strategic talent management thinking has been overly led by North American scholarship. We believe that while this North American scholarship has advanced our understanding considerably and provides an important base for academic inquiry, it is now important to integrate different international perspectives to make the study of talent management truly comparative, and to examine talent-management issues from different international perspectives, including those of Europe, Asia-Pacific, and the Middle East.

- However, in incorporating a more comparative perspective on the field, strategic talent-management researchers will need to ask some difficult questions of their comparative management colleagues. We cannot simply import ideas honed by the study of other phenomena to organizational practices that are themselves evolving and attempting to be innovative. Do existing convergence and divergence frameworks explain the diffusion of talent-management practices across regions and countries sufficiently well enough? We suspect that the complex interplay between business logics and new models for globalization means the answer might be no. Clearly, an important area of research is to explore issues related to designing and configuring global talent-management systems and the issues involved with the implementation of global talent-management systems in different contexts, such as across regions and specific countries. Moreover, as attitudes toward work are changing dramatically in some countries, will this impact the opportunities for global talent management?
- Future research should also focus particular attention on global talent-management issues at the macro level. As suggested by Schuler, Jackson, and Tarique (2011), it will be useful to examine how macro factors such as globalization, demographic changes, and economic cycles affect an organization's capability to ensure just the right amount of talent, at the right place, at the right price, and at the right time.
- As this book demonstrates, talent management has come a long way from just managing the elites. There is now a clear recognition that its activities must cut across all employees. This is an important development – it suggests that a primary unit of analysis in talent-management thinking is the appropriate employee group that is considered to be the "talent group or segment" – everything else then follows.
- Once we shift the unit of analysis to employees and employee groups, an interesting set of areas for future research emerges. For example, research is needed to further improve our knowledge of what it is that makes such talent segments talented in the first place,

how such segments are identified, and how they may be formed and developed. We need to examine the career paths or career progressions of such talented individuals or segments. What is the relative contribution made by their human, social, reputational, and business-model capital? To what extent and for how long can an individual sustain his or her talents to remain in the organization's talent pool? The same questions apply to employee groups that are seen to have value as strategic talent. There is also a need, as argued above, to move gender to a more central position in the talent-management debate and to develop links between diversity management and talent management.

- There is a need to move beyond the continuing calls for defining global talent management – it includes a wide collection of philosophies, tools, and techniques – and many definitions reflect the interests and educational traditions of the definer. In addition, we focus on defining the boundaries of the field, developing a number of important cross-disciplinary bridges, and strengthening our understanding of the different insights involved. Applying these lenses to the study of talent management will also open up an interesting set of studies. For example, looking at the bridge between talent management and strategic management, the resource-based view of the firm clearly has the potential to become a core theoretical anchor. Future research can use the resource-based view to determine both the antecedents and outcomes associated with the dynamics capability perspective.

- By thinking about talent management from a capabilities or knowledge-management perspective, attention could be given to important mechanisms discussed in these literatures such as the role of talent through the lens of knowledge acquisition, integration, recombination, and obsolescence. It could also be used to ask more fundamental questions about the strategic value (or otherwise) of key employee groups, and to think about better ways of creating a collective capability across talent segments.

- Looking to the bridge between talent management and operations management, it is evident that talent planning has become a critical component of talent-management systems. Future longitudinal research is needed to investigate the longitudinal relationships between talent supply and talent demand. Looking to the bridge between talent management and marketing, there is considerable research on corporate/employer reputation. An interesting line of research would be to examine the notion of "talent-management reputation," that is how organizations manage their most talented employees. It is possible that an organization ranks higher on talent-management reputation while being lower on organizational reputation. What would constitute such a reputation, and can such functional reputation be harnessed to good effect?

It is clear that thought leadership within the field of strategic talent management has come from two groupings, academics and practitioners, with not that much dialogue between the two. Research and practice need to be shaped and facilitated by the transfer of knowledge and agendas from academics to practitioners, and vice versa. As the book demonstrates, much practice seems to be ill conceived and under attack, yet it also brings with it the potential for innovative ways of managing. For academics, there is the possibility of addressing emerging problems that have been identified by organizations, while not compromising on theory building at the expense of pragmatic solutions. For practitioners, the time has come to step back from the pragmatic and to capitalize on the cross-disciplinary insights that can be brought to bear on the topic from all those who have a stake in strengthening their organization's capability.

References

Beaverstock, J. V. (2004). "Managing across borders": knowledge management and expatriation in professional legal service firms. *Journal of Economic Geography*, 4 (1), 157–79.

(2005). Transnational elites in the city: British highly skilled inter-company transferees in New York City's financial district. *Journal of Ethnic and Migration Studies*, 31 (2), 245–68.

Christopherson, S. (2007). Barriers to "US style" lean retailing: the case of Wal-Mart's failure in Germany. *Journal of Economic Geography*, 7, 451–69.

Coe, N. and Lee, Y.-S. (2006). The strategic localization of transnational retailers: the case of Samsung-Tesco in South Korea. *Economic Geography*, 82 (1), 61–88.

Currah, A. and Wrigley, N. (2004). Networks of organizational learning and adaptation in retail TNCs. *Global Networks*, 4 (1), 1–23.

Ewers, M. C. (2007). Migrants, markets and multinationals: competition among world cities for the highly skilled. *GeoJournal*, 68 (1), 119–30.

Faulconbridge, J. R. (2007). Relational spaces of knowledge production in transnational law firms. *Geoforum*, 38 (5), 925–40.

Faulconbridge, J. R., Beaverstock, J. V., Derudder, B., and Witlox, F. (2009a). Corporate ecologies of business travel in professional service firms: working towards a research agenda. *European Urban and Regional Studies*, 16, 295–308.

Faulconbridge, J. R., Beaverstock, J. V., Hall, S., and Hewitson, A. (2009b). The "war for talent": the gatekeeper role of executive search firms in elite labour markets. *Geoforum*, 40, 800–8.

Festing, M., Schäfer, L., and Scullion, H. (2013). Talent management in medium-sized German companies: an explorative study and agenda for future research. *International Journal of Human Resource Management*, 24 (9), 1872–93.

Goldman Sachs (2007). The Next-11: more than an acronym. *Global Economics Paper* 153.

Hartmann, E., Feisel, E., and Schober, H. (2010). Talent management of Western MNCs in China: balancing global integration and local responsiveness, *Journal of World Business*, 45 (2), 169–78.

Hewlett, S. A. and Rashid, R. (2010). The battle for female talent in emerging markets. *Harvard Business Review*, 88, 101–5.

Horváthová, P. and Durdová, I. (2011). Talent management and its use in the field of human resources management in the organization of the Czech Republic. *World Academy of Science, Engineering and Technology*, 53, 809–24.

Horwitz, F. M. and Mellahi, K. (2009). Human resource management in emerging markets. In D. G. Collings and G. Wood (eds.) *Human Resource Management: A Critical Approach*. New York and London: Routledge.

Hoskisson, R. E., Eden, L., Lau, C. M., and Wright, M. (2000). Strategy in emerging economies. *Academy of Management Journal*, 7, 276–84.

Jones, A. (2007). More than "managing across borders?". The complex role of face-to-face interaction in globalizing law firms. *Journal of Economic Geography*, 7 (3), 223–46.

Koser, K. and Salt, J. (1997). The geography of highly skilled international migration. *International Journal of Population Geography*, 3 (2), 285–303.

Lane, K. and Pollner, F. (2008). How to address China's growing talent shortage. *McKinsey Quarterly*, 3, 32–40.

ManpowerGroup Survey (2012). 2012 Talent shortage survey research results. Milwaukee, WI: ManpowerGroup.

Maskell, P., Bathelt, H., and Malmberg, A. (2006). Building global knowledge pipelines: the role of temporary clusters. *European Planning Studies*, 14 (8), 997–1013.

Mellahi, K. and Collings, D. G. (2010). The barriers to effective global talent management: the example of corporate elites in MNEs. *Journal of World Business*, 45 (2), 143–9.

Michaels, E., Handfield-Jones, H., and Axelrod, B. (2001). *The War for Talent*. Boston: Harvard Business School Press.

Millar, D. and Salt, J. (2008). Portfolios of mobility: the movement of expertise in transnational corporations in two sectors – aerospace and extractive industries. *Global Networks*, 8 (1), 25–50.

Parker, C. P., Baltes, B. B., Young, S. A., *et al.* (2003). Relationships between psychological climate perceptions and work outcomes: a meta-analytical review. *Journal of Organizational Behavior*, 24, 389–416.

Salt, J. and Wood, P. (2012). Recession and international corporate mobility. *Global Networks*, 12 (4), 425–543.

Schuler, R. S., Jackson, S. E., and Tarique, I. (2011). Global talent management and global talent challenges: strategic opportunities for IHRM. *Journal of World Business*, 46, 506–16.

Shi, Y. and Handfield, R. (2012). Talent management issues for multinational logistics companies in China: observations from the field. *International Journal of Logistics: Research and Applications*, 15, 163–79.

Skuza, A., Scullion, H., and McDonnell, A. (2013). An analysis of the talent management challenges in a post-communist country: the case of Poland. *International Journal of Human Resource Management*, 24 (3), 453–70.

Sparrow, P. R., Farndale, E., and Scullion, H. (2013). An empirical study of the role of the corporate HR function in global talent management in professional and financial service firms in the global financial crisis. *International Journal of Human Resource Management*, 24 (9), 1777–98.

Stahl, G., Björkmann, I., Farndale, E., *et al.* (2012). Six principles of effective global talent management. *MIT Sloan Management Review*, 53 (2), 25–32.

Tung, R. and Lazarova, M. (2006). Brain drain versus brain gain: an exploratory study of ex host country nationals in Central and Eastern Europe. *International Journal of Human Resource Management*, 17, 1853–72.

Tymon, W., Stumpf, S. A., and Doh, J. P. (2010). Exploring talent management in India: the neglected role of intrinsic rewards. *Journal of World Business*, 55, 109–21.

Vaiman, V. and Collings, D G. (2013). Talent management: advancing the field. *International Journal of Human Resource Management*, 24 (9), 1737–43.

Vaiman, V. and Holde, N. (2011). Talent management in Central and Eastern Europe. In H. Scullion and D. G. Collings (eds.) *Global Talent Management*. London: Routledge.

Valverde, M., Scullion, H., and Ryan, G. (2013). Talent management in Spanish medium-sized organizations. *International Journal of Human Resource Management*, 24 (9), 1832–52.

van den Brink, M., Fruytier, B., and Thunnissen, M. (2012). Talent management in academia: performance systems and HRM policies. *Human Resource Management Journal*, 23 (2), 180–95.

Williams, C. (2007). Transfer in context: replication and adaptation in knowledge transfer relationships. *Strategic Management Journal*, 28, 867–89.

Yeung, A. K., Warner, M., and Rowley, C. (2008). Growth and globalization: evolution of human resource practices in Asia. *Human Resource Management*, 47, 1–13.

Index